Meet Us
IN THE
Kitchen

JUNIOR LEAGUE OF ST. LOUIS

Mission Statement

The Junior League of St. Louis is an organization of women

committed to promoting voluntarism, developing the

potential of women, and improving the community through

the effective action and leadership of trained volunteers.

Its purpose is exclusively educational and charitable.

Meet Us

IN THE Kitchen

A COLLECTION OF RECIPES AND STORIES
FROM THE JUNIOR LEAGUE OF ST. LOUIS

This cookbook is a collection of favorite recipes, which are not necessarily original recipes. Published by the Junior League of St. Louis.

Meet Us in the Kitchen
A Collection of Recipes and Stories from the Junior League of St. Louis

Library of Congress Catalog Number: 99-098091
ISBN: 0-9638298-2-3

Edited, Designed, and Manufactured by Favorite Recipes® Press
an imprint of

FRP™

P.O. Box 305142, Nashville, Tennessee 37230
800-358-0560

Art Director: Steve Newman
Designer: David Malone
Book Project Manager: Linda A. Jones

Manufactured in the United States of America
First Printing: 2000 15,000 copies

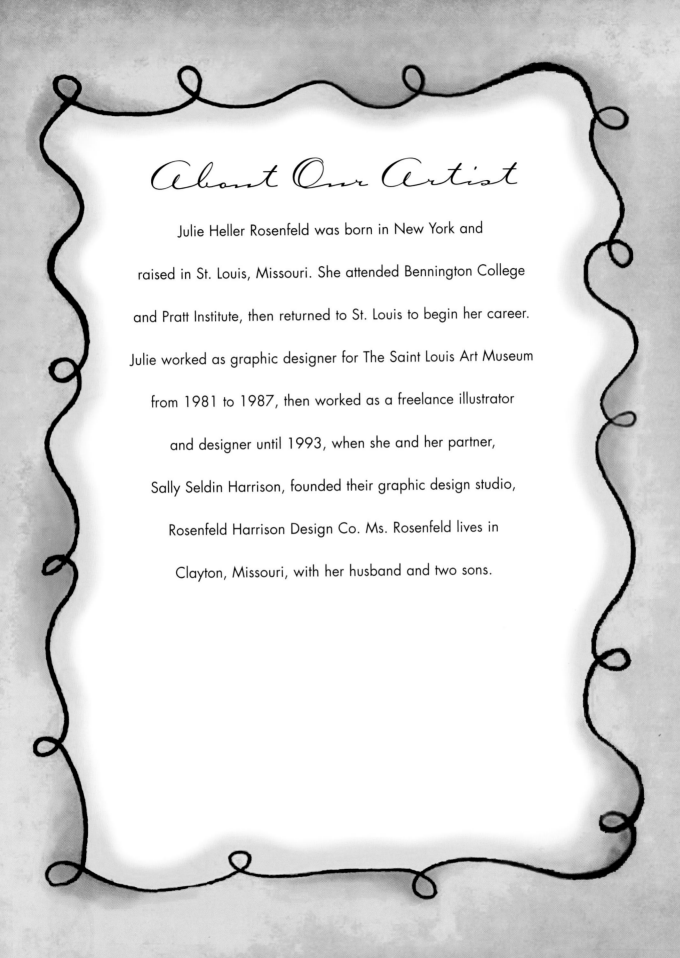

About Our Artist

Julie Heller Rosenfeld was born in New York and

raised in St. Louis, Missouri. She attended Bennington College

and Pratt Institute, then returned to St. Louis to begin her career.

Julie worked as graphic designer for The Saint Louis Art Museum

from 1981 to 1987, then worked as a freelance illustrator

and designer until 1993, when she and her partner,

Sally Seldin Harrison, founded their graphic design studio,

Rosenfeld Harrison Design Co. Ms. Rosenfeld lives in

Clayton, Missouri, with her husband and two sons.

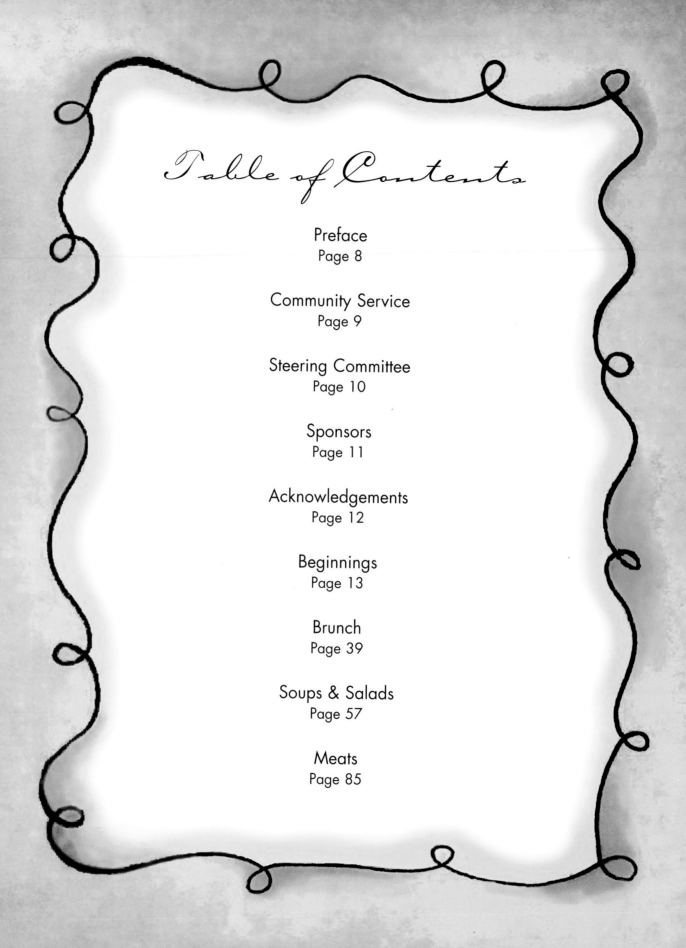

Table of Contents

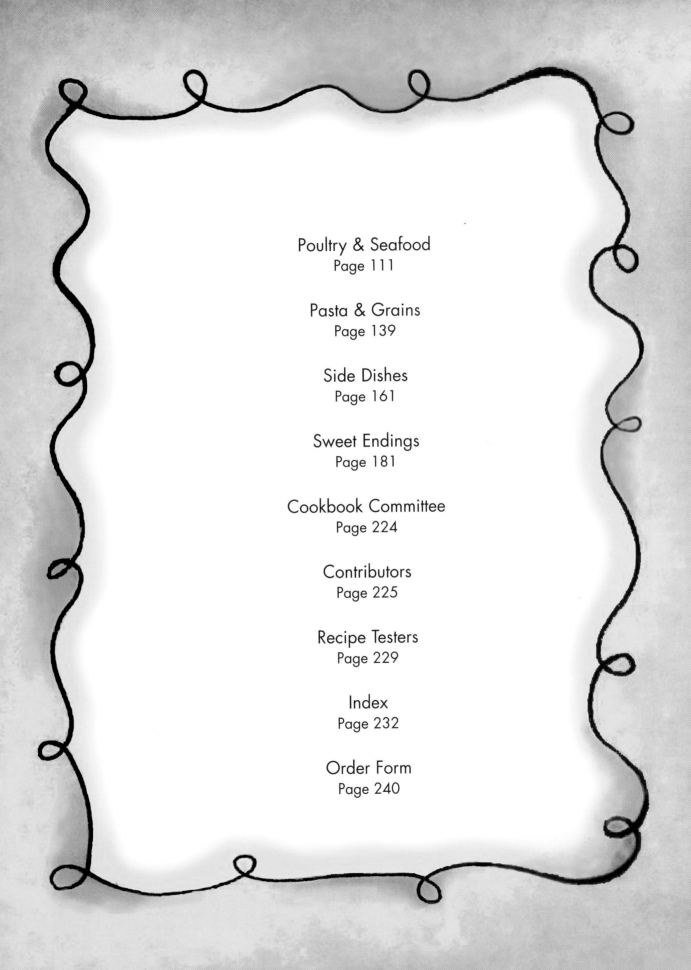

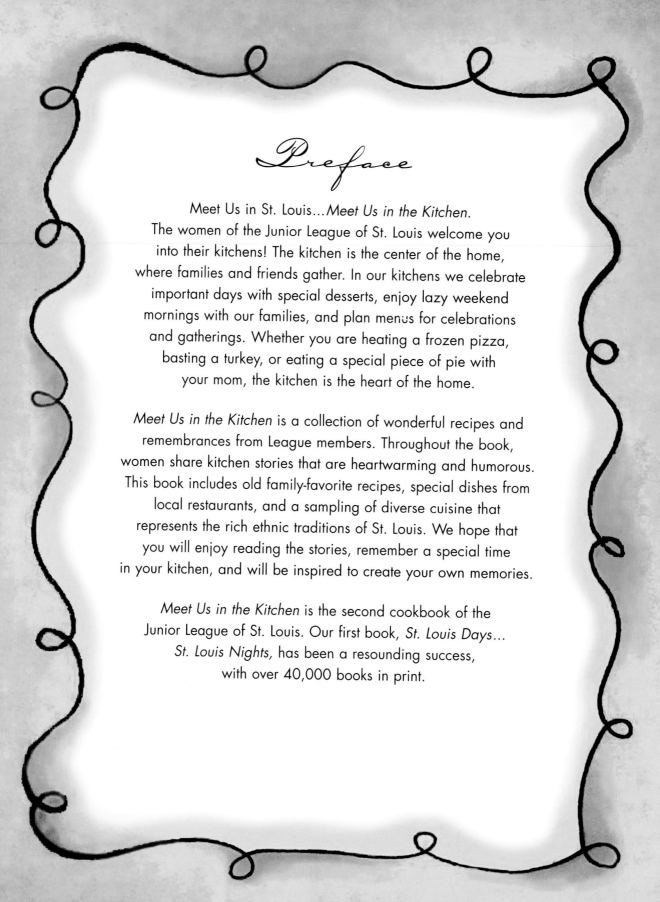

Preface

Meet Us in St. Louis...*Meet Us in the Kitchen.*
The women of the Junior League of St. Louis welcome you
into their kitchens! The kitchen is the center of the home,
where families and friends gather. In our kitchens we celebrate
important days with special desserts, enjoy lazy weekend
mornings with our families, and plan menus for celebrations
and gatherings. Whether you are heating a frozen pizza,
basting a turkey, or eating a special piece of pie with
your mom, the kitchen is the heart of the home.

Meet Us in the Kitchen is a collection of wonderful recipes and
remembrances from League members. Throughout the book,
women share kitchen stories that are heartwarming and humorous.
This book includes old family-favorite recipes, special dishes from
local restaurants, and a sampling of diverse cuisine that
represents the rich ethnic traditions of St. Louis. We hope that
you will enjoy reading the stories, remember a special time
in your kitchen, and will be inspired to create your own memories.

Meet Us in the Kitchen is the second cookbook of the
Junior League of St. Louis. Our first book, *St. Louis Days...
St. Louis Nights,* has been a resounding success,
with over 40,000 books in print.

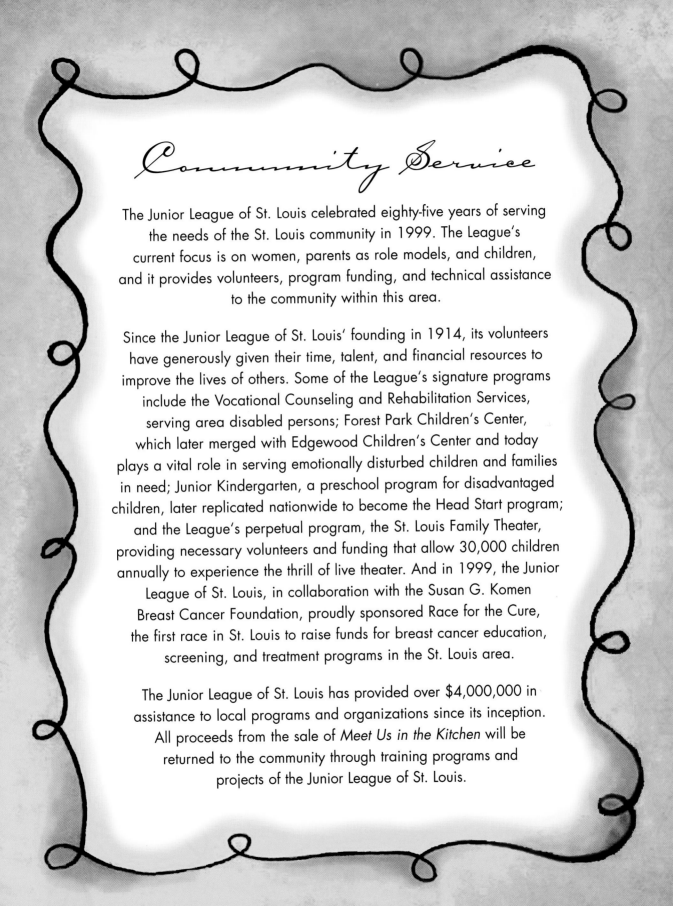

Community Service

The Junior League of St. Louis celebrated eighty-five years of serving the needs of the St. Louis community in 1999. The League's current focus is on women, parents as role models, and children, and it provides volunteers, program funding, and technical assistance to the community within this area.

Since the Junior League of St. Louis' founding in 1914, its volunteers have generously given their time, talent, and financial resources to improve the lives of others. Some of the League's signature programs include the Vocational Counseling and Rehabilitation Services, serving area disabled persons; Forest Park Children's Center, which later merged with Edgewood Children's Center and today plays a vital role in serving emotionally disturbed children and families in need; Junior Kindergarten, a preschool program for disadvantaged children, later replicated nationwide to become the Head Start program; and the League's perpetual program, the St. Louis Family Theater, providing necessary volunteers and funding that allow 30,000 children annually to experience the thrill of live theater. And in 1999, the Junior League of St. Louis, in collaboration with the Susan G. Komen Breast Cancer Foundation, proudly sponsored Race for the Cure, the first race in St. Louis to raise funds for breast cancer education, screening, and treatment programs in the St. Louis area.

The Junior League of St. Louis has provided over $4,000,000 in assistance to local programs and organizations since its inception. All proceeds from the sale of *Meet Us in the Kitchen* will be returned to the community through training programs and projects of the Junior League of St. Louis.

Steering Committee

Co-Chairs: Millicent Dohr
                                Becky Eggmann

Co-Vice Chairs: Tracee Holmes
                                Lisa Price

Treasurer: Laurie Zeveski

Story Editor: Leslie Hollander

Special Events Chair: Ronda Helton

Kick-Off Party Chair: Carole Bartnett

Distribution Chairs: Todd Higley
                                Laurie Zeveski

Sales Chair: Ann Brubaker

Sponsors

We recognize with gratitude the generosity and support
of the following *Meet Us in the Kitchen* sponsors:

Gourmet Chefs

Carole Bartnett	Mary Beth Hughes	Billie Rittendale
Ann Brubaker	Christine L. Norton	Jane Hoyt "GiGi" Sanders
Gretchen Gregory Davis	Heidi L. Oberman	Betty I. Williamson

Expert Cooks

Caroline Bean	Laura M. Heitland	Lisa Price
Elizabeth Bohlman	Tracee J. Holmes	Ann Rackers
Sharon Boranyak	Krista Hunt	Annette Ritchie
Sam Cocking	Ellen Jones	Jean T. Roessler
Jenifer Corbin	Sally Jones	Lee Quelsh Ross
JoAnne "Midge" Crider	Berry R. Lane	Gloria M. Smith
Mimi Denes	Sandy Lauschke	Sally Snavely
Claire Devoto	Margie Lazarus	Victoria Sonnenberg
Millicent Akin Dohr	Jane A. Mayfield	Laura Lynne Weinshenker
Anita Eftimoff	Mason Schott McMullin	Vicki Wilding
Mary Belle Eggers	Alison F. Pass	Heather G. Winsby
Becky Rowe Eggmann		Cheri L. Wuertz
Suzanne B. Gunter		Rita Mary Wylie

Acknowledgements

We want to thank all of the women of the Junior League

of St. Louis who contributed to *Meet Us in the Kitchen*.

The League is comprised of over 2,000 active women with

families, homes, careers, and volunteer activities.

Over 1,300 recipes were contributed and tested by League

members and friends. Thank you to everyone who had

tasting parties, sampled recipes at meetings, and recruited

family members for taste testing. We also want to thank

the local restaurants who enthusiastically submitted a

variety of recipes. We are grateful to those League members

for their inspiring stories and rich traditions, which enhance

the personality of *Meet Us in the Kitchen*. And finally,

a very special thank you to Cookbook Committee members and

our families for their support and encouragement.

Beginnings

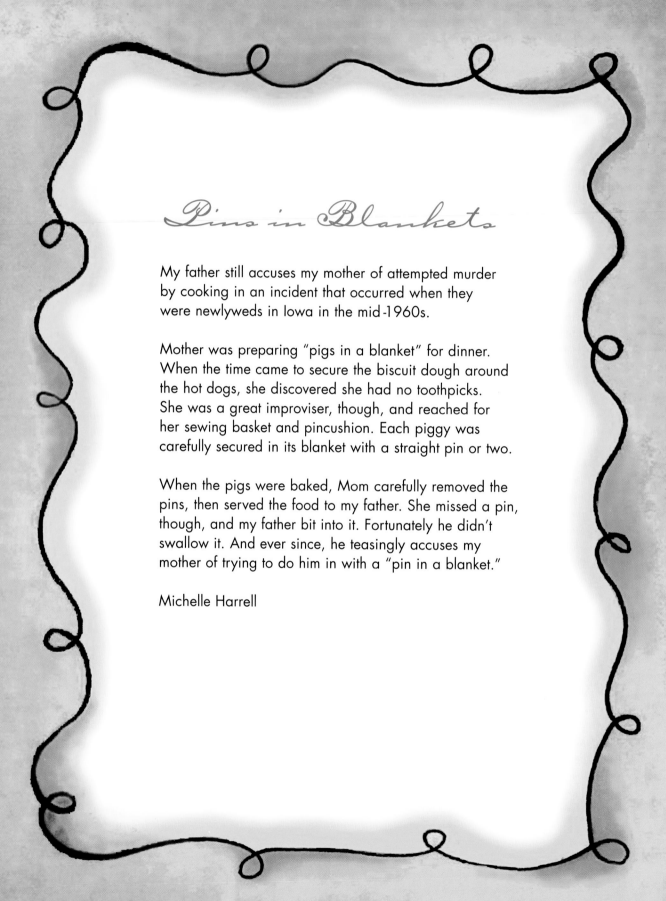

Pins in Blankets

My father still accuses my mother of attempted murder
by cooking in an incident that occurred when they
were newlyweds in Iowa in the mid-1960s.

Mother was preparing "pigs in a blanket" for dinner.
When the time came to secure the biscuit dough around
the hot dogs, she discovered she had no toothpicks.
She was a great improviser, though, and reached for
her sewing basket and pincushion. Each piggy was
carefully secured in its blanket with a straight pin or two.

When the pigs were baked, Mom carefully removed the
pins, then served the food to my father. She missed a pin,
though, and my father bit into it. Fortunately he didn't
swallow it. And ever since, he teasingly accuses my
mother of trying to do him in with a "pin in a blanket."

Michelle Harrell

Pigs in a Blanket

Try this gourmet version of an old favorite recipe.

INGREDIENTS

8 ounces cream cheese, softened
2 tablespoons Dijon mustard
1 tablespoon prepared horseradish
Chopped fresh chives to taste
2 sheets puff pastry, at room temperature
1 egg
$\frac{1}{4}$ cup cold water
48 smoked cocktail frankfurters

Beat the cream cheese, Dijon mustard and horseradish in a bowl until smooth. Stir in the chives. Cut each puff pastry sheet into thirds. Cut each piece into 8 strips. Beat the egg and water in a bowl to form an egg wash. Brush over the puff pastry strips. Spread with the cream cheese mixture. Wrap each frankfurter with a puff pastry strip, pinching ends to seal. Brush with the egg wash. Place on a baking sheet. Bake at 400 degrees for 12 to 14 minutes or until golden brown.

Makes 4 dozen

"Always a Favorite" Party Dip

This simple dip received rave reviews from our recipe testers.

INGREDIENTS 8 ounces cream cheese, softened
        1 package Carl Buddig beef, chopped
        8 to 12 large black olives, chopped
        2 tablespoons chopped onion
        2 tablespoons mayonnaise
        Sherry to taste (optional)
        Melba toast

  Beat the cream cheese in a mixing bowl until creamy. Add the beef, olives, onion, mayonnaise and sherry and mix well. Serve with melba toast.

Serves 6 to 8

Note: The flavor of this recipe is enhanced if prepared the day before serving.

Asiago Cheese Dip

INGREDIENTS 1/2 cup sun-dried tomatoes
        1 cup hot water
        1 cup mayonnaise
        1 cup sour cream
        1/2 cup shredded asiago cheese
        1/2 cup chopped fresh mushrooms
        1/4 cup chopped green onions
        1 tablespoon shredded asiago cheese
        Toasted French bread

  Reconstitute the tomatoes in hot water in a small bowl. Squeeze out any excess water. Cut the tomatoes into julienne strips.

  Combine the tomatoes, mayonnaise, sour cream, 1/2 cup cheese, mushrooms and green onions in a bowl and mix well. Spoon into an 8x8-inch baking dish or pie plate. Sprinkle with 1 tablespoon cheese. Bake at 350 degrees for 25 minutes or until bubbly. Serve with toasted French bread.

Serves 8

Bacon and Swiss Dip

INGREDIENTS

8 ounces cream cheese, softened
1/2 cup mayonnaise
1 tablespoon prepared horseradish
6 ounces shredded Swiss cheese
2 green onions, chopped
6 slices bacon, cooked, crumbled
Assorted crackers

Beat the cream cheese, mayonnaise and horseradish in a mixing bowl until blended. Add the Swiss cheese and green onions and mix well. Spoon into a microwave-safe bowl. Microwave on High for 2 minutes; stir.
Microwave for 2 minutes longer. Spoon into a serving dish. Sprinkle with crumbled bacon. Serve with crackers.

Serves 8

Raspberry Cheese Dip

INGREDIENTS

2 cups finely shredded Cheddar cheese
2 cups finely shredded Monterey Jack cheese
6 to 10 green onions, chopped
1 cup chopped pecans
6 tablespoons mayonnaise
1 1/2 cups raspberry preserves
Assorted crackers

Line a pie plate with plastic wrap. Combine the Cheddar cheese, Monterey Jack cheese, green onions, pecans and mayonnaise in a bowl and mix well. Press into the prepared pie plate. Chill, covered, for 1 hour or longer. Invert onto a serving tray and discard the plastic wrap. Spread raspberry preserves over the top and side just before serving. Serve with crackers.

Serves 8

Spicy Roasted Red Bell Pepper Dip with Crispy Pita Chips

DIP	1 (12-ounce) jar roasted red bell peppers, drained
	1/2 cup coarsely ground blanched almonds
	1/2 cup chopped fresh cilantro leaves
	1 jalapeño pepper, chopped, or to taste
	1 tablespoon tomato paste
	1 tablespoon balsamic vinegar
	1 tablespoon lemon juice
	1 1/2 teaspoons minced garlic
	1 teaspoon salt
	1/2 teaspoon chili powder
	1/2 teaspoon paprika
	1/4 teaspoon cayenne pepper
PITA CHIPS	1/2 teaspoon paprika
	1/2 teaspoon ground fennel seeds
	1/2 teaspoon onion powder
	1/2 teaspoon ground cumin seeds
	1/2 teaspoon salt
	1 (6-count) package pita bread
	1/4 cup vegetable oil

For the dip, process the red peppers, almonds, cilantro, jalapeño pepper, tomato paste, vinegar, lemon juice, garlic, salt, chili powder, paprika and cayenne pepper in a food processor until blended. Spoon into a serving bowl. Chill, covered, for 8 to 12 hours to enhance the flavor.

For the pita chips, combine the paprika, fennel seeds, onion powder, cumin seeds and salt in a small bowl. Cut each pita bread into halves horizontally. Brush the rough side of each pita round with oil. Sprinkle with the spice mixture. Cut each round into 8 wedges. Place on baking sheets. Bake at 350 degrees for 9 minutes or until crisp and golden brown.

Serves 8

Note: May store the chips in a sealable plastic food storage bag for up to 1 week.

Baked Pesto Brie

The red and green colors make it a perfect appetizer for the holidays.

INGREDIENTS

1 (16-ounce) wheel Brie cheese
1/2 cup ricotta cheese
1/4 cup pesto
1/4 cup sun-dried tomatoes, rehydrated
5 sheets phyllo dough, thawed
Melted butter

Place the wrapped Brie cheese in the freezer. Freeze for 1 hour or until firm. Unwrap the Brie cheese and cut into halves horizontally.

Combine the ricotta cheese, pesto and tomatoes in a bowl and mix well. Spread on the cut side of the bottom half of the cheese. Replace the top half of the cheese. May cover tightly with plastic wrap and chill until ready to use.

Place 1 phyllo sheet on a clean work surface, keeping the remaining phyllo sheets covered with a damp cloth. Brush with butter. Top with another phyllo sheet and brush with butter. Continue stacking the phyllo sheets and brushing with butter until all of the phyllo sheets are used. Place the cheese in the center of the stacked phyllo sheets and wrap as for a package. Brush the outside with butter. Place folded side down on a parchment-lined baking sheet. Brush the top and side with butter.

Bake at 375 degrees for 20 to 25 minutes or until golden brown and the cheese feels soft to the touch and begins to flow out of the wrapper. Serve immediately.

Serves 8 to 10

Kahlúa Pecan Brie

INGREDIENTS

3 tablespoons brown sugar
1/4 cup Kahlúa or strong-brewed coffee, cooled
3/4 cup pecan halves, toasted
1 (16-ounce) wheel Brie cheese
Assorted crackers or fresh apple or pear wedges

Combine the brown sugar and Kahlúa in a medium skillet. Heat until blended, stirring constantly. Add the pecans. Simmer until thickened and heated through. Remove from heat.

Place the cheese on a microwave-safe serving plate. Spoon the warm pecan mixture on top. Microwave on High for 1 to 2 minutes or until the cheese softens. Watch carefully because the cheese will melt quickly. Serve with crackers or fresh apple or pear wedges.

Serves 8 to 10

Brie Cheese

Try serving Brie cheese and other soft-ripening cheeses with assorted fresh seasonal fruits and thinly sliced French bread. When choosing a wine, consider cabernet sauvignon, merlot, petite sirah, fine-age ports, and other full-bodied vintages.

Wild Mushroom and Chive Pâté

INGREDIENTS

1 pound assorted mushrooms, coarsely chopped
2 tablespoons butter, melted
1 1/2 tablespoons brandy
8 ounces Louis Bien garlic and herb cream cheese,
     softened
1 tablespoon finely chopped fresh chives
1 teaspoon cracked pepper
Butter crackers or toasted bread slices

Sauté the mushrooms in the butter in a skillet over medium-high heat for 3 minutes. Add the brandy. Sauté until all of the liquid is absorbed. Remove from heat. Let stand until cool.

Process the cream cheese and chives in a food processor fitted with a knife blade until blended. Add the mushroom mixture and pepper and process until smooth. Spoon into a round bowl lined with plastic wrap and sprayed with nonstick cooking spray. Chill, covered, for 2 hours or up to 2 to 3 days. Unwrap and unmold on a serving plate. Serve with butter crackers or toasted bread slices.

Serves 8

Note: May use button, shiitake, cremini or portobello mushrooms, but be sure to remove the dark gill first.

Elegant Lobster Pâté

INGREDIENTS

1 pound cooked lobster meat
1 garlic clove, pressed
1/4 cup lemon juice
1/4 teaspoon freshly ground white pepper
1/8 teaspoon paprika
1/8 teaspoon salt
1 cup olive oil
Toast rounds or assorted crackers

Process the lobster in a food processor until finely minced. Add the garlic, lemon juice, white pepper, paprika and salt and blend thoroughly. Add the olive oil in a fine stream, processing constantly to form a smooth paste. Pack into a crock or small soufflé dish. Chill, covered, for 8 to 12 hours.

To serve, set the dish in hot water for 1 minute, loosening the edge from the side of the dish with a knife. Invert onto a serving plate. Serve with toast rounds or crackers.

Serves 8

Artichoke Hearts with Caviar

INGREDIENTS
8 ounces cream cheese, softened
2 tablespoons sour cream
2 teaspoons mayonnaise
1 teaspoon lemon juice
1 (8-ounce) can artichoke hearts, drained,
    chopped
2 teaspoons grated onion
1/8 teaspoon garlic salt
1/8 teaspoon white pepper
3 ounces caviar, drained
Assorted crackers

Blend the cream cheese, sour cream, mayonnaise and lemon juice in a bowl. Add the artichokes, onion, garlic salt and white pepper and mix well. Shape into a mound on a serving plate, flattening the top slightly. Spread the caviar on top. Serve with crackers.

Serves 8

Caviar

Caviar should be firm, fresh, shiny, and perfectly whole. Keep fresh caviar refrigerated, never frozen, until 15 minutes before serving. When serving caviar, avoid using silver containers or utensils, as they can give caviar a metallic taste.

Summer Salsa

INGREDIENTS
1 cup chopped red seedless grapes
1 cup chopped green seedless grapes
1 cup chopped green bell pepper
1/2 cup chopped scallions, or 3 to 4 green onions,
    chopped
1/4 cup chopped fresh cilantro
2 tablespoons olive oil
2 tablespoons fresh lime juice
4 teaspoons finely chopped seeded jalapeño
    pepper
2 teaspoons salt
1/2 teaspoon hot pepper sauce
Tortilla chips

Combine the red grapes, green grapes, green pepper, scallions, cilantro, olive oil, lime juice, jalapeño pepper, salt and hot pepper sauce in a bowl and mix well. Chill, covered, for 1 hour or longer for enhanced flavor. Drain well before serving. Serve with tortilla chips.

Serves 8

New England Clams Casino

INGREDIENTS

½ cup chopped onion
½ cup chopped celery
¼ cup chopped green bell pepper
¼ cup (½ stick) butter
2 tablespoons flour
1 tablespoon grated Parmesan cheese
¼ teaspoon Worcestershire sauce
¼ teaspoon Tabasco sauce
1 tablespoon white wine
⅛ teaspoon oregano
¼ cup dry bread crumbs
2 (7-ounce) cans minced clams, drained
¼ cup dry bread crumbs
1 tablespoon butter, melted
Cleaned clam/mussel shell halves (optional)
Assorted crackers

Sauté the onion, celery and green pepper in ¼ cup butter in a skillet until the onion is tender. Stir in the flour, Parmesan cheese, Worcestershire sauce, Tabasco sauce, wine and oregano. Add ¼ cup bread crumbs and mix well. Add the drained clams. Cook until thick and bubbly, adding additional wine if needed. Spoon into clam shells or into a 9-inch pie plate.

Mix ¼ cup bread crumbs with 1 tablespoon butter in a bowl. Sprinkle over the clam mixture. Bake at 350 degrees for 15 minutes. Serve with crackers.

Serves 6 to 8

Mushroom Bleu Cheese Spread

INGREDIENTS

1 pound mushrooms, sliced
1/4 cup (1/2 stick) butter
1/8 teaspoon nutmeg
1/8 teaspoon garlic powder
1/8 teaspoon pepper
2 tablespoons Dijon mustard
2 tablespoons white wine or vermouth, or to taste
8 ounces cream cheese, softened
3 ounces cream cheese with chives
Crumbled bleu cheese to taste
Chopped fresh parsley to taste
Assorted crackers or French bread

Sauté the mushrooms in the butter in a skillet until tender. Sprinkle with the nutmeg, garlic powder and pepper. Stir in the Dijon mustard and wine. Add the cream cheese and cream cheese with chives.

Cook over low heat until softened and blend well. Stir in the bleu cheese. Adjust the seasonings and add additional wine if needed for the desired consistency. Spoon into a serving bowl. Sprinkle with parsley. Chill, covered, in the refrigerator until 1 hour before serving time. Serve with crackers or French bread.

Serves 8 to 12

Beer Cheddar Spread

INGREDIENTS

8 ounces shredded Cheddar cheese
3 ounces cream cheese, softened
1 garlic clove, crushed
1 tablespoon Worcestershire sauce
1/2 teaspoon dry mustard
1/2 cup beer
Melba rounds, bagel chips or other crisp crackers

Process the Cheddar cheese, cream cheese, garlic, Worcestershire sauce, dry mustard and beer in a food processor until smooth. Spoon into a crock. Chill in the refrigerator for 1 week to allow flavors to fully blend before serving. Serve with melba rounds, bagel chips or other crisp crackers.

Serves 8

Garlic Feta Cheese Spread

INGREDIENTS

4 ounces feta cheese, crumbled
4 ounces cream cheese or reduced-fat cream
    cheese, softened
1/3 cup mayonnaise or reduced-fat mayonnaise
1 garlic clove, minced
1/4 teaspoon basil
1/4 teaspoon oregano
1/8 teaspoon dillweed
1/8 teaspoon dried thyme
Chopped fresh thyme to taste (optional)
Unsalted crackers or cracked pepper crackers
Assorted fresh vegetables

Combine the feta cheese, cream cheese, mayonnaise, garlic, basil, oregano, dillweed, dried thyme and fresh thyme in a bowl and mix well. The mixture will be lumpy. Spoon into a serving dish. Serve with crackers and assorted vegetables for dipping.

Serves 8 to 10

Zesty Sun-Dried Tomato Spread

INGREDIENTS

16 ounces cream cheese, softened
1/3 cup coarsely chopped, drained, oil-pack
    sun-dried tomatoes
3 green onions, chopped
3/4 teaspoon chopped fresh basil
3/4 teaspoon chopped fresh thyme
1/4 teaspoon oregano
Toasted French bread, melba rounds or bagel chips

Process the cream cheese, sun-dried tomatoes, green onions, basil, thyme and oregano in a food processor until blended. Spoon into a container with a lid. Store, covered, in the refrigerator for up to 1 week before serving.

To serve, spoon into a serving dish. Serve with toasted French bread, melba rounds, bagels or bagel chips.

Makes 2 cups

Pesto Tomato Bruschetta

INGREDIENTS
1 loaf French bread
1 (7-ounce) jar pesto
1 or 2 small tomatoes, seeded, chopped
12 ounces shredded mozzarella cheese

Cut the bread into slices 1/2 inch thick. Place on an ungreased baking sheet. Spread each slice with a scant tablespoon of pesto. Top each with tomatoes. Sprinkle with cheese.
Bake at 375 degrees for 8 minutes or until the cheese is melted.

Serves 8

Bacon Tomato Cups

INGREDIENTS
8 slices bacon, cooked, coarsely crumbled
1 medium tomato, seeded, coarsely chopped
3 or 4 green onions, coarsely chopped
4 ounces sharp Cheddar cheese, shredded
1/2 cup mayonnaise
1 teaspoon basil
1 (10-count) can flaky biscuits

Combine the bacon, tomato and green onions in a bowl and mix well. Add the cheese, mayonnaise and basil and mix well.
Separate each biscuit dough round into 3 layers. Lay each layer over a miniature muffin cup; press into the cup with a floured wooden shaper or tamper. Fill each with the tomato mixture.
Bake at 375 degrees for 10 to 12 minutes or until golden brown. Serve immediately.

Serves 6

Artichoke-Stuffed Mushrooms

INGREDIENTS

1 (14-ounce) can water-pack artichokes
2 tablespoons olive oil
4 garlic cloves, minced
8 ounces cream cheese, softened
3 tablespoons ricotta cheese
6 large portobello mushrooms
3 tablespoons balsamic vinegar
4 ounces asiago or romano cheese

Rinse the artichokes in cold water; drain. Cut the artichokes into quarters. Heat the olive oil in a skillet. Add the garlic. Cook until the garlic begins to brown. Add the artichokes. Cook for 2 to 3 minutes. Add to the cream cheese and ricotta cheese in a bowl. Mix with a fork until the mixture is a uniform consistency.

Remove the stems from the mushrooms and reserve for another purpose. Brush the mushroom caps inside and outside with the vinegar. Place on a grill rack. Grill until heated through. Let stand until cool. Store, covered, in the refrigerator until ready to use.

Shave the asiago cheese with a vegetable peeler. Stuff the mushroom caps with the cream cheese mixture. Sprinkle with asiago cheese.

Place the stuffed mushroom caps on a baking sheet. Bake at 400 degrees until the asiago cheese is golden brown.

Serves 6

Savory Stuffed Mushroom Caps

INGREDIENTS

1 pound medium mushrooms
1/4 cup chopped green onions
1 garlic clove, finely chopped
1/4 cup (1/2 stick) butter or margarine
1/2 cup dry bread crumbs
1/4 cup grated Parmesan cheese
2 tablespoons chopped fresh parsley
1/2 teaspoon each basil and pepper
1/4 teaspoon salt
1 tablespoon butter or margarine

Remove the stems from the mushrooms and reserve the caps. Chop the mushroom stems finely. Sauté the chopped mushroom stems, green onions and garlic in 1/4 cup butter in a skillet for 5 minutes or until tender. Remove from heat. Stir in the bread crumbs, Parmesan cheese, parsley, basil, pepper and salt.

Melt 1 tablespoon butter in a shallow baking pan. Fill the mushroom caps with the mushroom stem mixture. Place stuffed side up in the melted butter. Bake, uncovered, at 350 degrees for 15 minutes. Serve hot.

Makes 3 dozen

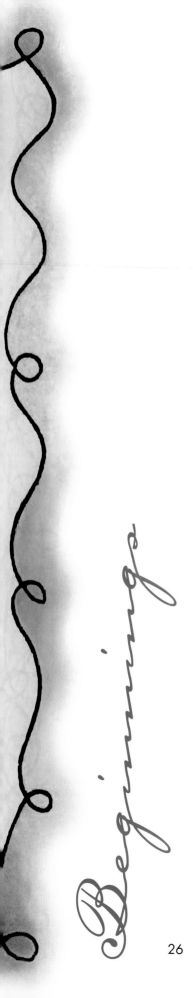

Beginnings

Seafood-Stuffed Grilled Portobello Mushroom

MUSHROOM	¼ cup (½ stick) butter, melted
	1 shallot, chopped
	2 tablespoons chopped fresh tarragon
	1 teaspoon fennel seeds (optional)
	½ teaspoon Worcestershire sauce
	½ teaspoon granulated garlic
	½ teaspoon salt
	½ teaspoon pepper
	⅛ teaspoon hot pepper sauce
	1 large (6-ounce) portobello mushroom cap
SEAFOOD STUFFING	2 tablespoons butter
	½ cup chopped leeks
	½ cup chopped shiitake mushroom caps
	½ teaspoon crushed garlic
	1 teaspoon pesto
	4 ounces (about ½ cup) tiny shrimp
	½ cup small bay scallops
	½ cup imitation crab meat
	¼ cup dry white wine
	½ cup chicken stock
	¼ cup grated Parmesan cheese
	1 tablespoon sesame oil
ASSEMBLY	Grated Parmesan cheese (optional)
	Chopped fresh parsley (optional)
	French bread

For the mushroom, combine the butter, shallot, tarragon, fennel seeds, Worcestershire sauce, garlic, salt, pepper and hot pepper sauce in a bowl and mix well. Spread the portobello mushroom cap with seasoned butter. Place on a grill rack. Grill over low coals for 7 minutes on each side or until tender, brushing frequently with the seasoned butter. Can place the mushroom cap on a baking sheet and bake at 350 degrees for 15 minutes, brushing with the seasoned butter every 5 minutes.

For the seafood stuffing, combine the butter, leeks, shiitake mushroom caps, garlic, pesto, shrimp, bay scallops and crab meat in a skillet. Sauté over high heat until the shrimp turns pink. Add the wine, stirring to deglaze the skillet. Add the chicken stock. Bring to a boil. Cook until the liquid is reduced by ⅓. Stir in the Parmesan cheese. Remove from heat. Stir in the sesame oil.

To assemble, fill the grilled portobello mushroom with the seafood stuffing. Sprinkle with Parmesan cheese and parsley. Cut into wedges. Serve with French bread.

Serves 2 to 4

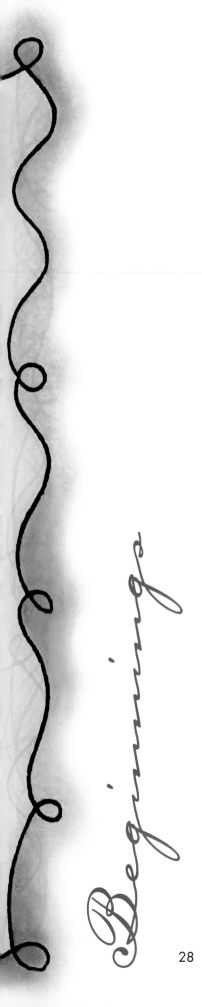

Sophisticated Salmon Mousse

MOUSSE	1 tablespoon unflavored gelatin
	1/4 cup cold water
	2 tablespoons fresh lemon juice
	1 small onion
	1/2 cup boiling water
	1/2 cup mayonnaise
	1 teaspoon dillweed
	1/2 teaspoon paprika
	1 (16-ounce) can boneless, skinless red salmon, flaked
	1 cup heavy cream
CUCUMBER SAUCE	2 cups sour cream
	3 tablespoons white wine vinegar
	3 tablespoons dillweed, or to taste
	1 tablespoon fresh lemon juice
	2 teaspoons grated onion
	1 teaspoon salt
	1/2 teaspoon cayenne pepper
	1 cup chopped, seeded, peeled cucumber

For the mousse, soften the gelatin in the cold water in a cup. Process the gelatin mixture, lemon juice, onion and boiling water in a blender until puréed. Add the mayonnaise, dillweed, paprika and salmon and blend well. Add the cream gradually, processing constantly for a few more seconds. Pour into an oiled 4-cup mold or individual ramekins. Chill until set.

For the cucumber sauce, combine the sour cream, white wine vinegar, dillweed, lemon juice, onion, salt and cayenne pepper in a bowl and blend well. Stir in the cucumber. Chill, covered, in the refrigerator until ready to serve.

To serve, unmold the mousse onto a serving dish or individual serving plates. Serve with the cucumber sauce.

Serves 4

Mussels Steamed with Saffron Curry Cream

CAFÉ CAMPAGNARD

INGREDIENTS

1 small yellow onion, finely chopped
2 garlic cloves, minced
1 Braeburn apple, finely chopped
1 1/2 tablespoons grated fresh gingerroot
1 tablespoon butter
1/4 cup brandy
2 cups white wine
2/3 cup unsweetened apple juice
1 teaspoon mild curry powder
1 teaspoon lemon zest
1 teaspoon thyme
1 small bay leaf
1 small dried chile, such as santaka or pasilla
2 teaspoons fresh lemon juice
1/8 teaspoon saffron
1 cup heavy cream
Salt and pepper to taste
5 1/3 pounds Prince Edward Island mussels
Crusty bread for dipping

Sweat the onion with the garlic, apple and ginger in the butter in a covered saucepan over low heat until soft. Increase heat. Add the brandy, stirring to deglaze the saucepan. Watch carefully, brandy may ignite; continue once flames subside. Add the wine, apple juice, curry powder, lemon zest, thyme, bay leaf, chile, lemon juice and saffron. Bring to a boil and reduce heat. Simmer until the mixture is reduced by half. Add the cream. Simmer for 5 minutes. Season with salt and pepper.

Rinse the mussels in cold water and discard the beards. Add the mussels to the sauce. Cook until the mussels open. Discard any mussels that do not open and the bay leaf. Serve immediately with crusty bread for dipping.

Serves 8

Note: Allow 2/3 pound Prince Edward Island mussels per serving.

Café Campagnard

This neighborhood bistro features French country cuisine in a casual, comfortable atmosphere. The menu includes some classic French fare, but mainly centers around rustic, hearty dishes that are inspired by decades of French home cooking.

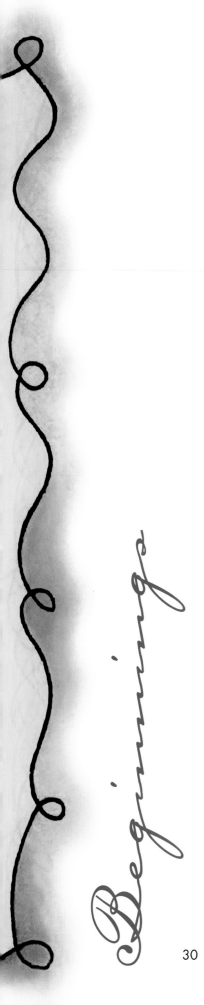

Crab Cakes with Mango Chutney

CRAB CAKES
- ½ cup finely chopped onion
- ¼ cup finely chopped celery
- 2 garlic cloves, finely chopped
- ¼ cup finely chopped green bell pepper
- 6 tablespoons butter
- 1 teaspoon thyme
- 1 teaspoon oregano
- 2 tablespoons finely chopped green onions
- 1 pound crab meat, flaked
- ½ cup chicken stock
- Cayenne pepper to taste
- Salt and black pepper to taste
- 2 eggs
- ¾ cup bread crumbs
- Flour
- 1 egg yolk
- 1 to 2 tablespoons water or milk
- 2 tablespoons vegetable oil

MANGO CHUTNEY
- ½ red bell pepper, julienned
- ½ green bell pepper, julienned
- ¼ white onion, julienned
- 1 ripe mango, peeled, julienned
- 2 tablespoons cider vinegar
- 1½ teaspoons sugar
- ½ teaspoon lime juice
- ½ teaspoon lemon juice
- ½ teaspoon honey
- ½ teaspoon curry powder
- ⅛ teaspoon salt
- 1½ teaspoons apricot preserves

For the crab cakes, sauté the onion, celery, garlic and green pepper in the butter in a skillet until transparent. Add the thyme, oregano, green onions, crab meat, chicken stock, cayenne pepper, salt and black pepper. Sauté for 3 to 5 minutes. Remove from heat; cool slightly. Add 2 eggs and ½ of the bread crumbs and mix well. Shape into 2-ounce patties. Sprinkle with flour. Brush with a mixture of the egg yolk and water. Coat with the remaining bread crumbs. Fry in the oil in a skillet until brown, turning once. Place on a baking sheet. Bake at 350 degrees for 5 minutes.

For the mango chutney, combine the red pepper, green pepper and onion in a heavy saucepan. Cook over low heat until transparent, stirring frequently. Add the mango, cider vinegar, sugar, lime juice, lemon juice, honey, curry powder and salt. Bring just to a boil, stirring frequently. Stir in the apricot preserves. Turn off heat. Let stand until cool. Spoon into a serving container. Chill in the refrigerator. Serve cold or at room temperature.

To serve, spoon the mango chutney on the hot crab cakes.

Serves 4

Scallop Puffs

INGREDIENTS

3 tablespoons unsalted butter
1 pound bay scallops, quartered
2 teaspoons finely chopped onion
3 garlic cloves, finely chopped
2 teaspoons lemon zest
3 tablespoons chopped fresh dill
2 cups grated Swiss or Gruyère cheese
2 1/4 cups mayonnaise
Freshly ground pepper to taste
12 dozen (1-inch) thin white bread rounds,
    lightly toasted
Paprika to taste

GARNISHES

Lemon slices
Sprigs of fresh dill

Melt the butter in a skillet over medium-high heat. Add the scallops, onion, garlic and lemon zest. Cook for 2 to 3 minutes or until the scallops are just barely cooked through, stirring constantly. Add the dill, cheese, mayonnaise and pepper and stir to mix well. Spoon into a container. Chill, covered, until ready to serve or for up to 1 week.

Spoon the scallop mixture onto each toasted bread round. Sprinkle with paprika. Place on a baking sheet. Broil 5 inches from the heat source for 2 to 3 minutes or until light brown.

To serve, place on a serving platter. Garnish with lemon slices and sprigs of fresh dill.

Makes 12 dozen

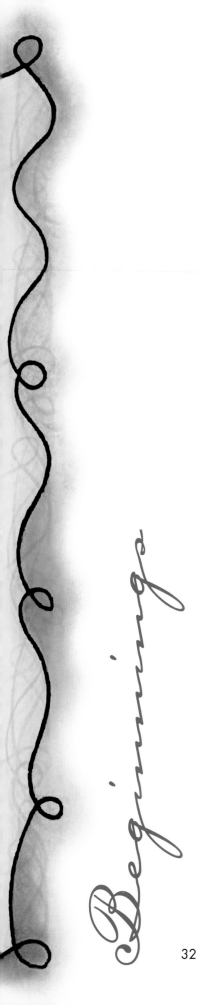

Spicy Glazed Scallops on Cucumber Disks

A refreshing summer appetizer with a spicy kick!

INGREDIENTS	1½ pounds sea scallops
	½ cup soy sauce
	¼ cup water
	3 tablespoons fresh orange juice
	5 pickled jalapeño peppers, finely chopped
	3 garlic cloves, minced
	1 teaspoon sugar
	¼ teaspoon salt
	1 tablespoon vegetable oil
	2 large cucumbers, cut into ¼-inch-thick slices
GARNISH	Fresh coriander leaves

Rinse the scallops and pat dry. Cut each scallop horizontally into halves.

Combine soy sauce, water, orange juice, jalapeño peppers, garlic, sugar and salt in a bowl and mix well. Add the scallops and stir to coat. Marinate, covered, in the refrigerator for 8 to 12 hours, stirring occasionally. Drain the scallops, discarding the marinade.

Heat 1 teaspoon of the oil in a heavy skillet over medium-high heat until hot but not smoking. Add ⅓ of the scallops. Cook for 4 to 5 minutes or until golden brown, stirring constantly. Remove to a warm platter. Repeat 2 times with the remaining scallops and oil.

To serve, arrange a scallop on each slice of cucumber. Garnish each with a coriander leaf.

Makes about 4½ dozen

Zesty Shrimp Sauté

ST. LOUIS STEAKHOUSE

GARLIC BUTTER	1 1/4 cups (2 1/2 sticks) butter, softened
	1/4 cup chopped garlic
	1/2 tablespoon (heaping) Worcestershire sauce
	3/4 teaspoon chopped rosemary
	1 teaspoon paprika
	1/2 teaspoon black pepper
	1/4 teaspoon salt
	1/4 teaspoon Tabasco sauce
	1/4 teaspoon cayenne pepper
	1/4 teaspoon Italian seasoning
SHRIMP	1 tablespoon extra-virgin olive oil
	20 jumbo shrimp, peeled
	1/2 tablespoon water
	1 tablespoon chopped green onions or chives

For the garlic butter, combine the butter, garlic, Worcestershire sauce, rosemary, paprika, black pepper, salt, Tabasco sauce, cayenne pepper and Italian seasoning in a bowl and blend well.

For the shrimp, spoon the olive oil into a hot sauté pan. Add the shrimp. Cook for 3 minutes on each side. Add the water and green onions. Cook for 1 minute. Reduce heat. Add 3 tablespoons of the garlic butter. Cook until creamy, stirring constantly. Arrange in a serving dish.

To serve, heat the remaining garlic butter in a saucepan. Pour over the shrimp. Serve immediately.

Serves 4

St. Louis Steakhouse

Although relatively new to the city, the St. Louis Steakhouse has quite a story to tell. The restaurant, located in historic Court Square and listed on the National Register of Historic Places, was built in 1902, and remains the first building west of the Mississippi to be completely financed by a woman. Although turmoil threatened the destruction of this building, it still stands today. The St. Louis Steakhouse symbolizes the pride, perseverance, and tradition of this great city.

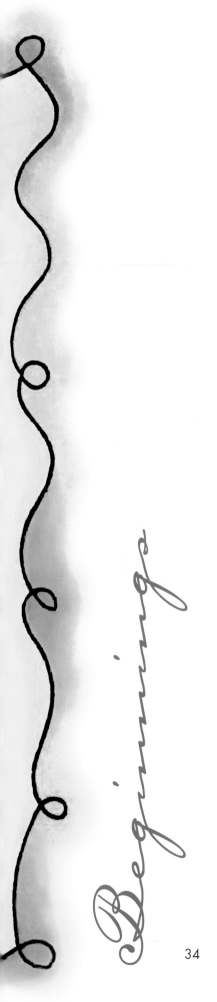

Shrimp and Pepper Won Tons

INGREDIENTS

Olive oil
1 (16-ounce) package won tons
8 ounces shrimp, cooked, peeled, chopped
1 yellow bell pepper, roasted, peeled, chopped
1 red bell pepper, roasted, peeled, chopped
½ cup chopped fresh cilantro
1 chipotle pepper in adobo sauce, drained, finely
    chopped (optional)
8 ounces fontina cheese, shredded

Brush miniature muffin cups with olive oil. Press 1 won ton into each cup. Bake at 350 degrees for 10 minutes or until golden brown. Remove from the oven and cool slightly.

Combine the shrimp, yellow pepper, red pepper, cilantro, chipotle pepper and cheese in a large bowl and mix well.

Remove the cooled won tons from the muffin cups and place on a baking sheet. Fill each won ton cup with the shrimp mixture. Bake at 350 degrees for 7 to 10 minutes or until the cheese melts.

Makes 2½ dozen

Mediterranean Marinated Shrimp

Try serving these shrimp on a bed of lettuce for a refreshing salad entrée.

INGREDIENTS

2 pounds shrimp, boiled, peeled
1 lemon, sliced
1 red onion, sliced
½ cup pitted kalamata olives
2 tablespoons chopped pimentos
½ cup lemon juice
¼ cup vegetable oil
1 tablespoon wine vinegar
1 garlic clove, chopped
½ bay leaf
1 tablespoon dry mustard
1 teaspoon salt
¼ teaspoon red pepper
¼ teaspoon black pepper
French bread slices

Place the shrimp in a large bowl. Combine the lemon, red onion, olives, pimentos, lemon juice, oil, wine vinegar, garlic, bay leaf, dry mustard, salt, red pepper and black pepper in a separate bowl and mix well. Pour over the shrimp. Chill, covered, for 2 to 12 hours.

To serve, discard the bay leaf. Serve with French bread for dipping.

Serves 8 to 10

Cucumber Sandwiches

INGREDIENTS
8 ounces cream cheese, softened
1 envelope Italian salad dressing mix
1 1/2 to 2 cucumbers
1 loaf party rye bread
Paprika to taste

Beat the cream cheese and Italian salad dressing mix in a mixing bowl until smooth.

Score the cucumbers with the tines of a fork. Cut the cucumbers into 1/4-inch slices.

Spread the cream cheese mixture onto each bread slice. Top each with a cucumber slice. Sprinkle with paprika. Chill, covered, until ready to serve.

Makes about 3 dozen

Pimento Cheese Party Sandwiches

INGREDIENTS
2 cups shredded extra-sharp Cheddar cheese
1/4 cup plus 2 tablespoons chopped pecans
1/4 cup plus 2 tablespoons mayonnaise
1 (2-ounce) jar chopped pimentos, drained
6 pimento-stuffed olives, chopped
1 tablespoon dry sherry
1/4 teaspoon hot sauce
1/4 teaspoon pepper
3 (2-pound) loaves sliced sandwich bread

GARNISH
Pimento-stuffed olives

Combine the cheese, pecans, mayonnaise, pimentos, olives, sherry, hot sauce and pepper in a bowl and mix well. Refrigerate, covered, until chilled through.

Cut the bread slices with a 2-inch daisy-shaped cutter. Spread the cheese mixture over 1/2 of the bread shapes; top with the remaining bread shapes. Garnish each with a stuffed olive in the center.

Makes 4 dozen

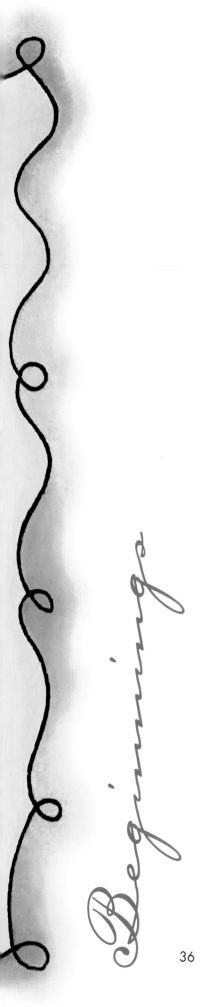

Jalapeño Bites

Spicy and unusual. Like a jalapeño popper without the deep-frying.

INGREDIENTS

8 ounces cream cheese, softened
8 ounces grated Parmesan cheese
3 tablespoons chopped jalapeño peppers
2 egg yolks
2 cups bread crumbs

Combine the cream cheese, Parmesan cheese, jalapeño peppers and egg yolks in a bowl and mix to form a paste. Shape 1/2 tablespoonful at a time into 1/4-inch rounds. Dip both sides in the bread crumbs. Place on an ungreased baking sheet. Bake at 350 degrees for 10 to 15 minutes or until golden brown. Serve warm.

Serves 6 to 8

Regal Seasoned Olives

INGREDIENTS

2 cups black or green pitted olives
4 large garlic cloves
2 teaspoons red wine vinegar
1/2 teaspoon crushed red pepper
1 tablespoon olive oil
1/2 teaspoon oregano

Combine the olives, garlic, red wine vinegar, red pepper and olive oil in a bowl and mix well. Crush the oregano and stir into the olive mixture. Spoon into a container with a lid. Chill, covered, for 24 hours or longer, shaking occasionally. Bring to room temperature before serving.

Serves 6 to 8

Celebration Punch

For an added touch, make a ginger ale ice ring and add cranberries at holiday time. Substitute lemon slices for the cranberries during the summertime.

INGREDIENTS
1 (32-ounce) bottle cranberry juice cocktail
1 (46-ounce) can unsweetened pineapple juice
2 cups orange juice
1 small can frozen lemonade concentrate, or
⅔ cup lemon juice
½ cup sugar
2 teaspoons almond extract
1 (32-ounce) bottle ginger ale, chilled

Combine the cranberry juice cocktail, pineapple juice, orange juice, lemonade concentrate, sugar and almond extract in a large container with a lid and mix well. Chill, covered, in the refrigerator.

To serve, pour ¼ of the mixture into a punch bowl. Add ¼ of the ginger ale and stir to mix well. Replenish the punch as needed.

Makes 4½ quarts

Peach Smoothie

INGREDIENTS
½ gallon vanilla ice cream or frozen yogurt
1 cup half-and-half
1 (10-ounce) package frozen peaches
4 jiggers peach brandy

GARNISHES
Fresh peach slices
Fresh mint leaves

Process the ice cream, half-and-half, peaches and brandy in a blender until smooth. Pour into champagne glasses. Garnish each serving with a peach slice and mint leaf.

Serves 6

Festive Wine Slush

INGREDIENTS

1 bottle lambrusco or other wine
1 (32-ounce) bottle ginger ale
1 (10-ounce) package frozen strawberries
2 tablespoons grenadine
9 ounces frozen orange juice concentrate
3 ounces frozen lemonade concentrate

Combine the lambrusco, ginger ale, strawberries, grenadine, orange juice concentrate and lemonade concentrate in a freezer container with a lid and mix well. Freeze, covered, for 8 to 12 hours or until firm. Thaw for about 20 minutes before serving.

Serves 8 to 10

Hot Buttered Rum Mix

INGREDIENTS

2 cups (4 sticks) butter, softened
1 (1-pound) package dark brown sugar
1 (1-pound) package confectioners' sugar
2 teaspoons cinnamon
1 teaspoon nutmeg
1 quart vanilla ice cream, softened
Dark rum
Boiling water

GARNISH

Whipped cream

Beat the butter, brown sugar and confectioners' sugar in a large mixing bowl until creamy. Stir in the cinnamon and nutmeg. Fold in the ice cream. Place in a freezer container with a lid. Freeze, covered, until firm.

To serve, place 2 tablespoons of the mix in a mug. Add 1 jigger of dark rum and enough boiling water to fill the mug and stir to mix well. Garnish each serving with whipped cream.

Makes 2 quarts mix

Brunch

Waffle Off to Buffalo

One of my favorite childhood memories is of making waffles for breakfast on our monthly visits to my grandparents, Nana and Papa.

Nana was four feet ten inches tall, with cat-eye glasses and curly white hair. Dressed in her silk bathrobe and pajamas, her look was crowned by sparkly slip-on house shoes with hard soles and a little heel.

To make the time pass quickly while the waffles cooked, Nana did a dance she called "Shuffle Off to Buffalo." The hard soles of her iridescent shoes tapped out the rhythm on the linoleum. My sister and I, around four and six years old, were delighted, and before we knew it, the waffles were ready.

My mother uses this same recipe to make waffles for her five grandchildren when they visit her. But at her house, there's no dancing, just waffles.

Jodi Luetkemper

Nana's Gourmet Waffles

INGREDIENTS

2 cups flour
1 tablespoon baking powder
2 egg yolks
$1\frac{3}{4}$ cups milk
$\frac{1}{4}$ cup melted shortening
4 egg whites

Combine the flour and baking powder in a large bowl and mix well. Add the egg yolks, milk and shortening and mix well. Beat the egg whites in a mixing bowl until stiff peaks form. Fold into the batter. Pour $\frac{1}{2}$ cup batter at a time onto a hot waffle iron. Bake using the manufacturer's directions.

Makes 4 to 6 servings

Cozy Cinnamon Waffles with Butter Pecan Sauce

WAFFLES	1 cup flour
	2 teaspoons baking soda
	1/4 cup sugar
	1 teaspoon cinnamon
	2 eggs
	1 1/4 cups skim milk
	2 tablespoons butter, melted
BUTTER PECAN SAUCE	1/4 cup (1/2 stick) butter, softened
	1 cup packed brown sugar
	1 cup half-and-half, heated
	1/4 cup brandy (optional)
	1/3 cup chopped pecans

For the waffles, mix the flour, baking soda, sugar and cinnamon in a mixing bowl. Add the eggs, milk and butter and blend well. Pour 1/2 cup batter at a time onto a hot waffle iron. Bake using the manufacturer's directions.

For the butter pecan sauce, beat the butter and brown sugar in a saucepan until creamy. Add the half-and-half gradually, stirring constantly. Cook over low heat until the mixture comes to a light boil, stirring constantly. Remove from heat. Add the brandy and whisk until smooth. Stir in the pecans.

To serve, pour the butter pecan sauce over the hot waffles.

Serves 4

French Toast Filled with Homemade Fresh Cranberry Sauce

CRANBERRY SAUCE	12 ounces fresh cranberries 1 cup cold water 1 cup sugar 1/2 teaspoon orange zest
FRENCH TOAST	8 (1-inch-thick) diagonal slices Italian or French bread 4 large eggs 1 cup milk 1/8 teaspoon salt 2 tablespoons butter Confectioners' sugar Butter Maple syrup

For the cranberry sauce, combine the cranberries, water, sugar and orange zest in a medium saucepan. Bring to a boil over medium-high heat. Boil for 5 minutes or until the cranberries pop open. Remove from heat and cool. This recipe makes 4 cups of sauce.

For the French toast, cut each bread slice horizontally to within 1/4 inch of the opposite side to form a pocket. Spoon 1 tablespoon of the cranberry sauce into each pocket and gently press closed. Beat the eggs, milk and salt in a shallow dish using a wire whisk. Add the stuffed bread slices in a single layer, turning 1 or 2 times. Let stand for 15 minutes or until the egg mixture is absorbed.

Melt 2 tablespoons butter in a 10-inch skillet over medium heat. Cook the stuffed bread slices for 5 to 7 minutes on each side or until golden brown.

To serve, sprinkle with confectioners' sugar. Serve with butter and warm maple syrup.

Serves 4

Sausage and Pepper Quiche

INGREDIENTS

1 (1-crust) pie pastry
12 ounces hot or sweet Italian sausage
1 red bell pepper, minced
1 green bell pepper, minced
¼ teaspoon salt
½ cup shredded Cheddar cheese
¼ cup freshly grated Parmesan cheese
2 eggs
½ cup heavy cream
3 tablespoons milk

Line a 9-inch quiche dish with the pie pastry, trimming the edge. Bake at 400 degrees for 9 minutes. Remove from the oven and let stand until cool.

Remove the casings from the sausage and discard. Crumble the sausage into a large skillet. Add the red pepper and green pepper. Cook over medium-high heat for 7 minutes or until the sausage is brown and crumbly, stirring constantly; drain.

Combine the sausage mixture, salt, Cheddar cheese and Parmesan cheese in a bowl and mix well. Spread in the partially baked quiche shell.

Beat the eggs, cream and milk in a bowl with a wire whisk. Pour over the sausage mixture. Place the quiche dish on a baking sheet. Bake at 425 degrees for 15 minutes. Reduce the oven temperature to 350 degrees. Bake for 10 minutes longer or until set.

Serves 8

Sunday Morning Scramble

INGREDIENTS
4 slices bacon
1 potato, peeled, cubed
1 onion, chopped
4 eggs
1 tablespoon milk
1 cup shredded Cheddar cheese
Salt and pepper to taste

Fry the bacon in a skillet until crisp. Remove the bacon to paper towels to drain, reserving the bacon drippings in the skillet. Add the potato to the skillet. Fry until golden brown. Add the onion. Sauté until the onion is tender, but not brown.

Beat the eggs and milk in a bowl. Stir in the cheese. Season with salt and pepper. Pour over the potato mixture.

Cook, covered, until set. Crumble the bacon and sprinkle over the top. Serve immediately.

Serves 4 to 6

Southwestern Eggs

INGREDIENTS
1 onion, chopped
1 pound pork sausage, crumbled
8 ounces sliced mushrooms
Salt and pepper to taste
6 eggs
3 tablespoons sour cream
1 (10-ounce) can tomatoes with green chiles
6 ounces shredded Cheddar cheese
6 ounces shredded Mozzarella cheese
6 ounces shredded Monterey Jack cheese

GARNISH
Salsa

Sauté the onion in a nonstick skillet until translucent. Add the sausage, mushrooms, salt and pepper. Cook until the sausage is brown and cooked through, stirring frequently; drain.

Beat the eggs and sour cream in a mixing bowl for 1 minute. Pour into a greased 9x13-inch baking dish. Bake at 400 degrees for 5 minutes. Remove from oven and reduce the oven temperature to 350 degrees. Spread the drained tomatoes and sausage mixture over the top. Sprinkle with the Cheddar cheese, Mozzarella cheese and Monterey Jack cheese. Bake for 20 minutes. Garnish with salsa.

Serves 10

Note: May assemble ahead of time and chill in the refrigerator until ready to bake. Bake at 350 degrees for 45 minutes.

Sunshine Sunday Morning Brunch

Fresh Fruit Compote, page 70

Sunshine Muffins, page 52

Blueberry Graham Coffee Cake, page 48

Sunday Morning Scramble, at left

Coffee, hot tea and assorted fruit juices

Country Breakfast Tart

This hearty dish is ideal for holiday mornings since it can be prepared the night before!

INGREDIENTS

1 (2-crust) pie pastry
1 cup shredded Cheddar cheese
12 ounces thinly sliced ham
1½ cups thinly sliced, unpeeled red potatoes
1 medium onion, thinly sliced
1 (10-ounce) package frozen spinach, thawed, drained
1 egg
1 tablespoon water

Let the pie pastry stand at room temperature for 15 to 20 minutes. Line a 10-inch deep-dish pie plate with 1 pastry. Sprinkle with ⅓ cup of the cheese. Layer ½ of the ham, ½ of the potatoes and ½ of the onion over the cheese. Spread the spinach over the onion. Sprinkle with ½ of the remaining cheese. Layer the remaining ham, remaining potatoes and remaining onions over the cheese. Sprinkle with the remaining cheese. Press the layers down gently.

Top with the remaining pastry, folding over the bottom pastry and pressing the edges to seal. Cut vents in the top. Brush with a mixture of the egg and water. At this point may refrigerate, covered, overnight. Place on a baking sheet preheated to 375 degrees.

Bake at 375 degrees for 50 to 60 minutes or until the pastry is golden brown and the filling is heated through. Bake for an additional 5 to 10 minutes if prepared ahead.

Serves 8

Note: Make vents in the top of the tart by using a very small cookie cutter. Brush the backs of the cutouts with the egg mixture and arrange decoratively on top of the tart.

Apple Cream Cheese Coffee Cake

This coffee cake received outstanding reviews from our recipe testers. It is well worth the effort.

BATTER	2$\frac{1}{2}$ cups flour
	$\frac{3}{4}$ cup sugar
	$\frac{3}{4}$ cup butter
	$\frac{1}{2}$ teaspoon baking powder
	$\frac{1}{2}$ teaspoon baking soda
	$\frac{1}{4}$ teaspoon salt
	$\frac{3}{4}$ cup sour cream
	1 egg
	1 teaspoon vanilla extract
CREAM CHEESE FILLING	11 ounces cream cheese, softened
	$\frac{1}{2}$ cup sugar
	1 tablespoon lemon juice
	1 teaspoon vanilla extract
	1 egg
APPLE FILLING	1$\frac{1}{2}$ cups thinly sliced peeled apples
	$\frac{3}{4}$ cup raisins
	1 tablespoon lemon juice
	$\frac{1}{2}$ cup sugar
	1 tablespoon cinnamon
TOPPING	$\frac{1}{2}$ cup chopped pecans

For the batter, combine the flour and sugar in a large bowl. Cut in the butter until crumbly. Reserve 1 cup of the mixture for the topping. Add the baking powder, baking soda, salt, sour cream, egg and vanilla to the remaining mixture and mix well.

For the cream cheese filling, beat the cream cheese, sugar, lemon juice and vanilla in a mixing bowl until blended. Add the egg and mix well.

For the apple filling, combine the apples, raisins, lemon juice, sugar and cinnamon in a bowl and toss to mix well.

For the topping, combine the reserved mixture and pecans in a bowl and mix well.

To assemble, spread the batter over the bottom and 2 inches up the side of a greased and floured 9-inch springform pan. Batter should be $\frac{1}{2}$ inch thick on the side. Pour the cream cheese filling in the prepared pan. Spoon the apple filling over the cream cheese filling. Sprinkle with the topping.

Bake at 350 degrees for 70 minutes or until the cream cheese filling is set and the apples are tender. Cool for 15 minutes. Remove the side of the springform pan and serve.

Serves 16

Blueberry Graham Coffee Cake

CINNAMON FILLING	½ cup graham cracker crumbs
	½ cup packed brown sugar
	1 teaspoon cinnamon
BATTER	½ cup (1 stick) butter or margarine, softened
	1 cup sugar
	1 cup sour cream
	3 eggs
	1 teaspoon vanilla extract
	2 cups flour
	1 teaspoon baking soda
	½ teaspoon salt
BLUEBERRIES	2 cups fresh blueberries
	1 tablespoon flour
GARNISH	Sifted confectioners' sugar

For the cinnamon filling, combine the graham cracker crumbs, brown sugar and cinnamon in a bowl and mix well.

For the batter, beat the butter, sugar, sour cream, eggs and vanilla at low speed in a mixing bowl until blended. Add the flour, baking soda and salt. Beat at low speed until moistened. Beat at medium speed for 2 minutes longer.

For the blueberries, combine the blueberries and flour in a bowl and toss to coat well.

To assemble, spread ½ of the batter in a greased and floured 9x13-inch baking pan. Sprinkle the cinnamon filling evenly over the batter. Spread the remaining batter over the cinnamon filling. Spoon the floured blueberries over the top. Bake at 350 degrees for 40 to 50 minutes or until the coffee cake springs back when lightly touched in the center. Cool on a wire rack.

To serve, garnish with confectioners' sugar. Cut into squares.

Serves 12 to 15

Brunch

Cinnamon Pecan Breakfast Ring

INGREDIENTS

6 ounces cream cheese
2 (10-count) cans biscuits
1/2 cup sugar
1 teaspoon cinnamon
3 tablespoons butter, melted
1/3 cup chopped pecans

Cut the cream cheese into 20 pieces and shape into balls. Roll each biscuit into a 3-inch circle. Mix the sugar and cinnamon in a bowl.

Place 1 ball of cream cheese and 1 teaspoon cinnamon mixture on each circle. Bring up the edge of the circle to the top and pinch to seal.

Pour the melted butter into a 5-cup ring mold. Sprinkle with 1/2 of the pecans and 1/2 of the remaining cinnamon mixture. Place 1/2 of the rolls seam side up in the prepared pan. Sprinkle with the remaining pecans and cinnamon mixture. Top with the remaining rolls seam side up.

Bake at 375 degrees for 20 minutes or until brown. Cool in the pan for 5 minutes. Invert onto a serving plate. Serve warm.

Serves 4 to 6

Banana Blueberry Muffins

For chocolate lovers, substitute one cup chocolate chips for the blueberries.

INGREDIENTS

3 ripe bananas, mashed
1/3 cup milk
1/3 cup vegetable oil
1/3 cup packed brown sugar
1 egg
2 cups flour
1 1/2 tablespoons baking powder
1/2 teaspoon salt
1 cup blueberries

Combine the bananas, milk, oil, brown sugar and egg in a large bowl and whisk with a wire whisk until blended. Stir in the flour, baking powder and salt. Fold in the blueberries. Spoon into paper-lined muffin cups. Bake at 400 degrees for 20 minutes or until golden brown.

Makes 1 dozen

Recipe for
Cinnamon Toast

Years ago, I visited my boyfriend (now my husband) and his family for the first time in St. Louis. He was so proud one morning when he woke me for a breakfast that he had prepared himself. I could tell by his expression that he really wanted to impress me, and consequently, as we went down to the kitchen, I was expecting a lavish spread. Imagine my surprise when I sat down and was presented with "Cinnamon and Sugar Toast"! It is still a family favorite.

Karen Boehme

Pumpkin Date Muffins

INGREDIENTS

2½ cups flour
2½ teaspoons baking powder
⅛ teaspoon salt
½ teaspoon cinnamon
⅛ teaspoon nutmeg
2 eggs
2 cups sugar
½ cup vegetable oil
1 teaspoon vanilla extract
1 (15-ounce) can pumpkin
1 cup coarsely chopped pitted dates

Combine the flour, baking powder, salt, cinnamon and nutmeg in a bowl and whisk with a wire whisk. Beat the eggs, sugar, oil and vanilla at medium speed in a mixing bowl until smooth. Add the pumpkin. Beat at low speed until blended. Add the flour mixture gradually, beating constantly. Stir in the dates. Fill paper-lined muffin cups almost full. Bake at 350 degrees for 25 to 30 minutes or until light brown and a wooden pick inserted in the center comes out clean. Cool on a wire rack.

Makes 1½ dozen

Note: Muffins may be wrapped and stored in the refrigerator for 3 to 4 days or stored in the freezer for up to 6 months. Reheat before serving.

Fresh Raspberry Muffins with Streusel Topping

BATTER	1 1/2 cups flour
	1/4 cup sugar
	1/4 cup packed brown sugar
	2 teaspoons baking powder
	1/4 teaspoon salt
	1 1/4 teaspoons cinnamon
	1 egg, lightly beaten
	1/2 cup (1 stick) butter, melted
	1/2 cup milk
	1 1/4 cups fresh raspberries, rinsed, drained
	1 teaspoon lemon zest
STREUSEL TOPPING	3/4 cup packed brown sugar
	1/4 cup flour
	1 teaspoon ground cinnamon
	1 teaspoon lemon zest
	2 tablespoons butter, melted
LEMON GLAZE	1/2 cup confectioners' sugar
	1 tablespoon fresh lemon juice

For the batter, sift the flour, sugar, brown sugar, baking powder, salt and cinnamon into a medium bowl and make a well in the center. Add the egg, butter and milk. Stir just until the ingredients are combined. Stir in the raspberries and lemon zest immediately.

For the streusel topping, mix the brown sugar, flour, cinnamon and lemon zest in a small bowl. Stir in the butter.

For the lemon glaze, mix the confectioners' sugar and lemon juice in a bowl until smooth.

To assemble, spoon the batter into paper-lined muffin cups, filling 3/4 full. Sprinkle the streusel topping evenly over the batter. Bake at 350 degrees for 20 to 25 minutes or until brown.

Drizzle the lemon glaze over the warm muffins.

Makes 1 dozen

Raspberries

Fresh raspberries are a local favorite and a hallmark of summer in St. Louis. When choosing raspberries, select solid, plump berries that have a good color. Raspberries with the caps intact may be underripe. Raspberries crush easily, so when cleaning these delicate berries, rinse them carefully with a light spray and lay them on paper towels to dry.

Sunshine Muffins

A basket of Sunshine Muffins will brighten any brunch or luncheon buffet.

INGREDIENTS

2 cups flour
1 cup sugar
2 teaspoons baking powder
1/2 teaspoon cinnamon
1/4 teaspoon ginger
1/2 cup shredded carrot
1/2 cup each raisins and chopped pecans
1 (8-ounce) can crushed pineapple
2 eggs
1/2 cup (1 stick) margarine, melted
1 teaspoon vanilla extract
Dark brown sugar to taste

Combine the flour, sugar, baking powder, cinnamon and ginger in a large bowl and mix well. Stir in the carrot, raisins and pecans.

Combine the undrained pineapple, eggs, margarine and vanilla in a small bowl and mix well. Add to the dry ingredients and stir until blended. Spoon into 12 greased 2 1/2-inch muffin cups. Bake at 375 degrees for 20 to 25 minutes or until golden brown. Remove from the pan to a wire rack to cool. Sprinkle the muffins with brown sugar.

Makes 1 dozen

French Breakfast Puffs

INGREDIENTS

1 1/2 cups sifted flour
1 1/2 teaspoons baking powder
1/2 teaspoon salt
1/4 teaspoon nutmeg
1 cup sugar
1/2 cup (1 stick) butter or margarine, softened
1 egg
1/2 cup milk
1 teaspoon cinnamon
6 tablespoons butter or margarine, melted

Sift the flour, baking powder, salt and nutmeg together. Beat 1/2 cup of the sugar, 1/2 cup butter and egg in a mixing bowl until creamy. Add the flour mixture alternately with the milk, beating well after each addition. Fill 12 greased or paper-lined muffin cups 2/3 full.

Bake at 350 degrees for 20 to 25 minutes or until the puffs test done.

Mix remaining 1/2 cup sugar and cinnamon in a bowl. Dip hot puffs in 6 tablespoons melted butter; coat with the cinnamon sugar. Serve warm.

Makes 1 dozen

Cheesy Artichoke Bread

This delicious cheesy bread is great with a salad or as an appetizer.

INGREDIENTS

1/4 cup (1/2 stick) butter or margarine
2 to 3 garlic cloves, minced
2 teaspoons sesame seeds
1 (14-ounce) can artichoke hearts, drained, chopped
1 cup shredded Monterey Jack cheese
1 cup grated Parmesan cheese
1/2 cup sour cream
1 (16-ounce) loaf French bread
1/2 cup shredded Cheddar cheese

Melt the butter in a large skillet. Add the garlic and sesame seeds. Cook until light brown, stirring constantly. Remove from heat. Place in a large bowl.

Stir in the artichoke hearts, Monterey Jack cheese, Parmesan cheese and sour cream.

Cover and chill until ready to use. Let stand at room temperature for 10 minutes before using.

Cut the bread into halves lengthwise. Scoop out the center of each half and reserve, leaving a 1-inch shell.

Crumble the reserved bread into the artichoke mixture and stir to mix well. Spoon evenly into the bread shells. Sprinkle with Cheddar cheese. Place each half on a baking sheet.

Bake, covered with foil, at 350 degrees for 25 minutes. Bake, uncovered, for 5 minutes longer or until the Cheddar cheese melts. Cut into slices and serve immediately.

Serves 12

Doughnuts in the Snow

My mother-in-law, a local St. Louisan, always makes doughnuts on the day of the first snow. You never know for sure when that will be, and the anticipation is always great. When the call goes out that Mom is making doughnuts, the whole family heads to her house. There is always a pot of soup or chili on the stove, and as soon as dinner is over the doughnuts begin. The rule is that if you do not help make them, you can't eat them! We all share the jobs of cutting, frying, and coating the doughnuts either with glaze or cinnamon and sugar. Those doughnuts are warm and delicious and make a cold, snowy day worth celebrating. Ten people in the kitchen are always a lot of fun, and as you can imagine, there are rarely any doughnuts left.

Jenifer Corbin

Glazed Lemon Thyme Bread

BREAD

2 cups flour
1 1/2 teaspoons baking powder
1/4 teaspoon salt
3/4 cup milk
1 tablespoon chopped fresh lemon balm or
  lemon juice
1 tablespoon chopped fresh lemon thyme, or
  1 teaspoon dried thyme
1/2 cup (1 stick) butter or margarine, softened
1 cup sugar
2 eggs
1 tablespoon lemon zest

LEMON GLAZE

1 cup confectioners' sugar
2 tablespoons lemon juice

For the bread, mix the flour, baking powder and salt together. Combine the milk, lemon balm and lemon thyme in a saucepan. Bring to a boil and remove from heat. Let stand, covered, until cool.

Beat the butter in a mixing bowl until creamy. Add the sugar gradually, beating constantly until light and fluffy. Add the eggs 1 at a time, beating well after each addition.

Add the flour mixture alternately with the milk mixture, beginning and ending with the flour mixture and beating well after each addition. Stir in the lemon zest. Pour into a greased and floured 5x9-inch loaf pan.

Bake at 325 degrees for 50 minutes or until a wooden pick inserted in the center comes out clean. Cool in the pan for 10 minutes. Remove to a wire rack to cool completely.

For the lemon glaze, combine the confectioners' sugar and lemon juice in a bowl and stir until smooth.

To assemble, pour the lemon glaze over the cooled bread. Cut into slices to serve.

Serves 12 to 14

Blue Ribbon Banana Bread

INGREDIENTS

1 cup (2 sticks) margarine, softened
2 cups sugar
4 eggs, lightly beaten
2 teaspoons baking soda
6 tablespoons buttermilk
4 cups flour
6 bananas, mashed
1 cup chopped walnuts, or to taste
1 cup raisins, or to taste

Beat the margarine and sugar in a mixing bowl until creamy. Add the eggs and beat well. Dissolve the baking soda in the buttermilk in a small bowl. Add to the creamed mixture and mix well. Beat in the flour and bananas. Stir in the walnuts and raisins. Spoon into 2 greased loaf pans. Bake at 300 degrees for 1 1/4 hours or until a wooden pick inserted in the centers comes out clean.

Makes 2 loaves

Note: This banana bread freezes well.

Quick and Easy Dill Rolls

INGREDIENTS

1/2 cup milk
1/4 cup water
2 cups flour
1 1/2 tablespoons sugar
1/2 teaspoon salt
1 envelope dry yeast
2 teaspoons dillweed
2 tablespoons butter, chilled

Heat the milk and water in a saucepan to 120 to 130 degrees on a cooking thermometer. Process the flour, sugar, salt, yeast and dillweed in a food processor fitted with a steel blade for 5 seconds. Add the butter. Process for 10 seconds. Add enough of the hot milk mixture in a fine stream to form a ball, processing constantly. Continue to pulse about 50 times to knead the dough. Place the dough in a greased bowl, turning to coat the surface. Cover with plastic wrap. Let rise for 15 minutes. Shape into balls. Place on a lightly greased baking sheet. Let rise for 15 minutes. Bake at 425 degrees for 12 minutes or until golden brown.

Makes 1 dozen

Buttermilk Substitution

If buttermilk is unavailable, try adding 1 tablespoon lemon juice or vinegar to 1 cup milk. Stir the mixture and let stand for 5 to 10 minutes before adding to your recipe.

Parmesan Herb Bread

This moist bread is a wonderful accompaniment to Tortellini Soup (page 68) and a fresh green salad.

INGREDIENTS

1 cup sour cream
1/3 cup milk
3 tablespoons butter, melted
2 1/2 cups flour
1 tablespoon sugar
1 teaspoon baking soda
1/2 teaspoon salt
1/3 cup grated Parmesan cheese
1 tablespoon minced onion
2 teaspoons Italian seasoning
1 egg white, lightly beaten
Grated Parmesan cheese to taste
Italian seasoning to taste

Combine the sour cream, milk and butter in a small bowl and mix well. Combine the flour, sugar, baking soda, salt, 1/3 cup Parmesan cheese, onion and 2 teaspoons Italian seasoning in a large bowl and mix well. Add the sour cream mixture and stir until moistened. Knead on a lightly floured surface for 1 minute or until smooth. Divide the dough into 2 equal portions. Shape each portion into a round loaf. Place the loaves on a greased baking sheet. Brush the tops with egg white. Sprinkle with Parmesan cheese and Italian seasoning to taste. Cut an "X" 1/2 inch through the top of each loaf. Bake at 350 degrees for 30 to 35 minutes or until golden brown.

Makes 2 loaves

Soups & Salads

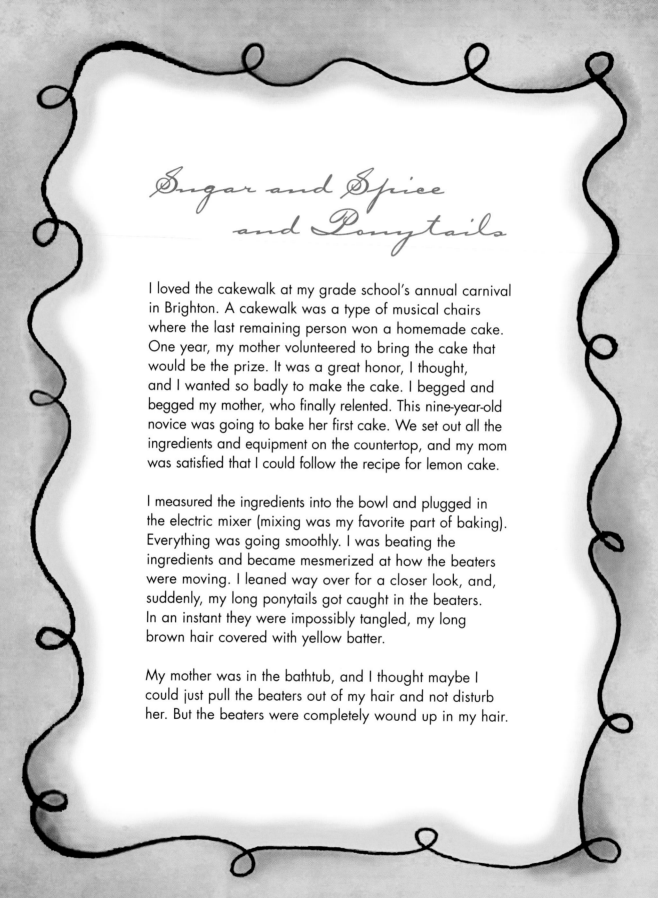

Sugar and Spice and Ponytails

I loved the cakewalk at my grade school's annual carnival in Brighton. A cakewalk was a type of musical chairs where the last remaining person won a homemade cake. One year, my mother volunteered to bring the cake that would be the prize. It was a great honor, I thought, and I wanted so badly to make the cake. I begged and begged my mother, who finally relented. This nine-year-old novice was going to bake her first cake. We set out all the ingredients and equipment on the countertop, and my mom was satisfied that I could follow the recipe for lemon cake.

I measured the ingredients into the bowl and plugged in the electric mixer (mixing was my favorite part of baking). Everything was going smoothly. I was beating the ingredients and became mesmerized at how the beaters were moving. I leaned way over for a closer look, and, suddenly, my long ponytails got caught in the beaters. In an instant they were impossibly tangled, my long brown hair covered with yellow batter.

My mother was in the bathtub, and I thought maybe I could just pull the beaters out of my hair and not disturb her. But the beaters were completely wound up in my hair.

So I picked up the whole mess, bowl, batter, beaters, and hair, and walked to the bathroom to show her what happened. Of course she rescued me, but there was no cake for the cakewalk, unfortunately. And you can bet I have done all future baking with my hair far from the beaters' reach.

Christine Blazevic

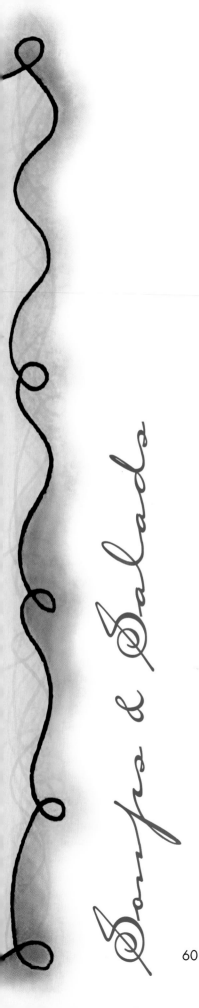

Portuguese Sausage Bean Soup

INGREDIENTS

2 cups dried kidney or pinto beans
4 meaty ham hocks
14 cups water
1 large onion, sliced
1 garlic clove, minced
4 pounds Portuguese or Italian sausage, cut into
    1-inch pieces
1 tablespoon olive oil
1 (24-ounce) can whole tomatoes
1 (8-ounce) can tomato sauce
1 small head cabbage, sliced
½ cup uncooked elbow macaroni
Salt and pepper to taste

Rinse and sort the beans. Soak the beans in water to cover in a bowl for 8 to 12 hours. Drain the beans and place in a large stockpot. Add the ham hocks and 14 cups water. Simmer until tender.

Sauté the onion, garlic and sausage in olive oil in a skillet until the sausage is cooked through. Add the tomatoes and tomato sauce and mix well. Stir into the bean mixture. Simmer for 15 minutes. Add the cabbage, macaroni, salt and pepper. Cook for 20 minutes. Serve immediately.

Serves 16

Spicy Black Bean Soup

Serve with corn bread and a green salad for a hearty meal with a southwestern flair.

INGREDIENTS

1 onion, chopped
2 tablespoons olive oil
2 garlic cloves, minced
1 (15-ounce) can diced tomatoes
1 jalapeño pepper, seeded, chopped
1/2 teaspoon oregano
1/4 teaspoon salt
1/4 teaspoon freshly ground black pepper
Juice of 1 lime
1 (15-ounce) can black beans, rinsed, drained
1 cup chicken stock

Sauté the onion in the olive oil in a medium skillet until tender. Add the garlic. Sauté for 1 minute. Stir in the undrained tomatoes, jalapeño pepper, oregano, salt, pepper and lime juice. Cook for 5 minutes, stirring frequently. Add the beans and mix well. Simmer, covered, for 25 minutes, stirring occasionally. Remove from heat. Cool to room temperature.

Purée the bean mixture 1/2 at a time in a blender or food processor and pour into a large saucepan. Add the chicken stock. Cook until heated through, stirring frequently.

Serves 2

Garnishes for Soup

Sour cream

Chopped fresh tomato

Lime wedges

Chopped green onions

Shredded Cheddar cheese

Crumbled bacon

Salsa

Cilantro

Carrot Ginger Soup

INGREDIENTS

4 carrots, chopped
2 garlic cloves, chopped
2 ribs celery, chopped
1 yellow onion, chopped
1 red bell pepper, chopped
2 tablespoons olive oil
6 cups chicken stock
1 1/2 teaspoons coriander seeds, toasted
2 tablespoons minced gingerroot
1/2 cup uncooked rice
3 bay leaves
1/3 cup honey
Salt and pepper to taste

Sauté the carrots, garlic, celery, onion and red pepper in the olive oil in a stockpot until the onion is translucent. Add the chicken stock, coriander seeds, gingerroot, rice and bay leaves. Simmer until the carrots and rice are tender. Cool to room temperature. Discard the bay leaves.

Process in batches in a blender or food processor until smooth and return to the stockpot. Cook over low heat until heated through, adding additional chicken stock if needed for the desired consistency. Stir in the honey, salt and pepper.

Serves 6 to 8

Pumpkin Corn Soup with Ginger Lime Cream

SOUP	6 cups fresh or frozen whole kernel corn
	3 cups water
	4 garlic cloves, minced
	1 1/2 teaspoons salt
	1 teaspoon ground white pepper
	6 to 7 cups chicken broth
	6 cups mashed cooked pumpkin or canned pumpkin
GINGER LIME CREAM	1/2 cup fresh lime juice
	2 tablespoons grated fresh gingerroot
	1 tablespoon lime zest
	1 cup whipping cream
GARNISH	Lime zest

For the soup, combine the corn and water in a stockpot. Cook, covered, over medium-high heat for 10 minutes or until tender. Process in a food processor for 2 minutes or until smooth. Pour through a wire-mesh strainer into a bowl, discarding the pulp. Combine the strained mixture, garlic, salt, white pepper and 6 cups of the chicken broth in a Dutch oven. Bring to a boil over medium-high heat. Reduce heat to low. Stir in the pumpkin. Simmer for 10 minutes, adding the remaining chicken broth as needed for the desired consistency and stirring constantly.

For the ginger lime cream, combine the lime juice and ginger in a small saucepan. Cook over medium heat for 2 minutes. Remove from heat. Pour through a wire-mesh strainer into a small mixing bowl, discarding the pulp. Add the lime zest and whipping cream. Beat at medium speed until soft peaks form.

To assemble, ladle into soup bowls. Dollop with ginger lime cream. Garnish with lime zest.

Serves 8

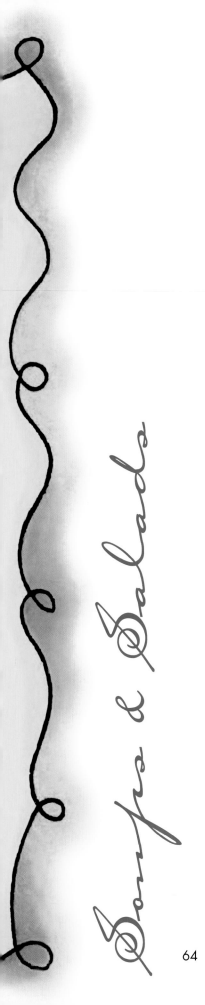

Cream of Red Bell Pepper Soup

Makes a beautiful scarlet soup with a mellow flavor and adds a festive touch to your holiday celebrations. It may be served hot or cold.

INGREDIENTS	
	6 medium red bell peppers
	1½ cups chopped onions
	½ cup chopped carrot
	2 tablespoons unsalted butter
	2 garlic cloves, minced
	1 cup dry white wine
	6 cups chicken stock
	1 bay leaf
	Salt and cayenne pepper to taste
	2 cups heavy cream
GARNISH	1 tablespoon chopped fresh herbs, such as parsley, chives, chervil or basil, or roasted red bell pepper slices

Place the red peppers on a baking sheet. Broil close to the heat source until charred and blistered on all sides. Place the red peppers in a nonrecyled paper bag. Cool for 10 minutes. Peel the red peppers, discarding the seeds. Cut the red peppers into pieces.

Sauté the onions and carrot in the butter in a large skillet for 5 minutes or until tender, but not brown. Add the garlic. Cook for 2 minutes. Add the roasted red peppers and wine. Bring to a boil. Cook until the liquid is reduced by half. Add the chicken stock and bay leaf. Season with salt and cayenne pepper to taste. Simmer for 20 minutes or until the vegetables are tender. Discard the bay leaf.

Purée the mixture in batches in a blender or food processor until smooth. Pour through a sieve into a saucepan, discarding the pulp. Add the cream. Boil for 2 to 3 minutes. Adjust the seasonings to taste.

To serve, ladle into soup bowls. Garnish with chopped fresh herbs or roasted red pepper slices.

Serves 8

Note: May prepare the roasted red peppers up to 1 day ahead.

Butternut Bisque

INGREDIENTS

1 pound butternut squash
2 green apples, peeled, sliced
1 medium onion, chopped
4 cups chicken stock
2 slices white bread, trimmed, cubed
1/8 teaspoon rosemary
1/8 teaspoon marjoram
Salt and freshly ground pepper to taste
2 egg yolks
1/4 cup whipping cream

Peel the squash. Cut into halves and discard the seeds. Cut the squash into large pieces. Combine the squash, apples, onion, chicken stock, bread, rosemary, marjoram, salt and pepper in a heavy 3-quart stockpot.

Simmer, uncovered, for 35 to 45 minutes or until the squash is tender. Purée the squash mixture in batches in a blender until smooth and return to the stockpot.

Beat the egg yolks and cream in a small bowl. Whisk in a small amount of the hot soup with a wire whisk; add to the soup in the stockpot. Reheat the soup, but do not boil. Serve immediately.

Serves 4

Butternut Squash

Butternut squash is shaped like a large pear with buttery-tan skin and weighs two to three pounds. The pulp is moist and sweet. When choosing, look for a squash that is firm and heavy with no cracks or soft spots.

Spicy Chicken Chili

INGREDIENTS	2½ to 3 pounds chicken breasts
	6 cups chicken broth
	2 tablespoons extra-virgin olive oil
	2 medium onions, chopped
	3 large garlic cloves, chopped
	3 or 4 (3-inch) fresh red or green chiles, finely chopped (about ¼ cup)
	1 tablespoon cumin
	1 tablespoon Mexican oregano
	½ teaspoon cinnamon
	2 (15-ounce) cans Great Northern beans, rinsed, drained
	1 tablespoon kosher salt (optional)
	Tabasco sauce or hot pepper sauce to taste
	1 cup shredded Monterey Jack cheese
	1 pound macaroni, cooked (optional)
	3 cups shredded Monterey Jack cheese
GARNISHES	Sour cream
	Salsa
	Lime wedges

Combine the chicken and chicken broth in a large stockpot. Bring to a simmer. Cook, uncovered, for 20 minutes or until cooked through. Cool the chicken in the broth for 15 minutes or longer.

Drain the chicken, reserving the broth. Pour the reserved broth through a strainer into a large bowl. Skim the broth and set aside. Let chicken cool. Shred or chop the chicken in a bowl, discarding the skin and bones. Chill, covered, in the refrigerator.

Heat the olive oil in the stockpot over medium heat. Add the onions. Sauté for 8 to 10 minutes or until light brown. Add the garlic. Sauté for 30 seconds. Add the red chiles, cumin, oregano, cinnamon and strained broth and stir to mix well. Cover the stockpot partially and reduce heat. Simmer for 1 hour. Stir in the beans. Simmer for 20 minutes. Stir in the chicken. Simmer for 5 minutes. Season with kosher salt and Tabasco sauce. Stir in 1 cup cheese.

To serve, ladle the chili over the macaroni in soup bowls. Sprinkle with the remaining cheese. Garnish with sour cream, salsa and lime wedges.

Serves 8

Cajun Jambalaya

THREE-PEPPER SEASONING	2 tablespoons salt
	1 tablespoon red pepper
	1 teaspoon white pepper
	1 teaspoon black pepper
	1 teaspoon garlic powder
JAMBALAYA	8 ounces andouille, sliced
	2 tablespoons olive oil
	1 (14-ounce) can tomatoes
	1 large onion, chopped
	1/2 cup chopped celery
	1/2 cup chopped green bell pepper
	2 garlic cloves, minced
	1/4 cup (1/2 stick) butter or margarine
	1/2 (6-ounce) can tomato paste
	1/2 cup water
	4 boneless skinless chicken breasts, cut into bite-size pieces
	1/4 teaspoon hot pepper sauce
	1 cup long grain rice, cooked

For the three-pepper seasoning, combine the salt, red pepper, white pepper, black pepper and garlic powder in a container with a tight-fitting lid. Cover and shake well. Store at room temperature. Use to season jambalaya, meats, fish, vegetables and soups. This recipe makes 1/4 cup.

For the jambalaya, sauté the sausage in the olive oil in a skillet for 4 to 5 minutes or until cooked through. Drain the tomatoes, reserving the juice. Chop the tomatoes.

Sauté the onion, celery, green pepper and garlic in the butter in a 3-quart saucepan until tender. Stir in the tomatoes, reserved tomato juice, tomato paste, sausage, water and 1 1/4 teaspoons of the three-pepper seasoning. Bring to a boil and reduce heat. Simmer, covered, for 30 minutes. Stir in the chicken and hot pepper sauce. Simmer, covered, for 15 minutes or until the chicken is cooked through and tender. Stir in the rice. Cook until heated through, stirring occasionally.

Serves 6

Tortellini Soup

An intriguing combination of balsamic vinegar and fresh basil complement this soup.

INGREDIENTS

4 cups canned chicken broth
1 (9-ounce) package fresh cheese, chicken or portobello mushroom tortellini
1 (15-ounce) can cannellini, drained
1 (15-ounce) can diced Italian-seasoned tomatoes
1/2 cup shredded fresh basil
2 tablespoons balsamic vinegar
Salt to taste

GARNISHES

1/3 cup grated Parmesan cheese or asiago cheese
1 1/2 teaspoons freshly ground pepper

Bring the chicken broth to a boil in a large stockpot. Add the tortellini. Cook for 4 minutes. Stir in the beans and tomatoes and reduce heat. Simmer for 5 minutes. Remove from heat. Stir in the basil, balsamic vinegar and salt.

To serve, ladle into soup bowls. Garnish with the Parmesan cheese and pepper.

Serves 4 to 6

Chicken Tortilla Soup

INGREDIENTS
4 corn tortillas, cut into 1/2x2-inch strips
6 garlic cloves, crushed
1/2 cup chopped fresh cilantro
1 bunch green onions, chopped
1/4 cup vegetable oil
1 (14-ounce) can diced tomatoes
1 (10-ounce) can diced tomatoes and green chiles
1 (4-ounce) can chopped green chiles
2 tablespoons cumin
1 tablespoon chili powder
3 bay leaves
6 cups chicken stock
1 to 2 cups shredded or chopped cooked
   chicken breasts
1 tablespoon fresh lime juice

GARNISHES
Lime slices
Chopped tomatoes
Sliced avocados
Shredded Monterey Jack or Cheddar cheese
Sprigs of cilantro
Sour cream

Cover a baking sheet with parchment paper and spray with nonstick cooking spray. Place the tortilla strips evenly on the prepared baking sheet. Coat the tortilla strips with nonstick cooking spray. Bake at 350 degrees for 10 minutes or until crisp. Watch carefully to prevent burning.

Sauté the garlic, cilantro and green onions in hot oil in a skillet. Remove as much of the oil as possible with a spoon. Add the tomatoes, tomatoes with green chiles, green chiles, cumin, chili powder and bay leaves. Simmer for 15 minutes. Add the chicken stock and chicken. Simmer for 15 minutes. Stir in the lime juice. Discard the bay leaves.

To serve, ladle into soup bowls. Top with the toasted tortilla strips. Garnish with lime slices, tomatoes, avocados, cheese, cilantro and/or sour cream.

Serves 6

Southwest Supper

Summer Salsa and chips, page 21

Chicken Tortilla Soup, at left

Spicy Green Enchiladas, page 178

Key Lime Pie with Chocolate Crust, page 222

Frozen margaritas and assorted flavored iced teas

Sweet Melon Soup

This soup is a refreshing addition to any summer menu. Serve in hollowed-out melon halves.

INGREDIENTS	1 large cantaloupe
	1/4 cup orange juice
	1/4 cup honey, or to taste
	1/4 cup whipping cream
GARNISH	Cinnamon to taste

Cut the cantaloupe into halves, discarding the seeds. Scoop out the pulp and place in a blender or food processor container, reserving the shells. Process the pulp until puréed. Add the orange juice, honey and whipping cream. Process until blended. Pour into a container with a lid. Chill, covered, for 1 hour.

To serve, ladle into the reserved shells or serving bowls. Garnish with cinnamon.

Serves 2

Fresh Fruit Compote

INGREDIENTS	1 cup white grape juice
	1/2 cup orange marmalade
	1/4 cup orange liqueur or orange juice
	10 cups fresh fruit in any combination
GARNISH	Fresh mint leaves

Combine the grape juice, marmalade and liqueur in a bowl and blend well. Place the fresh fruit in a large bowl. Add the grape juice mixture and stir gently. Chill, covered, for 1 to 2 hours, stirring 1 to 2 times. Spoon into a carved melon or large serving bowl. Garnish with mint leaves.

Serves 10 to 12

Note: Use fresh fruit such as strawberries, honeydew melon balls, cantaloupe balls, watermelon balls, grapes, blueberries or raspberries.

Walnut Orange Spinach Salad

DIJON MUSTARD
VINAIGRETTE
4 teaspoons balsamic vinegar
1 1/2 teaspoons Dijon mustard
1/4 teaspoon salt
1/4 teaspoon freshly ground pepper
1/4 cup extra-virgin olive oil

SALAD
8 ounces spinach leaves, trimmed
1 (7-ounce) can mandarin oranges
1/4 cup chopped walnuts
1/4 cup sliced red onion
1/4 cup crumbled feta cheese

For the vinaigrette, blend the vinegar, Dijon mustard, salt and pepper in a bowl. Add the olive oil in a fine stream, whisking constantly with a wire whisk until blended.

For the salad, combine the spinach, mandarin oranges, walnuts and onion in a large serving bowl. Add the vinaigrette and toss gently to evenly coat. Sprinkle with feta cheese.

Serves 4

Spicy Cumin Vinaigrette

INGREDIENTS
1 teaspoon minced garlic
1/2 teaspoon kosher salt
3 tablespoons red wine vinegar
2 tablespoons Dijon mustard
1 teaspoon cumin
1/2 teaspoon oregano
Freshly ground pepper to taste
2/3 cup olive oil

Mix the garlic and kosher salt in a bowl to form a paste. Add the vinegar, Dijon mustard, cumin, oregano and pepper and blend well. Add the olive oil gradually, whisking constantly with a wire whisk to blend. May serve over a salad of chilled mixed greens, chopped avocado, peppers, tomato and star fruit.

Makes about 1 cup

Cranberry and Pecan Salad

CRANBERRY VINAIGRETTE
½ cup fresh or thawed frozen cranberries
½ cup balsamic vinegar
1 tablespoon chopped red onion
2 tablespoons sugar
2 teaspoons prepared mustard
2 cups vegetable oil

SALAD
2 heads Bibb lettuce, torn
1 cup dried cranberries
½ cup chopped pecans
1 cup crumbled goat cheese

For the vinaigrette, purée the cranberries in a food processor. Add the vinegar, onion, sugar and mustard. Process until blended. Add the oil in a fine stream, processing constantly until blended. The vinaigrette will be thick and can be made 1 to 2 days ahead of time and chilled. Mix before using.

For the salad, combine the lettuce, cranberries and pecans in a serving bowl. Add the vinaigrette and toss to coat well. Sprinkle with goat cheese.

Serves 8

Autumn Salad

APPLE CIDER VINAIGRETTE
3 tablespoons olive oil
3 tablespoons apple cider vinegar

SALAD
1 head Bibb lettuce, torn
1 (10-ounce) package baby spinach
3 green onions, chopped
1 green apple, sliced
½ cup seedless red grapes, cut into halves
¼ cup coarsely chopped walnuts

For the vinaigrette, whisk the olive oil and vinegar in a bowl with a wire whisk until blended.

For the salad, combine the lettuce, spinach, green onions, apple, grapes and walnuts in a large serving bowl. Add the vinaigrette just before serving and toss to coat well.

Serves 8

Mixed Greens with Warm Chèvre Toasts

TANGY VINAIGRETTE	3 tablespoons balsamic vinegar
	1½ tablespoons Dijon mustard
	2 green onions, minced
	¾ cup extra-virgin olive oil
	Salt and pepper to taste
CHÈVRE TOASTS	2 (4-ounce) logs chèvre
	½ cup sesame seeds, lightly toasted
	16 (¼-inch-thick) slices thin French baguette, lightly toasted
SALAD	6 to 8 cups mixed salad greens
	16 ounces kalamata olives, drained, pitted

For the vinaigrette, combine the vinegar, Dijon mustard and green onions in a small bowl. Add the olive oil gradually, whisking constantly with a wire whisk until blended. Season with salt and pepper. Chill, covered, until serving time. The vinaigrette can be stored in the refrigerator for up to 2 weeks.

For the chèvre toasts, cut each log of the goat cheese into 8 even slices. Coat each slice with sesame seeds. Place 1 slice chèvre on each baguette slice on a baking sheet. Bake at 400 degrees for 7 to 8 minutes or until warm.

For the salad, place the mixed salad greens in a serving bowl. Add enough of the vinaigrette to coat, tossing gently. Divide among 8 salad plates. Top each salad with an equal number of olives and 2 chèvre toasts. Serve immediately.

Serves 8

Chèvre

There are a wide variety of different chèvres, or cheeses made from goat's milk, available today. The more popular include Montrachet, Bûcheron, and Valencay. Try them paired with an assertive zinfandel or chilled chardonnay.

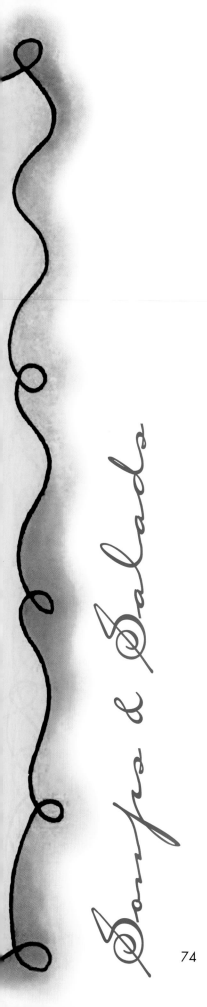

Mixed Baby Greens with Poppy Seed Watermelon Dressing

POPPY SEED	1 1/2 teaspoons white wine vinegar
WATERMELON	1/2 teaspoon unflavored gelatin
DRESSING	1 3/4 cups cubed seeded watermelon
	1/2 teaspoon dry mustard
	2 teaspoons poppy seeds
	2 tablespoons honey
SALAD	4 to 6 cups mixed baby salad greens

For the poppy seed watermelon dressing, combine the vinegar and gelatin in a saucepan. Let stand for 1 minute. Cook over low heat until thickened, stirring constantly. Remove from heat. Let stand until cool. Purée the watermelon in a blender. Add the gelatin mixture, dry mustard, poppy seeds and honey and blend well. Chill, covered, for 8 hours.

For the salad, place the salad greens in a serving bowl. Shake the dressing and pour over the salad greens. Toss until the salad greens are coated. Serve immediately.

Serves 4

Note: May serve the dressing over fresh fruit.

Roquefort and Mixed Green Salad with Balsamic Vinaigrette

BALSAMIC VINAIGRETTE	1/2 cup extra-virgin olive oil
	3 1/2 tablespoons balsamic vinegar
	2 teaspoons minced green onions
	1 tablespoon water
	1 1/2 teaspoons sugar
	1/8 teaspoon cumin
	Salt and freshly ground pepper to taste
SALAD	1 small head red leaf lettuce
	1 small head endive
	1 medium head Boston or Bibb lettuce
	1/2 bunch watercress
	12 button mushrooms, sliced
	3 tomatoes, cut into wedges
	1/2 cup walnut pieces
	3 ounces Roquefort or bleu cheese

For the balsamic vinaigrette, combine the olive oil, vinegar, green onions, water, sugar, cumin, salt and pepper in a glass jar with a lid. Cover and shake until blended. Chill until ready to serve. This recipe makes 1 cup.

For the salad, rinse the red leaf lettuce, endive, Boston lettuce and watercress and drain well. Chill in the refrigerator until ready to assemble the salad. Tear the red leaf lettuce, endive and Boston lettuce into bite-size pieces. Trim the watercress.

Combine the salad greens in a large salad bowl. Top with the mushrooms. Add enough of the balsamic vinaigrette to coat the salad greens, tossing gently. Divide among 6 salad plates. Top each salad with tomato wedges, walnut pieces and cheese. Serve immediately.

Serves 6

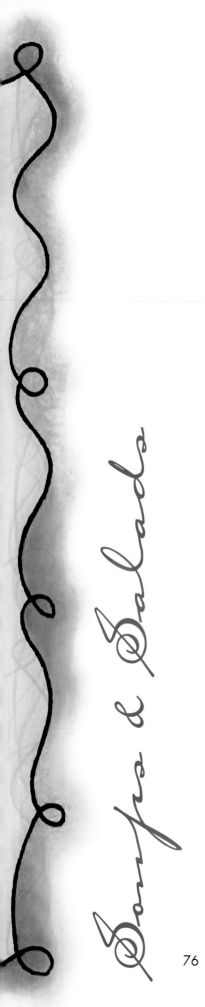

Hearts of Palm Salad with French Vinaigrette

A guaranteed hit at any dinner party.

FRENCH VINAIGRETTE	
	1/4 cup chopped fresh parsley
	1 garlic clove, finely minced
	1/2 cup olive oil
	1/2 cup vegetable oil
	2 tablespoons lemon juice
	1/4 cup red wine vinegar
	2 tablespoons Dijon mustard
	1 teaspoon sugar
	1/4 teaspoon salt
	1/8 teaspoon freshly ground pepper

SALAD	
	1 tablespoon vegetable oil
	1/2 cup slivered almonds
	1 head red leaf lettuce
	1 head Boston or Bibb lettuce
	1 (14-ounce) can hearts of palm, drained, cut crosswise into bite-size pieces
	8 ounces mushrooms, sliced

For the French vinaigrette, combine the parsley, garlic, olive oil, vegetable oil, lemon juice, red wine vinegar, Dijon mustard, sugar, salt and pepper in a 1-pint jar with a lid. Cover and shake until blended. Store the vinaigrette in the refrigerator. May be prepared in a food processor fitted with a knife blade.

For the salad, heat the oil in a small skillet over medium heat. Add the almonds. Sauté until light brown. Drain on paper towels. Let stand until cool.

Rinse the red leaf lettuce and Boston lettuce and drain well. Tear into bite-size pieces and place in a salad bowl. Add the hearts of palm and mushrooms. Chill until serving time. Add the almonds and toss to combine. Add the French vinaigrette 1 spoonful at a time, tossing until the salad greens are lightly coated. Serve immediately.

Serves 8

Black Bean and Corn Salad

INGREDIENTS

1 (15-ounce) can black beans, drained
1 (15-ounce) can whole kernel corn, drained
1 (4-ounce) can chopped green chiles, drained
3 green onions, thinly sliced
1 green bell pepper, chopped
3 tablespoons fresh lime juice
2 tablespoons minced fresh parsley
2 tablespoons olive oil
1/8 teaspoon salt
Pepper to taste
Lettuce leaves or tomato cups

GARNISH

Sprigs of cilantro

Combine the black beans, corn, green chiles, green onions and green pepper in a large bowl. Add the lime juice, parsley, olive oil, salt and pepper and mix well. Chill for 1 to 2 hours before serving.

To serve, spoon onto lettuce leaves or into tomato cups. Garnish each serving with a sprig of cilantro.

Serves 6 to 8

Portobello Mushroom Salad

INGREDIENTS

8 ounces portobello mushrooms
2 tablespoons butter or margarine
1 garlic clove, minced
8 to 10 lettuce leaves
2 tablespoons coarsely chopped red onion
6 to 8 fresh basil leaves, coarsely chopped
3 ounces Brie cheese, cut into small pieces
1 tablespoon balsamic vinegar
2 tablespoons olive oil
Salt and freshly ground pepper to taste

Cut the mushrooms into 1/4-inch slices. Melt the butter in a large skillet. Add the garlic. Cook for 20 seconds. Add the mushrooms. Sauté for 5 minutes.

Tear the lettuce into bite-size pieces. Divide among 2 serving plates. Spoon the onion and basil over the lettuce. Top with the sautéed mushrooms. Place the cheese over the hot mushrooms. The cheese will melt.

Combine the vinegar, olive oil, salt and pepper in a small bowl and whisk to blend. Drizzle over the salads. Serve immediately.

Serves 2

Potato Salad with Goat Cheese and Roasted Red Peppers

Take the time to roast the red peppers to enhance their flavor.

INGREDIENTS

3 pounds medium red or white potatoes
3 large red bell peppers
6 ounces soft goat cheese
1/3 cup olive oil
2 teaspoons salt
1 teaspoon freshly ground pepper
1/2 cup thinly sliced scallions
1/3 cup chopped drained oil-pack sun-dried
    tomatoes
1/3 cup chopped fresh basil
8 ounces bacon, cooked, crumbled

Scrub and rinse the unpeeled potatoes. Place in a steamer basket over water in a large saucepan. Steam over medium-high heat for 20 to 25 minutes or until tender. Drain and let stand until cool.

Roast the red peppers over a gas flame or under a broiler as close to the heat as possible until charred all over, turning frequently. Place in a nonrecyled paper bag and seal the bag. Steam for 10 minutes. Scrape off the charred skins and discard the stems and seeds. Cut the red peppers into thin strips lengthwise; cut crosswise into 1/2-inch pieces. Reserve 1 tablespoon of the juices.

Peel the potatoes and cut into halves lengthwise. Cut into slices 1/3 inch thick. Combine the goat cheese, olive oil, reserved red pepper juice, salt and pepper in a large bowl and mix well. Add the potatoes, red peppers, scallions, sun-dried tomatoes, basil and bacon and stir gently. Serve at room temperature.

Serves 6 to 8

Greek Pasta Salad with Oregano Dressing

OREGANO DRESSING	1/3 cup olive oil
	1/4 cup lemon juice
	1 1/2 teaspoons crushed oregano leaves
	1 teaspoon garlic powder
	1 teaspoon dry mustard
	3/4 teaspoon salt
	1/4 teaspoon coarsely ground pepper
SALAD	12 ounces rotini
	4 cups bite-size spinach pieces
	1 cup cherry tomato halves
	1 cup crumbled feta cheese
	1/4 cup pitted kalamata olives

For the oregano dressing, combine the olive oil, lemon juice, oregano, garlic powder, dry mustard, salt and pepper in a small bowl. Whisk with a wire whisk until blended.

For the salad, cook the pasta using the package directions. Rinse under cold running water and drain. Place in a large bowl. Add the spinach and tomatoes. Add the oregano dressing and toss to coat. Sprinkle with feta cheese and olives.

Serves 6

Note: May prepare ahead of time, but add the spinach just before serving.

Italian Pasta Salad

A summer treat for picnics or barbecues.

DRESSING	1 cup vinegar
	1/2 cup grated Parmesan cheese
	3 tablespoons garlic powder
	1 1/2 tablespoons oregano
	2 tablespoons salt
	2 tablespoons pepper
	1 1/2 cups vegetable oil

SALAD	30 ounces tri-color rotini
	1 large head cauliflower, cut into florets
	2 bunches broccoli, cut into florets
	1 pound carrots, thinly sliced
	1 1/2 pounds Roma tomatoes, chopped
	12 ounces provolone cheese, thinly sliced
	8 ounces hot pepper cheese, finely chopped
	8 ounces shredded mozzarella cheese
	2 medium onions, finely chopped
	2 green bell peppers, finely chopped
	12 ounces hard salami, thinly sliced, cut into strips
	8 ounces pepperoni, chopped
	1 large can sliced black olives, drained

For the dressing, combine the vinegar, Parmesan cheese, garlic powder, oregano, salt and pepper in a bowl and blend well. Add the oil in a fine stream and whisk with a wire whisk to blend.

For the salad, cook the pasta using package directions until al dente; drain. Place in a large bowl. Blanch the cauliflower, broccoli and carrots in 3 separate batches in a saucepan. Add the cauliflower, broccoli, carrots, tomatoes, provolone cheese, hot pepper cheese, mozzarella cheese, onions, green peppers, salami, pepperoni and black olives to the pasta and toss to mix. Add the dressing and toss until coated. Marinate, covered, in the refrigerator for 4 hours or longer before serving.

Serves 15 to 20

Orzo Salad Florentine

INGREDIENTS

16 ounces orzo
Chicken stock
2 tablespoons olive oil
1 bunch green onions, chopped
1 bunch fresh spinach, julienned
1 cup julienned fresh basil
1 1/2 cups crumbled feta cheese
3/4 cup toasted pine nuts
1 1/2 teaspoons fresh lemon juice
1/4 cup olive oil
Salt and freshly cracked pepper to taste

Cook the orzo using the package directions, substituting chicken stock for the water; drain. Add 2 tablespoons olive oil and toss well. Combine the orzo, green onions, spinach, basil, feta cheese and pine nuts in a large bowl and mix gently.

Whisk the lemon juice and 1/4 cup olive oil with a wire whisk in a small bowl until blended. Add to the orzo mixture and toss to coat. Season with salt and pepper.

Serves 6

Caribbean Chicken Salad

INGREDIENTS

5 cups chopped cooked chicken or turkey
2 cups drained pineapple chunks
1 cup sliced water chestnuts
1 cup sliced celery
1/2 cup chopped green onions
1/2 cup slivered almonds
1 cup sour cream
3 to 4 tablespoons Major Grey chutney
1 teaspoon curry powder
1 teaspoon mayonnaise

GARNISH

Chinese noodles

Combine the chicken, pineapple, water chestnuts, celery, green onions and almonds in a large bowl and mix well. Blend the sour cream, chutney, curry powder and mayonnaise in a small bowl. Add to the chicken mixture and mix well. Spoon into a serving dish. Garnish with Chinese noodles.

Serves 6 to 8

Sesame Peanut Chicken Pasta Salad

INGREDIENTS

8 ounces spaghetti or linguini
2 cups broccoli florets
6 carrots, thinly sliced
2 large garlic cloves
1 (1-inch) piece fresh gingerroot, peeled
1/3 cup peanut butter
1 tablespoon honey
2 tablespoons soy sauce
3 tablespoons Worcestershire sauce
2 tablespoons fresh lemon juice
3/4 cup chicken or vegetable stock
1 tablespoon sesame oil
4 scallions, diagonally sliced
1 (8-ounce) can sliced water chestnuts, drained
1 1/2 cups chopped cooked chicken
4 large Napa cabbage leaves
2 cups thinly shredded Napa cabbage

GARNISH

1/2 cup mandarin oranges

Cook the pasta using the package directions. Add the broccoli and carrots to the pasta about 8 minutes before the pasta is al dente. Cook for 4 minutes longer; drain and rinse in cold water. Place in a large bowl.

Purée the garlic, gingerroot, peanut butter, honey, soy sauce, Worcestershire sauce, lemon juice, stock and sesame oil in a food processor or blender until smooth. Pour over the pasta mixture. Reserve 1/4 cup of the scallions. Add the remaining scallions, water chestnuts and chicken to the pasta mixture and toss to mix well.

To serve, line individual serving plates with a cabbage leaf. Sprinkle each leaf with 1/2 cup shredded cabbage. Mound the pasta mixture on top. Sprinkle with the reserved scallions. Garnish with mandarin oranges. Serve immediately.

Serves 4

Spanish Paella Salad

BRANDIED MAYONNAISE	3/4 cup mayonnaise
	1 tablespoon brandy
	1 teaspoon lemon juice
SALAD	4 boneless skinless chicken breasts
	3 tablespoons olive oil
	1/4 cup white wine
	1 1/2 teaspoons salt
	1 pound shrimp, peeled, deveined
	1/4 teaspoon saffron
	2 teaspoons lemon juice
	2 cups chicken broth
	1 medium onion, chopped
	1 garlic clove, minced
	3 tablespoons olive oil
	1 1/2 cups uncooked rice
	1 1/2 cups sliced green olives
	Salt to taste
GARNISHES	1 ripe avocado, cut into wedges
	Tomato wedges

For the brandied mayonnaise, blend the mayonnaise, brandy and lemon juice in a bowl. Chill, covered, until serving time.

For the salad, brown the chicken in 3 tablespoons olive oil in a skillet. Add the wine and 1 1/2 teaspoons salt. Simmer for 10 minutes. Turn over the chicken. Add the shrimp. Simmer, covered, for 10 minutes. Remove the chicken and shrimp to a heated platter. Pour the pan drippings into a glass measure; skim. Stir in the saffron and lemon juice. Add enough of the chicken broth to measure 2 1/2 cups.

Sauté the onion and garlic in 3 tablespoons olive oil in the skillet until tender. Add the rice. Cook until opaque, stirring constantly. Add the broth mixture. Bring to a boil and reduce heat. Simmer for 12 to 15 minutes or until the liquid is absorbed.

Cut each chicken breast into 2 or 3 slices. Cut the shrimp into halves lengthwise. Add the chicken, shrimp and olives to the rice mixture and toss to mix. Season with salt to taste. Let stand until cool. Chill, covered, for several hours before serving.

To serve, garnish with avocado and tomato wedges. Serve with the brandied mayonnaise on the side.

Serves 6 to 8

Cajun Crab Toss

DRESSING

1 egg, pasteurized
1 tablespoon Dijon mustard
1 tablespoon lemon juice
¼ cup tarragon vinegar
2 tablespoons minced fresh tarragon leaves, or
    1 teaspoon dried tarragon
¼ teaspoon salt
Freshly ground pepper to taste
¾ cup olive oil
¾ cup vegetable oil

SALAD

1 pound crab meat
6 ounces small salad shrimp
1 cucumber, seeded, cut into chunks
1 green bell pepper, chopped
1 small red onion, chopped
2 tomatoes, peeled, chopped
3 ribs celery, chopped
¼ cup minced parsley
Lettuce leaves

For the dressing, process the egg, Dijon mustard and lemon juice in a food processor until blended. Add the tarragon vinegar, tarragon, salt and pepper and process well. Add a mixture of the olive oil and vegetable oil, processing constantly until all of the oil mixture is incorporated. Process for 10 seconds longer. Store, covered, in the refrigerator.

For the salad, rinse the crab meat and shrimp and drain well. Combine the crab meat, shrimp, cucumber, green pepper, onion, tomatoes, celery and parsley in a bowl and mix well. Stir in enough of the dressing for the desired consistency. Spoon into a large bowl lined with lettuce leaves.

Serves 6

Note: May omit the egg in the dressing, but the dressing will not be as smooth.

Meats

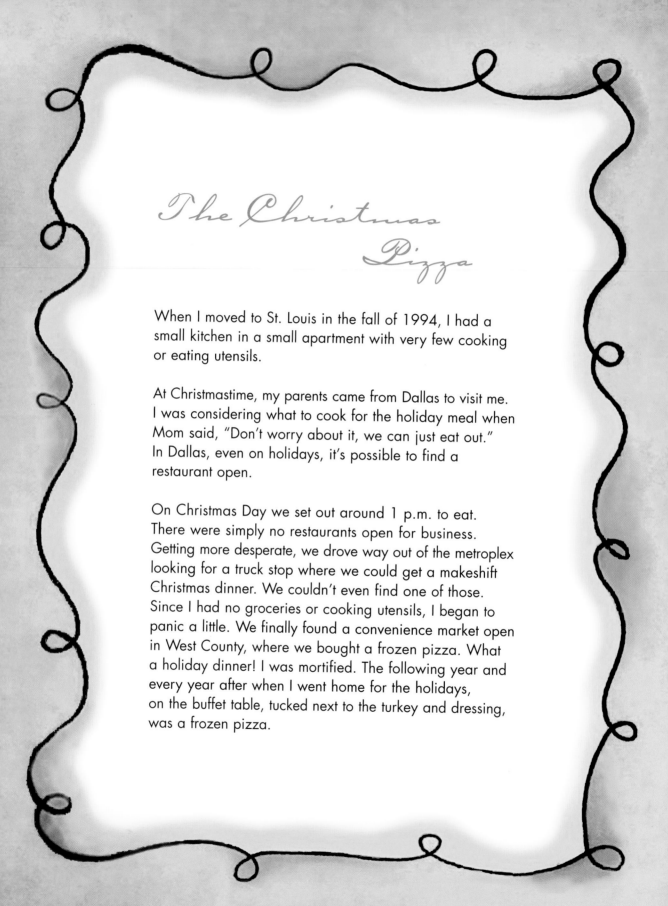

The Christmas Pizza

When I moved to St. Louis in the fall of 1994, I had a small kitchen in a small apartment with very few cooking or eating utensils.

At Christmastime, my parents came from Dallas to visit me. I was considering what to cook for the holiday meal when Mom said, "Don't worry about it, we can just eat out." In Dallas, even on holidays, it's possible to find a restaurant open.

On Christmas Day we set out around 1 p.m. to eat. There were simply no restaurants open for business. Getting more desperate, we drove way out of the metroplex looking for a truck stop where we could get a makeshift Christmas dinner. We couldn't even find one of those. Since I had no groceries or cooking utensils, I began to panic a little. We finally found a convenience market open in West County, where we bought a frozen pizza. What a holiday dinner! I was mortified. The following year and every year after when I went home for the holidays, on the buffet table, tucked next to the turkey and dressing, was a frozen pizza.

Last year, my husband and I hosted my parents and his family for Christmas in our new home. As part of our buffet, we included a frozen pizza, cooked to perfection. My parents were thrilled and my new in-laws were introduced to a new tradition. (The pizza was great; the turkey...needs work.)

Jenni Chambers-Smith

Filet Mignon with Roquefort Sauce

To complement this hearty beef entrée, serve with roasted new potatoes and sautéed carrots and snow peas.

ROQUEFORT SAUCE	2 tablespoons butter
	1/3 cup finely chopped shallots
	2 teaspoons flour
	1/2 cup dry white wine
	2/3 cup Roquefort cheese (3 ounces)
	1/4 cup heavy cream
	Salt and pepper to taste
FILET MIGNONS	2 tablespoons butter
	4 (6- to 8-ounce) filet mignons, 1 inch thick
	Salt and pepper to taste

For the Roquefort sauce, melt the butter in a medium saucepan over medium heat. Add the shallots. Sauté for 5 minutes or until the shallots are just beginning to brown. Add the flour. Cook for 1 minute, stirring constantly. Stir in the wine. Boil for 5 minutes or until the liquid is reduced to 1/4 cup, stirring frequently. Reduce heat to low. Add the cheese. Cook until the cheese is melted, stirring frequently. Add the cream. Simmer for 2 minutes or until thickened to a sauce consistency, stirring constantly. Season with salt and pepper.

For the filet mignons, melt the butter in a large heavy skillet over medium-high heat. Season the filet mignons with salt and pepper. Place in the hot butter in the skillet. Cook on each side for 5 minutes for medium-rare.

To serve, place the filet mignons on a serving plate. Spoon the Roquefort sauce over the top and serve.

Serves 4

Pepper Fillet with Bordelaise Sauce

BUSCH'S GROVE

BORDELAISE SAUCE	4 1/2 to 5 cups water
	3 tablespoons red wine
	2 tablespoons white wine
	4 ounces powdered demi-glace mix
	2 ounces chopped onion
	2 ounces diced pimentos or red bell pepper
	1/4 cup sugar
	2 ounces fresh mushrooms
PEPPER FILLET	1/2 cup virgin olive oil
	2 1/4 ounces cracked pepper
	1 ounce garlic powder
	8 ounces beef fillet, about 2 inches thick

For the bordelaise sauce, bring the water to a boil in a large saucepan. Add the red wine, white wine, demi-glace mix, onion and pimentos. Cook until thickened, stirring frequently. Add additional demi-glace if needed for the desired consistency. Remove from heat slowly. Stir in the sugar and mushrooms.

For the pepper fillet, heat the olive oil in a medium skillet to 350 to 375 degrees on a meat thermometer. Mix the pepper and garlic powder together. Coat the fillet with the pepper mixture. Place in the heated oil. Fry on each side for 5 to 7 minutes for medium-rare.

To serve, place the fillet on a serving plate. Top with 4 to 6 ounces of the bordelaise sauce.

Serves 1

Note: May find powdered demi-glace mix at Allen Foods specialty store.

Busch's Grove

The "clubby" atmosphere and semi-private outdoor cabana dining of Busch's Grove have made it a St. Louis favorite for years. Regulars and newcomers alike come to relax and enjoy the American-Continental fare of this old-time restaurant and watering hole.

Beef Tenderloin with Roasted Shallots and Port

INGREDIENTS

1 1/2 pounds large shallots, peeled, cut into halves lengthwise (about 24)
3 tablespoons olive oil
Salt and pepper to taste
6 cups canned beef broth
1 1/2 cups tawny port
1 tablespoon tomato paste
2 (3-pound) beef tenderloins, trimmed
2 teaspoons thyme
7 slices bacon, chopped
6 tablespoons butter
1 1/2 tablespoons flour

GARNISH

Watercress

Toss the shallots in the olive oil in a 9-inch pie plate. Season with salt and pepper. Bake at 375 degrees for 30 minutes or until the shallots are deep brown and tender, stirring occasionally. Set aside.

Bring the broth and port to a boil in a large saucepan. Boil for 30 minutes or until reduced to 3 3/4 cups. Whisk in the tomato paste with a wire whisk. Set aside.

Pat the beef dry. Sprinkle with thyme and salt and pepper. Sauté the bacon in a large roasting pan over medium heat for 4 minutes or until golden brown. Remove the bacon with a slotted spoon to paper towels to drain. Add the beef to the drippings in the pan. Cook over medium-high heat for 7 minutes or until brown on all sides. Insert a meat thermometer into the center of the beef. Bake at 375 degrees for 45 minutes or until the meat thermometer registers 125 degrees for medium-rare. Remove the beef to a warm platter and tent with foil.

Skim the pan drippings in the roasting pan. Place over high heat. Stir in the broth mixture. Bring to a boil, stirring to deglaze the pan. Pour into a medium saucepan. Bring to a simmer.

Mix 3 tablespoons of the butter and flour in a saucepan to form a paste. Cook over medium heat until light brown. Add the hot broth mixture gradually, whisking constantly with a wire whisk. Simmer for 2 minutes or until thickened, whisking constantly. Whisk in the remaining butter. Stir in the roasted shallots and bacon. Season with salt and pepper.

To serve, cut the beef into slices 1/2 inch thick. Spoon the sauce over the beef. Garnish with watercress. Serve with the remaining sauce.

Serves 12

Note: May prepare the shallots and broth mixture a day ahead. Cover each and chill until ready to use.

Filet Maison

VIVIAN'S VINEYARDS

INGREDIENTS

2 (10-ounce) beef tenderloin filets
1/2 cup clarified butter
1 tablespoon minced garlic
1 teaspoon cracked pepper
6 ounces sliced mushrooms
6 tablespoons brandy
6 tablespoons heavy cream
2 tablespoons Dijon mustard
8 ounces long grain and wild rice, cooked

Place the beef on a rack in a roasting pan. Place in a 500-degree oven. Reduce the oven temperature to 350 degrees. Bake until the desired degree of doneness. May grill if desired.

Heat the clarified butter in a saucepan. Add the garlic, pepper and mushrooms. Sauté until the mushrooms are tender. Do not brown the garlic. Remove from heat. Flambé with the brandy. Cook over medium heat until the sauce is reduced by one-third. Add the cream and Dijon mustard. Cook until the sauce is reduced and has a solid glossy texture around the edge.

To serve, place hot rice in the center of each serving plate. Arrange the beef over the rice. Spoon the sauce over the beef.

Serves 2

Editor's Note: To clarify butter, melt the butter in a small saucepan over low heat until foamy. Remove from heat and let stand until the milk solids settle to the bottom of the saucepan and the salt crystals settle on the top. Skim off the salt crystals and carefully pour the butter oil into a separate container. Discard the milk solids that have settled in the bottom.

Vivian's Vineyards

Located in St. Charles, this small family-owned business serves its guests in a turn-of-the-century two-story brick home that has been converted into an unforgettable dining atmosphere. Vivian's Vineyards is known for its fine food, cocktails, and camaraderie. The eclectic setting and occasional tune on the house accordion will make for a truly enjoyable evening.

Beef Tenderloin with Peppercorn Marsala Sauce

BEEF TENDERLOIN	1 (2-pound) beef tenderloin
	Kosher salt and freshly ground pepper to taste
	1 tablespoon vegetable oil
PEPPERCORN MARSALA SAUCE	2 green onions, finely chopped
	1 cup dry marsala
	1/2 cup beef broth
	1/4 cup dried green peppercorns
	2 teaspoons tomato paste
	12 button mushroom caps, sliced
	6 tablespoons butter
GARNISH	1/4 cup chopped fresh parsley

For the beef tenderloin, rinse the beef and pat dry. Rub with kosher salt and pepper. Heat the oil in a heavy skillet over high heat until hot. Add the beef. Cook for 2 to 3 minutes or until brown on all sides. Remove the beef to a roasting pan, reserving the drippings in the skillet. Bake at 350 degrees for 30 to 40 minutes or until a meat thermometer registers 135 degrees for rare, or until done to taste. Remove the beef to a warm platter, reserving the juices in the pan. Cool for 10 to 15 minutes.

For the peppercorn marsala sauce, sauté the green onions in the reserved drippings in the skillet for 2 minutes. Add the wine and mix well. Cook until the mixture is reduced by half, stirring frequently. Add the beef broth, stirring to deglaze the skillet. Stir in the peppercorns, tomato paste and the reserved juices in the roasting pan. Cook until reduced by half, stirring frequently. Add the mushrooms and butter, stirring until the butter is melted.

To serve, cut the beef into slices. Spoon the peppercorn marsala sauce over the beef. Garnish with parsley.

Serves 4

Sirloin Tip Roast with
Bleu Cheese Butter or Herb Butter

ROAST

1 (4- to 5-pound) sirloin tip roast
3 or 4 garlic cloves, split
2 tablespoons salt
1/2 teaspoon pepper
2 tablespoons crumbled thyme

BLEU CHEESE
BUTTER

1/2 cup (1 stick) butter, softened
2 tablespoons crumbled bleu cheese
2 tablespoons parsley
1 garlic clove, minced

HERB BUTTER

1/2 cup (1 stick) butter, softened
1 tablespoon chopped fresh chives
1 tablespoon chopped fresh parsley
1/2 tablespoon chopped fresh tarragon
1 teaspoon whole-grain mustard
Salt and freshly ground pepper to taste

For the roast, make incisions in the roast and insert the garlic. Rub with salt, pepper and thyme. Insert a meat thermometer into the center of the roast. Place on a grill rack. Grill, covered, for 1 1/2 hours or until the desired degree of doneness. Let stand for 15 minutes.

For the bleu cheese butter, beat the butter and bleu cheese in a mixing bowl until creamy. Add the parsley and garlic and mix well. Serve at room temperature.

For the herb butter, combine the butter, chives, parsley, tarragon, mustard, salt and pepper in a bowl and mix well. Chill, covered, for 1 hour or longer.

To serve, cut the beef into slices. Serve with bleu cheese butter or herb butter.

Serves 4 to 6

Sunday Pot Roast

Serve on a large platter with parslied buttered noodles and top with hot gravy.

INGREDIENTS

Flour for dredging
Salt and pepper to taste
1 (5- to 6-pound) rump or sirloin tip roast
Vegetable oil for browning
6 to 8 carrots, cut into sticks
3 large onions, sliced
1 cup water
1 cup sherry
1/2 cup chili sauce
2 garlic cloves, minced
2 bay leaves
1/2 teaspoon thyme
1/2 teaspoon marjoram
1/2 teaspoon dry mustard
1/2 teaspoon rosemary
Sliced fresh mushrooms
1/2 cup water
3 tablespoons cornstarch

Combine the flour, salt and pepper in a shallow dish. Dredge the beef in the flour mixture. Brown in the oil in a Dutch oven. Remove the beef to a baking sheet, reserving the drippings.

Add the carrots and onions to the reserved drippings. Sauté until the carrots and onions are brown. Stir in 1 cup water, sherry, chili sauce, garlic, bay leaves, thyme, marjoram, dry mustard and rosemary. Return the beef to the Dutch oven.

Bake, covered, at 300 degrees for 3 1/2 hours. Add the mushrooms. Bake for 30 minutes longer. Remove from the oven. Stir in a mixture of 1/2 cup water and cornstarch if needed for the desired consistency. Cook until thickened, stirring constantly. Discard the bay leaves before serving.

Serves 8

Robust Chianti Beef Stew

INGREDIENTS

2 tablespoons olive oil
2 pounds cubed beef
2 teaspoons (heaping) minced garlic
2 tablespoons flour
2 teaspoons salt
1/4 teaspoon pepper
1 (16-ounce) jar spaghetti sauce
2 cups chianti
2 cups water
1 teaspoon Worcestershire sauce
1 teaspoon oregano
2 bay leaves
1/2 teaspoon basil
1/2 teaspoon thyme
1/8 teaspoon crushed red pepper
2 medium yellow onions, quartered
5 carrots, sliced
5 potatoes, coarsely chopped

Heat the oil in a Dutch oven. Add the beef and garlic. Sauté until brown. Stir in the flour, salt and pepper. Add the spaghetti sauce, wine and water. Bring to a simmer, scraping the sides frequently.

Stir in the Worcestershire sauce, oregano, bay leaves, basil, thyme and red pepper. Add the onions, carrots and potatoes and mix well. Remove from heat.

Bake, covered, at 350 degrees for 3 hours or until the beef is cooked through and tender. Discard the bay leaves before serving.

Serves 6

Oriental Flank Steak

INGREDIENTS

1 1/2 pounds flank steak
1/4 cup soy sauce
2 tablespoons honey
1 tablespoon corn oil
1 teaspoon sesame oil
1/2 teaspoon ground ginger
1/8 teaspoon garlic powder

Score the steak. Combine the soy sauce, honey, corn oil, sesame oil, ginger and garlic powder in a sealable plastic food storage bag and mix well. Add the steak and seal the bag. Marinate in the refrigerator for 2 to 4 hours. Drain the steak, discarding the marinade.

Place the steak on a grill rack or on a rack in a broiler pan. Grill or broil for 8 to 10 minutes on each side or to the desired degree of doneness. Cut at a 45-degree angle cross grain into thin slices.

Serves 4 to 6

St. Paddy's Baked Corned Beef

INGREDIENTS

1 (3- to 4-pound) corned beef brisket
1/2 cup packed brown sugar
6 tablespoons prepared mustard
1 (12-ounce) can ginger ale
5 whole cloves

Place the corned beef lean side down on a rack in a roasting pan. Cover with foil. Bake at 350 degrees for 2 1/2 hours.

Combine the brown sugar and mustard in a bowl. Uncover the corned beef and baste with ginger ale. Stud with cloves. Brush the top and sides with the brown sugar mixture.

Bake, uncovered, for 30 to 45 minutes or until the corned beef is glazed. Cool for 15 minutes. Cut the corned beef cross grain into slices.

Serves 6 to 8

Vitello Pizzaiola

GIANFABIO RISTORANTE

INGREDIENTS
- 6 thin veal cutlets
- 1/4 cup flour
- 3 tablespoons olive oil
- 2 medium tomatoes, chopped
- 1 scallion, chopped
- 1/2 teaspoon oregano
- 1/8 teaspoon salt
- 1/8 teaspoon pepper
- 1/4 cup white wine

Dredge the veal lightly in the flour. Heat the olive oil in a skillet. Add the veal. Cook for 2 to 3 minutes on each side. Remove the veal to a warm platter.

Add the tomatoes, scallion, oregano, salt and pepper to the skillet. Stir in the wine. Simmer until the tomatoes are partially cooked through. Return the veal to the skillet. Cook until heated through. Serve with the sauce spooned over the veal.

Serves 2 or 3

Gianfabio Ristorante

This family-owned and -operated restaurant has been a landmark in the Chesterfield area since 1987. Gianfabio's addition of the Il Forno Cafe three years ago has given its guests several dining options. For special occasions or a quiet evening out, one may choose the tranquility of the main dining room. Others will surely enjoy the casual atmosphere of the Cafe or Patio. Regardless of the environment, Gianfabio Ristorante will please any palate.

Saltimbocca

INGREDIENTS

2 pounds veal scallopine
Flour for dredging
3 tablespoons butter
5 tablespoons olive oil
Chopped fresh or dried sage to taste
Salt and pepper to taste
1 1/4 pounds prosciutto, thinly sliced
1 pound fontina cheese, thinly sliced
1/2 cup white wine
1/4 cup dry marsala
1/2 cup chicken stock

Pound the veal 1/8 inch thick. Dredge in the flour and shake off the excess.

Melt 2 tablespoons of the butter and 2 tablespoons of the olive oil in a skillet over medium-high heat. Add enough veal to cover the bottom of the skillet. Cook for 20 seconds per side. Repeat with the remaining butter, olive oil and veal.

Arrange the veal on an ungreased baking sheet, reserving the drippings in the skillet. Sprinkle with sage, salt and pepper. Place prosciutto and cheese on each piece of veal. Bake at 350 degrees for 8 minutes or until the cheese melts.

Add the white wine, marsala and chicken stock to the drippings in the skillet. Cook until reduced by half.

To serve, place the veal on a serving platter. Pour the sauce over the veal.

Serves 6 to 8

Note: May cook the veal ahead of time and let stand until cool. Chill, covered, until ready to use.

Sautéed Stuffed Veal Chops

TONY'S

INGREDIENTS

2 fresh ripe plum tomatoes
4 veal rib chops, 1 inch thick
4 ounces fontina or mozzarella cheese,
  cut into 1/4-inch slices
4 fresh basil leaves
Freshly ground pepper to taste
1 tablespoon extra-virgin olive oil

Remove the skin from the tomatoes with a vegetable peeler. Cut the tomatoes lengthwise into 1/4-inch slices. Remove the seeds with the tip of a paring knife. Place the tomato slices in a strainer and shake 2 or 3 times to remove any juice.

Cut the veal chops horizontally to the bone, forming 2 parallel slices of veal attached to 1 bone. Fold back one of the slices; pound the other slice as thin as possible, moving the pounder outward from the bone. Turn over the chop. Fold back the flattened side and repeat with the other side. Be careful not to pound a hole through the veal. Repeat with the other veal chops.

Divide the tomatoes and cheese into 4 equal portions. Place a portion of tomato, cheese, basil and pepper between each chop, trimming away any excess protruding from the chop. Skewer each chop with 3 round wooden picks to seal the edges.

Heat the olive oil in a skillet. Add the stuffed veal chops. Cook until brown on both sides. Place on a baking sheet. Bake at 400 degrees for 15 minutes. Do not overcook.

Serves 4

Tony's

For a very special evening out, it is hard to top Tony's. The Bommarito family has provided their guests with first-rate food and service since 1946. Tony's is the only St. Louis restaurant to achieve the coveted Five Star Award and is known in culinary circles as one of the world's finest Italian restaurants.

Lamb Stuffed with Spinach and Chèvre

INGREDIENTS

1 tablespoon olive oil
2 tablespoons minced garlic
2 cups drained cooked spinach
8 ounces chèvre
Salt and pepper to taste
1 butterflied leg of lamb (about 5 pounds
    after boning)
2 garlic cloves, slivered
1/2 teaspoon kosher salt
1/2 teaspoon freshly ground pepper
2 tablespoons chopped fresh rosemary leaves

Heat the olive oil in a skillet. Add the minced garlic. Sauté over medium-low heat for 1 minute. Do not brown the garlic. Combine the sautéed garlic, spinach and chèvre in a bowl and mix well. Season with salt and pepper to taste.

Lay the lamb flat on a work surface. Spread evenly with the spinach mixture. Roll up lengthwise and tie at intervals with string. Make small slits in the surface and insert garlic slivers. Sprinkle with kosher salt, 1/2 teaspoon pepper and rosemary. Place in a shallow roasting pan.

Bake at 425 degrees for 1 hour (12 minutes per pound) for rare or until a meat thermometer inserted into the thickest portion registers 140 degrees. Let stand for 15 minutes before serving.

Serves 6 to 8

Note: For medium, bake the lamb for 15 minutes per pound or until the meat thermometer registers 155 degrees.

Zesty Grilled Lamb Chops

INGREDIENTS

6 loin lamb chops (about 1 1/2 pounds)
2 tablespoons water
2 tablespoons red wine vinegar
Juice of 1 lime
1 tablespoon vegetable oil
1 teaspoon grated onion
1/2 teaspoon lemon pepper
1/2 teaspoon coarse ground mustard
1/4 teaspoon ground red pepper
Mint jelly

Trim the lamb chops. Combine the water, vinegar, lime juice, oil, onion, lemon pepper, mustard and red pepper in a sealable plastic food storage bag. Add the lamb chops and seal the bag. Marinate in the refrigerator for 3 to 12 hours.

Drain the lamb chops, discarding the marinade. Place on a grill rack. Grill over medium-hot coals for 4 to 6 minutes per side for medium-rare. Serve with mint jelly.

Serves 2 or 3

Blueberry Pork Tenderloin

An attractive and unusual entrée.

TENDERLOIN	1 (1- to 1¾-pound) pork tenderloin
	2 to 4 slices bacon
BLUEBERRY SAUCE	2 tablespoons butter
	2 medium onions, sliced
	½ teaspoon salt
	¼ teaspoon pepper
	2 tablespoons sugar
	¼ cup sweet sherry, port or chicken broth
	2 tablespoons balsamic vinegar
	1 cup fresh or frozen blueberries
	1 cup cherry tomato halves

For the tenderloin, wrap the tenderloin in the bacon slices. Place on a rack in a broiler pan. Broil 4 to 5 inches from the heat source for 20 minutes or until a meat thermometer inserted into the thickest portion registers 160 degrees, turning occasionally. Remove the pork to a platter and keep warm.

For the blueberry sauce, melt the butter in a large skillet over medium heat. Add the onions, salt and pepper. Sauté for 10 minutes or until the onions are golden brown. Stir in the sugar. Cook for 3 minutes, stirring constantly. Stir in the wine and vinegar. Bring to a boil. Boil gently for 3 minutes. Stir in the blueberries and tomatoes. Cook until heated through.

To serve, cut the tenderloin into thin slices and place on a serving platter. Spoon the blueberry sauce over the top.

Serves 4

Note: May grill the tenderloin, covered, on a grill rack over a drip pan over medium-hot coals for 30 to 40 minutes.

Elegant Pork Tenderloin

Experiment with one or more of the exotic rices available as an attractive side dish.

INGREDIENTS
1 (3-pound) boneless pork tenderloin
1 (12-ounce) package dry fruit mix, chopped
Salt and pepper to taste
1 shallot, minced
1 tablespoon butter
3 tablespoons apricot preserves
1 tablespoon spicy mustard
¼ cup white wine

Hollow out the tenderloin using a round knife sharpener; widen with fingers. Stuff with dry fruit mix. Season with salt and pepper. Place on a grill rack. Grill for 25 to 30 minutes or until the pork tests done.

Sauté the shallot in the butter in a skillet until transparent. Add the preserves, mustard and wine and stir until blended.

To serve, cut the tenderloin into slices. Spoon the sauce over the sliced tenderloin.

Serves 4

Note: May bake at 300 degrees for 90 minutes or until a meat thermometer registers 145 degrees when inserted into the center.

Peppered Pork Tenderloins

This excellent dinner party entrée goes well with stuffed or mashed potatoes.

SOUR CREAM GARLIC SAUCE	¾ cup mayonnaise
	¾ cup sour cream
	⅓ teaspoon salt
	⅓ teaspoon pepper
	½ teaspoon garlic powder, or ½ teaspoon pressed garlic
	1 tablespoon Dijon mustard
	⅓ teaspoon Worcestershire sauce
PORK TENDERLOINS	2 cups vegetable oil
	⅓ cup soy sauce
	¼ cup honey
	1 teaspoon onion powder
	1 teaspoon garlic powder
	4 (8- to 12-ounce) pork tenderloins
	Seasoned salt to taste
	Freshly cracked pepper to taste

For the sour cream garlic sauce, combine the mayonnaise, sour cream, salt, pepper, garlic powder, Dijon mustard and Worcestershire sauce in a bowl and mix well. Chill, covered, in the refrigerator. Bring to room temperature before serving.

For the tenderloins, combine the oil, soy sauce, honey, onion powder and garlic powder in a large nonmetal bowl and mix well. Trim the tenderloins and place in the marinade. Marinate in the refrigerator for 6 hours or longer, turning occasionally.

Drain the tenderloins, discarding the marinade. Sprinkle the tenderloins with seasoned salt and pepper. Place on a grill rack or on a rack in a broiler pan. Grill over hot coals or broil for 3 to 4 minutes per side. Cut each tenderloin crosswise into 6 to 8 pieces ¾ inch thick. Return the slices to the grill or broiler rack. Grill or broil for 4 to 5 minutes or until cooked through.

To serve, arrange the tenderloin medallions on a serving plate. Serve with the sour cream garlic sauce.

Serves 4

Note: The sour cream garlic sauce makes twice as much as needed. It is also good served on baked potatoes or as a dipping sauce for fresh vegetables.

Meats

Pork Tenderloins with Raspberry Sauce

SOULARD'S RESTAURANT

RASPBERRY SAUCE | 18 ounces raspberry preserves
1/4 cup red wine vinegar
2 tablespoons soy sauce
1/2 tablespoon prepared horseradish
1/2 tablespoon catsup
1 tablespoon garlic powder

PORK TENDERLOINS | 4 cups vegetable oil
1/2 cup soy sauce
1/2 cup honey
1 tablespoon onion powder
6 (8-ounce) pork tenderloins
Seasoned salt to taste
Cracked pepper to taste

For the raspberry sauce, combine the preserves, vinegar, soy sauce, horseradish, catsup and garlic powder in a bowl and whisk with a wire whisk until blended. Serve warm or at room temperature.

For the tenderloins, combine the oil, soy sauce, honey and onion powder in a large bowl and whisk with a wire whisk to blend well. Season the tenderloins with seasoned salt and cracked pepper. Place in a sealable plastic food storage bag. Add the marinade and seal the bag. Marinate in the refrigerator for 6 hours or longer.

Drain the tenderloins, discarding the marinade. Place the tenderloins on a grill rack. Grill for 2 minutes on each side. Cut each tenderloin into 6 medallions. Grill the medallions for 2 minutes on each side or until cooked through.

To serve, place 6 medallions on each serving plate. Spoon the raspberry sauce over the top.

Serves 6

Soulard's Restaurant

Soulard's Restaurant is located one block south of the Historic Soulard Market, known as the oldest outdoor market west of the Mississippi and established in 1779. Owned and operated by two brothers for nearly twenty years, Soulard's has been named as the locale for the "Best Private Parties" by the St. Louis Riverfront Times for the last four years. The restaurant's specialties include fresh seafood, pasta dishes, steaks, and of course their renowned stuffed pork tenderloin!

Pepper and Sage Grilled Pork Tenderloin

INGREDIENTS	2 small dried red chiles, broken
	2 teaspoons black peppercorns
	1½ teaspoons coarse salt
	3 large garlic cloves, peeled
	3 tablespoons fresh sage leaves
	2 pork tenderloins, trimmed (1½ pounds total)
	2 tablespoons olive oil
GARNISH	Sage leaves

Process the chiles, peppercorns and salt in a small food processor until medium ground. Add the garlic and sage and process to form a paste. Rub on the tenderloins. Brush with olive oil. Place on a grill rack.

Grill over medium-hot coals for 5 minutes or until brown on all sides. Move the tenderloins to the side of the grill. Grill for 10 to 12 minutes or until a meat thermometer inserted into the thickest portion registers 145 to 150 degrees.

To serve, remove the tenderloins to a cutting board and let stand for 5 minutes. Cut cross grain into ½-inch slices. Place on a serving platter. Garnish with sage leaves. Serve hot or at room temperature.

Serves 4

Super Barbecue Sauce

SUPER SMOKERS BBQ

To make the sauce less spicy, eliminate or reduce the Pickapeppa sauce. This flavorful sauce can be used for just about any application.

INGREDIENTS
- 4 cups catsup
- 1 (10-ounce) bottle Heinz 57 sauce
- 1 (10-ounce) bottle A-1 steak sauce
- 1 1/2 cups apple juice
- 1/2 cup Pickapeppa sauce
- 1/3 cup Worcestershire sauce
- 1/3 cup dark corn syrup
- 2 teaspoons pepper
- 1 teaspoon granulated garlic

Combine the catsup, Heinz 57 sauce, A-1 steak sauce, apple juice, Pickapeppa sauce, Worcestershire sauce, corn syrup, pepper and garlic in a bowl and mix well. Use to brush on pork, beef or poultry during the last 10 minutes of grilling or baking.

Makes about 7 cups

All-Purpose Lemon Pepper Dry Rub

SUPER SMOKERS BBQ

This is a simple, yet flavorful, spice blend. It also works well sprinkled on vegetables just before baking or grilling.

INGREDIENTS
- 1 tablespoon lemon pepper
- 1 teaspoon garlic powder
- 1/2 teaspoon salt
- 1/2 teaspoon sugar
- 1/4 teaspoon cayenne pepper

Combine the lemon pepper, garlic powder, salt, sugar and cayenne pepper in a bowl and mix well. Use to rub on pork, beef or poultry. Refrigerate, covered, for 8 to 12 hours before smoking or grilling.

Makes about 2 tablespoons

Super Smokers BBQ

Super Smokers BBQ is the only St. Louis born company that has placed in the top ten at the World Barbecue Championships in Memphis five times since 1994. The National Pork Producers Association has named them one of the "Top Ten" restaurants in the nation. In addition to their original location in Eureka, Missouri, there are now others in O'Fallon, Illinois and Chesterfield, Missouri.

Pork with Spinach and Herb Stuffing

SPINACH AND HERB STUFFING	1 (10-ounce) package frozen chopped spinach, thawed, drained
	3 ounces cream cheese, softened
	4 green onions, chopped
	1/4 cup chopped fresh basil
	3 garlic cloves, finely chopped
	1 1/2 teaspoons chopped fresh tarragon
	1/4 teaspoon red pepper
PORK	1 (3- to 4-pound) boneless pork loin
	1/4 teaspoon salt
	1/8 teaspoon pepper

For the spinach and herb stuffing, combine the spinach, cream cheese, green onions, basil, garlic, tarragon and red pepper in a bowl and mix well.

For the pork, cut lengthwise to, but not through the pork; open to enlarge into a rectangle. Pound 1/2 inch thick with a meat mallet. Sprinkle with salt and pepper. Spread with the spinach and herb stuffing. Roll up the pork beginning at the long side. Secure at 2-inch intervals with string. Place on a greased rack in a shallow roasting pan.

Bake at 325 degrees for 1 1/4 hours or until a meat thermometer inserted into the thickest portion registers 160 degrees. Remove from the oven and let stand for 10 minutes.

To serve, remove the string and place the pork on a serving platter. Cut into slices to serve.

Serves 10

Pork and Pear Stir-Fry

INGREDIENTS

1 pound pork tenderloin
1/2 cup plum preserves
3 tablespoons soy sauce
2 tablespoons lemon juice
1 tablespoon prepared horseradish
2 teaspoons cornstarch
1/2 teaspoon crushed red pepper
1 tablespoon vegetable oil
2 teaspoons grated fresh gingerroot
1 medium yellow or red bell pepper, julienned
1 green bell pepper, julienned
2 medium pears, peeled, cored, thinly sliced
1 (8-ounce) can sliced water chestnuts, drained
2 tablespoons sliced almonds
Hot cooked rice

Cut the tenderloin into thin bite-sized pieces. Combine the plum preserves, soy sauce, lemon juice, horseradish, cornstarch and red pepper in a bowl and blend well.

Heat the oil in a wok or large skillet. Add the gingerroot. Stir-fry for 15 seconds; do not burn. Add the yellow pepper, green pepper and pears. Stir-fry for 2 minutes. Remove the peppers and pears to a bowl and keep warm.

Add the pork to the wok. Stir-fry for 2 to 3 minutes or until cooked through. Push the pork to the side of the wok. Add the plum preserve mixture. Cook until thickened and bubbly, stirring constantly. Return the peppers and pears to the wok. Stir to mix all the ingredients in the wok together. Add the water chestnuts. Cook until heated through. Add the almonds just before serving. Serve over hot rice.

Serves 2

Pork and Red Onion Kabobs

This marinade is also wonderful on lamb.

INGREDIENTS

1 1/2 pounds pork tenderloin, cut into
    16 equal pieces
1 red onion, cut into 16 equal pieces
1/3 cup vegetable oil
1/4 cup dry red wine
3 tablespoons red wine vinegar
3 tablespoons soy sauce
1 tablespoon chopped garlic
1 tablespoon chopped peeled fresh gingerroot
1 1/2 teaspoons sugar

Place the pork and red onion pieces in a glass dish. Combine the oil, wine, vinegar, soy sauce, garlic, gingerroot and sugar in a bowl and blend well. Pour over the pork mixture. Marinate for 2 hours at room temperature, turning occasionally or marinate, covered, in the refrigerator for up to 24 hours, turning occasionally.

Drain the pork mixture, discarding the marinade. Thread 2 pieces of pork and 2 pieces of onion alternately onto each skewer. Place on a grill rack. Grill until the pork is cooked through.

Serves 4

Spicy Pork Stew

INGREDIENTS

1 1/2 to 2 pounds boneless pork loin,
    cut into 1-inch pieces
1/4 cup olive oil
1 medium onion, cut into thin wedges
2 garlic cloves, minced
1 (2 1/2- to 3-pound) head cabbage,
    torn into chunks
1 (15-ounce) can tomatoes
2 tablespoons flour
1 tablespoon chili powder
1 teaspoon oregano
3/4 teaspoon salt
1/4 teaspoon red pepper flakes
1/2 to 3/4 cup water

Cook the pork in the olive oil in a Dutch oven over high heat for 3 to 5 minutes or until brown. Add the onion and garlic. Sauté for 1 to 2 minutes or until tender. Add the cabbage, undrained tomatoes, flour, chili powder, oregano, salt and red pepper flakes and mix well. Bring to a boil and reduce heat. Simmer, covered, for 10 minutes. Add enough water to almost cover. Simmer, covered, for 20 to 30 minutes or until the pork and cabbage are cooked through.

Serves 6 to 8

Poultry & Seafood

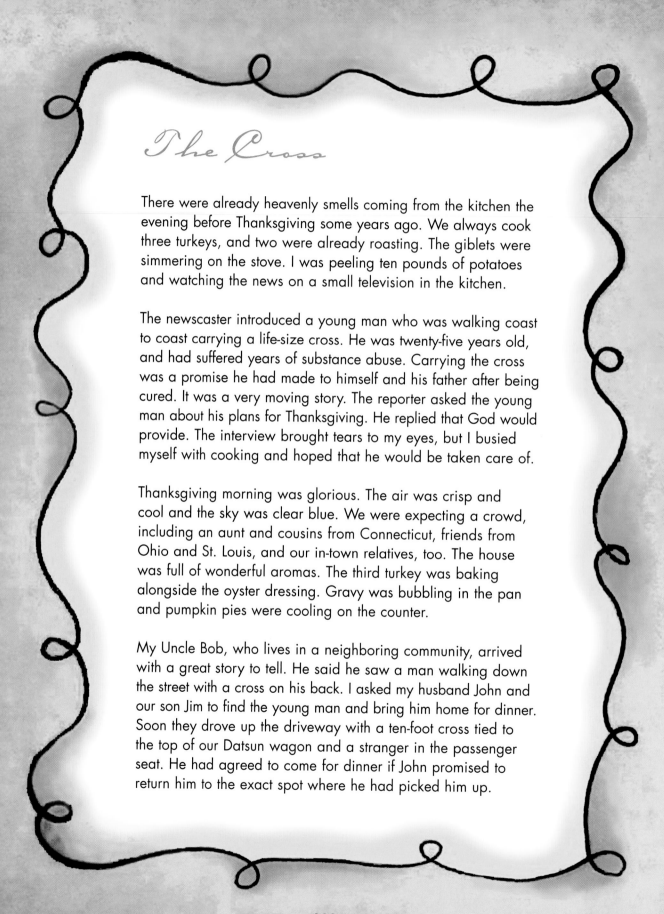

The Cross

There were already heavenly smells coming from the kitchen the evening before Thanksgiving some years ago. We always cook three turkeys, and two were already roasting. The giblets were simmering on the stove. I was peeling ten pounds of potatoes and watching the news on a small television in the kitchen.

The newscaster introduced a young man who was walking coast to coast carrying a life-size cross. He was twenty-five years old, and had suffered years of substance abuse. Carrying the cross was a promise he had made to himself and his father after being cured. It was a very moving story. The reporter asked the young man about his plans for Thanksgiving. He replied that God would provide. The interview brought tears to my eyes, but I busied myself with cooking and hoped that he would be taken care of.

Thanksgiving morning was glorious. The air was crisp and cool and the sky was clear blue. We were expecting a crowd, including an aunt and cousins from Connecticut, friends from Ohio and St. Louis, and our in-town relatives, too. The house was full of wonderful aromas. The third turkey was baking alongside the oyster dressing. Gravy was bubbling in the pan and pumpkin pies were cooling on the counter.

My Uncle Bob, who lives in a neighboring community, arrived with a great story to tell. He said he saw a man walking down the street with a cross on his back. I asked my husband John and our son Jim to find the young man and bring him home for dinner. Soon they drove up the driveway with a ten-foot cross tied to the top of our Datsun wagon and a stranger in the passenger seat. He had agreed to come for dinner if John promised to return him to the exact spot where he had picked him up.

We sat around the kitchen table enjoying stories about his trip across America and the kindness that people shared. We checked him into a downtown motel so he would have a warm place to stay that night. The next morning, John and another relative drove him to the previous day's stopping point. We heard from him once again when he called our Connecticut cousins as he passed through a nearby town. We all felt that the presence of this determined young stranger was a gift that none of us would ever forget.

Claire Devoto

Almond Chicken with Tarragon Tomato Sauce

INGREDIENTS

8 to 12 boneless skinless chicken breasts
3 tablespoons butter
2 tablespoons chopped onion
1 garlic clove, minced
2 tablespoons tomato paste
2 tablespoons flour
1 1/2 cups chicken broth
3 tablespoons dry sherry
3 tablespoons slivered almonds
1/2 teaspoon tarragon
Salt and pepper to taste
1 cup sour cream, at room temperature
1/2 cup shredded Gruyère cheese

Brown the chicken in the butter in a skillet. Remove the chicken to a platter and keep warm.

Add the onion and garlic to the skillet. Sauté for 2 to 3 minutes. Add the tomato paste and flour. Cook until blended, stirring constantly. Stir in the chicken broth and sherry gradually. Cook until smooth and slightly thickened, stirring constantly.

Return the chicken to the skillet. Add the almonds, tarragon, salt and pepper. Simmer, covered, over low heat for 25 to 30 minutes or until the chicken is cooked through.

Arrange the chicken in a shallow 9x13-inch baking dish. Stir the sour cream into the sauce in the skillet. Pour over the chicken. Sprinkle with cheese. Broil until brown.

Serves 8 to 12

Savory Chicken and Rice Bake

Try this make-ahead casserole with a green salad and crusty French bread.

INGREDIENTS

½ cup mushrooms, sliced
4 green onions, sliced
2 tablespoons butter
1⅓ cups milk
2 eggs, beaten
½ teaspoon dillweed
¼ teaspoon marjoram
¼ teaspoon salt
Pepper to taste
3 cups cooked long grain rice
1 cup cubed cooked chicken
1 cup cubed cooked ham
2¼ cups shredded Swiss cheese

Sauté the mushrooms and green onions in the butter in a saucepan over medium heat for 5 minutes. Remove from heat. Add the milk, eggs, dillweed, marjoram, salt and pepper to taste and mix well.

Combine the rice, chicken, ham and Swiss cheese in a large bowl and mix well. Spoon into a nonstick 9x13-inch baking dish. Spoon the sautéed mixture over the top. Bake, covered, at 350 degrees for 1 hour.

Serves 6 to 8

Chicken Cacciatore Casserole

Welcome a new neighbor with this easy dish, that freezes well.

INGREDIENTS

1 1/4 cups uncooked quick-cooking rice
6 chicken breast fillets, cooked, chopped
1 (14-ounce) can chicken broth
6 ounces sliced fresh mushrooms
1/2 cup water
1/2 cup dry white wine
1/2 cup chopped onion
1/2 cup chopped green bell pepper
1 tablespoon chopped fresh parsley
2 teaspoons basil
1 teaspoon garlic salt
1/2 teaspoon Italian seasoning
1/4 teaspoon pepper
1 cup grated Parmesan cheese
1 tablespoon chopped fresh parsley

Spread the rice in a lightly greased 9x13-inch baking dish. Combine the chicken, chicken broth, mushrooms, water, wine, onion, green pepper, 1 tablespoon parsley, basil, garlic salt, Italian seasoning and pepper in a bowl and mix well. Pour over the rice.

Bake, covered, at 350 degrees for 45 to 50 minutes or until the rice is tender. Uncover and sprinkle with Parmesan cheese. Bake for 5 minutes longer. Sprinkle with 1 tablespoon parsley just before serving.

Serves 6

Chicken Bozada

KEMOLL'S

Well worth the effort to impress your dinner party guests.

CHICKEN	8 (6-ounce) boneless skinless chicken breasts Olive oil
SHERRY SAUCE	2 tablespoons chopped fresh garlic 1/4 cup olive oil 2 cups medium dry sherry 1 (3-inch) piece fresh rosemary 1/2 cup lemon juice 4 cups 40% cream Salt and pepper to taste
ASSEMBLY	1 to 1 1/2 cups Italian bread crumbs 1/4 cup toasted pine nuts
GARNISH	8 sprigs fresh rosemary, or other garnish of choice

For the chicken, coat the chicken lightly with olive oil. Place on a grill rack. Grill until the chicken is cooked through. Cover and keep warm.

For the sherry sauce, sauté the garlic in the olive oil in a medium saucepan; do not brown. Add the sherry. Boil for 45 minutes or until reduced by half. Add the rosemary, lemon juice and cream. Boil until thick and creamy, scraping the side of the pan with a spatula. Season with salt and pepper.

To assemble, place the chicken in a baking pan. Sprinkle with the bread crumbs. Broil until slightly brown. Spoon the sherry sauce onto individual serving plates. Place the chicken in the sauce. Sprinkle with pine nuts. Garnish with rosemary.

Serves 8

Note: May use pork tenderloin instead of chicken breasts. If a grill is not accessible, pan sear the olive oil-coated chicken breasts, then bake at 350 degrees for 15 to 20 minutes or until cooked through.

Kemoll's

Originally located near the old Sportsman's Park, Kemoll's was frequented by the sports crowd with a passion for good Italian food, especially cannelloni and toasted ravioli. After sixty-two years on Grand Boulevard, Kemoll's moved to its present location in the heart of downtown St. Louis. Since 1927, this family-run restaurant has been a favorite for those who truly enjoy fine Italian food.

Caribbean Coconut Chicken

CHICKEN
6 boneless skinless chicken breasts
Salt and freshly ground pepper
6 tablespoons butter
2 medium sweet onions, thinly sliced
1 (2-ounce) jar pimentos
3 tablespoons dried currants
1 1/2 tablespoons fresh lemon juice
1 tablespoon brown sugar
1/4 teaspoon salt
1/8 teaspoon powdered saffron

COCONUT TOPPING
3 tablespoons butter, melted
1 1/2 tablespoons fresh lemon juice
3 tablespoons chopped fresh parsley
1/4 teaspoon salt
1/4 teaspoon freshly ground pepper
3/4 cup flaked coconut

For the chicken, season the chicken with salt and pepper to taste. Heat 3 tablespoons of the butter in a large skillet over medium heat until bubbly. Add the chicken. Cook for 10 to 12 minutes or until golden brown and almost opaque.

Arrange the chicken in a single layer in a shallow baking dish. Add the remaining 3 tablespoons butter to the skillet. Add the onions. Sauté until tender. Stir in the pimentos, currants, lemon juice, brown sugar, 1/4 teaspoon salt and saffron. Spoon over the chicken. Bake, covered, at 375 degrees for 10 minutes.

For the coconut topping, combine the melted butter, lemon juice, parsley, salt, pepper and coconut in a bowl and toss to mix well.

To assemble, sprinkle the coconut topping over the chicken. Bake, uncovered, for 10 minutes.

Serves 6

Herb-Marinated Chicken with Apricot Chutney

This versatile chutney is also delicious with pork or seafood.

CHICKEN	8 boneless skinless chicken breasts
	1/4 cup olive oil
	1 tablespoon white wine
	1 tablespoon lemon juice
	1 tablespoon Dijon mustard
	1 teaspoon salt
	1/2 teaspoon pepper
	1/2 teaspoon thyme

APRICOT CHUTNEY	2 tablespoons olive oil
	1/2 cup chopped onion
	2 tablespoons minced fresh gingerroot
	1 quart whole plum tomatoes, chopped, drained
	8 ounces dried Turkish apricots, chopped
	1/2 cup apricot preserves
	1/2 cup minced fresh cilantro
	1 tablespoon lemon juice
	1 cinnamon stick
	1 teaspoon ground coriander
	1 teaspoon white pepper
	1/2 teaspoon salt

For the chicken, place the chicken in a sealable plastic freezer bag. Combine the olive oil, wine, lemon juice, Dijon mustard, salt, pepper and thyme in a bowl and blend well. Pour over the chicken and seal the bag. Marinate in the refrigerator for 30 to 60 minutes. Drain the chicken, discarding the marinade. Place in a baking dish. Bake at 375 degrees for 15 minutes or until the chicken is cooked through, turning once.

For the apricot chutney, heat the olive oil in a skillet over medium heat. Add the onion and gingerroot. Sauté until the onion is tender. Add the tomatoes, apricots, preserves, cilantro, lemon juice, cinnamon, coriander, white pepper and salt. Simmer for 20 minutes, stirring occasionally. Spoon into a hot sterilized jar; seal with a 2-piece lid. Chill or freeze until ready to serve.

To serve, place the chicken on individual serving plates. Serve with the chilled or reheated apricot chutney.

Serves 8

Boursin-Stuffed Chicken

INGREDIENTS

5 ounces boursin cheese with herbs and garlic, softened
1 tablespoon flour
¼ cup shredded carrots
¼ cup coarsely chopped walnuts (optional)
2 tablespoons chopped fresh parsley
4 boneless skinless chicken breasts
⅓ cup dry bread crumbs
2 tablespoons grated Parmesan cheese
2 tablespoons chopped fresh parsley
2 tablespoons butter, melted

Combine the cheese, flour, carrots, walnuts and 2 tablespoons parsley in a bowl and blend well. Pound each chicken breast into a 5½-inch square. Place ¼ of the cheese mixture on each square. Fold in the sides and roll up; secure with wooden picks or skewers.

Mix the bread crumbs, Parmesan cheese and 2 tablespoons parsley in a shallow dish. Brush the chicken roll-ups with butter. Roll in the bread crumb mixture. Place on a wire rack sprayed with nonstick cooking spray. Place the rack in an 8x8-inch baking pan. Bake at 350 degrees for 40 minutes or until the chicken is cooked through.

Serves 4

Poultry & Seafood

Golden Cardamom Chicken

CHICKEN

8 chicken breasts
1/4 cup walnuts, coarsely ground
1/4 cup filberts, coarsely ground
1/4 cup (1/2 stick) butter
3 tart apples, cored, peeled
2/3 cup golden raisins
1/2 cup currants
1/2 teaspoon cinnamon
1/4 teaspoon finely crushed fresh rosemary
1/8 teaspoon thyme
7 cardamom pods, peeled, ground, or
    3/4 teaspoon crushed cardamom
1/2 teaspoon salt
1/4 cup fruity white wine
1/2 cup chicken broth

HONEY GLAZE

6 egg yolks
1/8 teaspoon saffron
2 tablespoons honey

Cardamom

Cardamom is a spice that is grown primarily in India and is a member of the ginger family. Loose and ground seeds lose flavor quickly, so it is best to buy whole pods. Discard the papery pods before grinding the seeds.

For the chicken, sauté the chicken, walnuts and filberts in the butter in a Dutch oven until the chicken is brown. Remove from heat.

Cut the apples into thin slivers. Combine with the raisins and currants in a bowl and mix well. Mix the cinnamon, rosemary, thyme, cardamom and salt in a small bowl. Add to the apple mixture and mix well. Spoon over the chicken. Add the wine and chicken broth. Bake at 350 degrees for 45 to 55 minutes or until the chicken is tender.

For the honey glaze, beat the egg yolks, saffron and honey in a mixing bowl until blended.

To assemble, pour the honey glaze evenly over the chicken to coat, or brush over the chicken with a pastry brush. Increase the oven temperature to 400 degrees. Bake for 5 to 7 minutes or until the glaze is set. Serve warm.

Serves 8

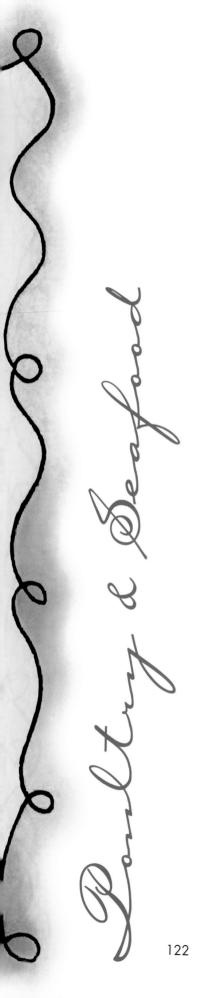

Crab-Stuffed Chicken with Hollandaise Sauce

CHICKEN	8 boneless skinless chicken breasts
	Salt and pepper to taste
	½ cup chopped onion
	½ cup chopped celery
	3 tablespoons butter
	3 tablespoons dry white wine
	1 (7-ounce) can crab meat, drained
	½ cup herb-seasoned stuffing mix
	2 tablespoons flour
	½ teaspoon paprika
	2 tablespoons butter, melted
HOLLANDAISE SAUCE	2 envelopes hollandaise sauce mix
	1½ cups milk
	¼ cup dry white wine
	1 cup shredded Swiss cheese

For the chicken, pound the chicken between 2 sheets of waxed paper to flatten. Season with salt and pepper.

Sauté the onion and celery in 3 tablespoons butter in a skillet until tender. Remove from heat. Add the wine, crab meat and stuffing mix and toss to mix well.

Spoon the stuffing mixture onto each chicken breast. Fold in the sides and roll up; secure with wooden picks.

Mix the flour and paprika in a shallow dish. Dredge the chicken roll-ups in the flour mixture. Arrange seam side down in a glass baking dish. Drizzle with 2 tablespoons melted butter. Bake, uncovered, at 375 degrees for 1 hour or until the chicken is cooked through.

For the hollandaise sauce, blend the hollandaise sauce mix and milk in a saucepan. Cook until thickened, stirring constantly. Add the wine and cheese. Cook until the cheese melts, stirring constantly.

To serve, place the chicken on individual serving plates. Spoon the hollandaise sauce over the chicken. Serve with additional stuffing if desired.

Serves 8

Chicken Prosciutto Medallions with Béarnaise Sauce

CHICKEN
⅓ cup extra-virgin olive oil
1 tablespoon chopped fresh parsley
1 tablespoon chopped fresh tarragon
1 tablespoon green peppercorns, crushed
1 garlic clove, minced
Salt and pepper to taste
8 boneless chicken breasts
8 slices prosciutto
½ cup chicken broth, heated
1 tablespoon chopped fresh parsley

BÉARNAISE SAUCE
1 cup (2 sticks) butter
5 green onions, finely chopped
3 tablespoons white wine vinegar
1 tablespoon chopped fresh tarragon
Salt and cracked pepper to taste
4 egg yolks

For the chicken, combine the olive oil, 1 tablespoon parsley, tarragon, peppercorns, garlic, salt and pepper in a bowl and mix well. Place the chicken between 2 sheets of waxed paper. Pound ¼ inch thick with a meat mallet or rolling pin. Place 1 slice prosciutto on each chicken breast.

Spoon about 1 tablespoon herb mixture over each. Fold in the sides of the chicken breasts and roll up; secure each with 2 wooden picks. Place seam side down in a baking dish. Spoon the remaining herb mixture over the chicken. Bake at 350 degrees for 15 minutes. Pour the hot chicken broth over the chicken. Bake for 20 to 25 minutes or until the chicken is cooked through, basting frequently. Add 1 tablespoon parsley to the baking dish and mix well.

For the béarnaise sauce, melt 1 tablespoon of the butter in a saucepan. Stir in the green onions, vinegar, tarragon, salt and pepper. Cook until reduced to 2 teaspoons, stirring constantly. Combine with the egg yolks in a stainless steel bowl. Place over a pan of hot water. Beat with a wire whisk until the consistency of whipped cream. Remove from heat. Melt the remaining butter in a saucepan. Stir into the sauce. Cover and keep warm.

To serve, remove the wooden picks from the chicken and cut into medallions. Fan the medallions on a serving platter or plate. Drizzle with the béarnaise sauce.

Serves 8

Curried Chicken Pitas with Grape Salsa

CURRIED CHICKEN	12 ounces boneless skinless chicken breasts, cut into 1/2-inch strips
	2 teaspoons curry powder
	2 teaspoons soy sauce
	1 tablespoon olive oil
GRAPE SALSA	1 1/2 cups coarsely chopped seedless red or green grapes
	1/3 cup finely chopped green onions
	1/3 cup finely chopped Anaheim or poblano chiles
	3 tablespoons chopped fresh cilantro
	1 tablespoon lime juice
	1/2 teaspoon hot sauce
ASSEMBLY	4 (7-inch) pita bread rounds, split, heated
	6 tablespoons sour cream

For the chicken, combine the chicken, curry powder and soy sauce in a medium bowl and toss to coat well. Marinate, covered, in the refrigerator for 30 to 60 minutes.

Heat the olive oil in a skillet sprayed with nonstick cooking spray over medium-high heat. Add the chicken mixture. Sauté for 8 to 10 minutes or until the chicken is cooked through.

For the grape salsa, combine the grapes, green onions, chiles, cilantro, lime juice and hot sauce in a bowl and mix well. Chill, covered, for 1 hour or up to 3 days.

To assemble, spoon the chicken mixture into the warm pita pockets. Top with the grape salsa and sour cream.

Serves 4

Maple-Barbecued Chicken

MAPLE BARBECUE SAUCE	2 large onions, finely chopped
	2½ tablespoons vegetable oil
	2½ tablespoons Worcestershire sauce
	1 tablespoon Dijon mustard
	1¼ cups catsup
	2½ cups chicken broth
	¾ cup cider vinegar
	½ cup plus 2 tablespoons pure maple syrup
CHICKEN	½ cup white wine vinegar
	1 tablespoon salt
	1 cup vegetable oil
	10 chicken breasts
	10 chicken thighs
	10 chicken wings
	10 chicken drumsticks

For the maple barbecue sauce, combine the onions, oil, Worcestershire sauce, Dijon mustard, catsup, broth, vinegar and maple syrup in a large heavy saucepan. Bring to a boil and reduce heat. Simmer for 50 minutes or until reduced to about 3⅓ cups, stirring frequently. Store, covered, in the refrigerator for up to 1 week.

For the chicken, beat the vinegar and salt in a bowl using a wire whisk. Add the oil in a fine stream, whisking constantly until emulsified. Divide the chicken between 2 large bowls. Pour the marinade over the chicken. Marinate, covered, in the refrigerator for 8 to 12 hours.

Pour some of the maple barbecue sauce into a small bowl, reserving the remaining maple barbecue sauce for serving with the chicken. Drain the chicken, discarding the marinade. Place on an oiled grill rack. Grill 4 inches above glowing coals for 10 minutes on each side or until cooked through, basting with the maple barbecue sauce. Grill for 2 minutes longer, turning frequently. Serve with the reserved maple barbecue sauce.

Serves 12

Labor Day Barbecue

Mixed Baby Greens with Poppy Seed Watermelon Dressing, page 74

Roasted corn on the cob

"Best of the Midwest" Baked Beans, page 165

Maple-Barbecued Chicken, at left

Apple Blueberry Crumble, page 186

Peanut Ginger Chicken with Fruit Salsa

CHICKEN

½ cup creamy peanut butter
½ cup hot water
1 tablespoon chili powder
¼ cup soy sauce
2 tablespoons vegetable oil
2 tablespoons vinegar
4 garlic cloves, minced
½ teaspoon ginger
¼ teaspoon ground red pepper
6 boneless skinless chicken breasts

FRUIT SALSA

1 cup chopped, peeled fresh fruit, such as plums, peaches, nectarines or pears
1 cup chopped, seeded, peeled cucumber
2 tablespoons thinly sliced green onions
2 tablespoons snipped parsley
1 tablespoon sugar
1 tablespoon vegetable oil
1 tablespoon vinegar

For the chicken, combine the peanut butter and hot water in a bowl and stir until the peanut butter is melted. Add the chili powder, soy sauce, oil, vinegar, garlic, ginger and red pepper and mix well. Pour into a 1-gallon sealable plastic food storage bag. Add the chicken and seal the bag.

Marinate in the refrigerator for 3 to 24 hours. Drain the chicken, discarding the marinade. Place the chicken on a grill rack. Grill over hot coals until the chicken is cooked through.

For the fruit salsa, combine the fruit, cucumber, green onions, parsley, sugar, oil and vinegar in a bowl and toss to mix well. Chill, covered, until 1 hour prior to serving.

To serve, arrange the chicken on a serving plate. Spoon the fruit salsa over the top.

Serves 6

Lemon Rosemary Turkey

The lemon and herbs really enhance the flavor of this turkey . . . and the leftovers are scrumptious.

INGREDIENTS
1 (10- to 12-pound) self-basting turkey
6 to 8 garlic cloves
2 large lemons, cut into halves
1/4 cup finely chopped fresh rosemary
1/4 cup finely chopped fresh sage
2 or 3 sprigs fresh rosemary
2 or 3 sprigs fresh sage

Cut 6 to 8 small slits in the turkey skin. Insert the garlic between the skin and turkey. Squeeze 2 lemon halves inside the turkey and place inside the cavity. Squeeze the remaining lemon halves over the outside of the turkey. Spray the outside of the turkey with nonstick cooking spray. Sprinkle with the chopped rosemary and sage. Place the sprigs of rosemary and sage inside the turkey cavity.

Place on a rack in a roasting pan. Bake, uncovered, at 325 degrees for 1 hour. Bake, covered with foil, for 3 to 3 1/2 hours longer or until golden brown and a meat thermometer inserted into the thickest portion of the leg registers 185 degrees. Let stand for 20 minutes before carving.

Serves 8

Turkey Piccata

INGREDIENTS
4 turkey cutlets
1 teaspoon crumbled marjoram
1/2 teaspoon salt
Flour
3 tablespoons butter
1 tablespoon vegetable oil
1 garlic clove, finely minced
Juice of 1 lemon
2 teaspoons parsley
1 tablespoon capers, drained

Pound the cutlets with a meat mallet until thin. Sprinkle both sides of the cutlets with marjoram and salt. Sprinkle lightly with flour. Heat the butter and oil in a skillet until the butter melts. Add the cutlets. Cook until brown and cooked through. Remove the cutlets from the skillet to a serving platter and keep warm.

Add the garlic to the skillet. Sauté until the garlic is soft, but not brown. Add the lemon juice, parsley and capers. Cook until heated through. Pour over the cutlets. Serve immediately.

Serves 4

Cornish Hens with Burgundy Cherry Sauce

Serve with a nutty brown or wild rice for an elegant holiday meal.

INGREDIENTS	4 Cornish hens
	1 teaspoon salt
	Pepper to taste
	1/4 cup (1/2 stick) butter, melted
	1 (17-ounce) can pitted, dark sweet cherries, drained
	1/2 cup burgundy
	1 teaspoon cornstarch
	1/4 cup water
	2 tablespoons currant jelly
GARNISH	Sprigs of fresh parsley

Sprinkle the hen cavities with salt and pepper. Place on a rack in a roasting pan. Bake at 350 degrees for 1 1/4 hours or until cooked through, basting every 15 minutes with melted butter and pan juices.

Combine the cherries and wine in a medium bowl and mix well. Arrange the hens on a serving platter and keep warm. Drain the cherries, reserving the wine. Skim the fat from the roasting pan. Add the reserved wine. Cook over medium heat until reduced, stirring to deglaze the pan.

Blend the cornstarch into the water in a 1-quart saucepan. Stir in the wine mixture and currant jelly. Cook over medium heat until slightly thickened, stirring constantly. Add the cherries. Cook until the cherries are heated through, stirring constantly. Pour over the hens. Garnish with parsley.

Serves 4

Sea Bass with Orange Soy Marinade

INGREDIENTS
- 1/2 cup soy sauce
- 1/2 cup orange juice
- 1/4 cup vegetable oil
- 1/4 cup catsup
- 2 garlic cloves, crushed
- 2 tablespoons lemon or lime juice
- 2 tablespoons minced parsley
- 2 teaspoons orange zest
- 1/2 teaspoon ground pepper
- 1 pound sea bass or salmon fillets

Combine the soy sauce, orange juice, oil, catsup, garlic, lemon juice, parsley, orange zest and pepper in a bowl and mix well. Pour over the fish in a sealable plastic food storage bag. Seal the bag. Marinate in the refrigerator for 1 to 2 hours.

Drain the fish, discarding the marinade. Place on a grill rack or a rack in a broiler pan. Grill or broil over medium coals or heat for 10 minutes per side per inch of thickness or until the fish flakes easily. Serve immediately.

Serves 2

Macadamia Dill Orange Roughy

INGREDIENTS
- 1/2 cup mayonnaise
- 2 pounds orange roughy or salmon fillets
- Fresh lemon juice
- Dill to taste
- 1 cup dry bread crumbs
- 2 tablespoons butter or margarine, melted
- 1/4 cup finely chopped macadamia nuts

GARNISHES
- Lemon wheels
- Sprigs of fresh dill

Spread the mayonnaise over the fish in a baking dish. Sprinkle with lemon juice and dill.

Mix the bread crumbs and butter in a bowl. Stir in the macadamia nuts. Sprinkle over the fish. Bake at 350 degrees for 15 minutes or until the fish flakes easily. Broil until brown, if desired. Garnish with lemon wheels and fresh dill.

Serves 4

Salmon Roulade en Croûte with Orange Ginger Beurre Blanc

CAFÉ DE FRANCE

SCALLOP MOUSSE	5 ounces sea or bay scallops 2½ ounces heavy cream 1 egg Salt and pepper and/or lemon juice to taste
SALMON ROULADE	1 (1½-pound) salmon fillet Salt and pepper to taste Juice of ½ lemon 8 ounces fresh spinach, rinsed, drained 12 ounces Brie cheese, rind removed, thinly sliced 1 puff pastry sheet Flour Melted butter Egg wash
ORANGE GINGER BEURRE BLANC	2 tablespoons minced fresh shallots 1 tablespoon minced fresh gingerroot 1 teaspoon olive oil Juice of 1 orange 1 tablespoon lemon juice 1 cup white wine ½ cup triple sec ½ cup heavy cream Salt and pepper to taste 1½ cups (3 sticks) butter, cut into pieces

For the scallop mousse, remove the muscle from the sea scallops. Process the scallops, cream, egg, salt and pepper and/or lemon juice in a food processor or blender until smooth.

For the salmon roulade, split the fillet down the center until approximately 1/4 inch from the bottom; cut horizontally from each side to form an upside down "T". Do not cut all the way through. Spread out the fillet on plastic wrap. Cover the top with plastic wrap. Pound the fillet lightly until 1/4 inch thick. Remove the top layer of plastic wrap. Sprinkle lightly with salt and pepper. Sprinkle with lemon juice. Spread the scallop mousse evenly over the fillet. Cover with whole spinach leaves. Spread the Brie cheese over the spinach. Roll up into a tight cylinder.

Sprinkle the puff pastry with flour and lightly roll with a rolling pin. Place the fillet roll-up in the center. Wrap the fillet roll-up from one end to the other in a tight roll. Chill for 15 minutes.

Brush a baking sheet with melted butter. Place the roulade on the baking sheet. Brush with egg wash. Place on the top oven rack. Bake at 375 degrees for 15 to 20 minutes or until golden brown.

For the orange ginger beurre blanc, place the shallots and gingerroot in olive oil in a stainless steel saucepan. Sweat, covered, over low heat until translucent. Add the orange juice, lemon juice, white wine and triple sec. Cook until reduced by 1/2, stirring to deglaze the saucepan. Add the cream. Season with salt and pepper. Bring to a low boil. Cook until the mixture begins to brown around the edge. Add the butter a small amount at a time, whisking constantly until the butter is melted after each addition. Cook until the sauce begins to thicken, whisking constantly. Remove from heat. Strain into a serving bowl. Serve immediately.

To assemble, place the salmon roulade on a serving platter. Cut into slices and serve with orange ginger beurre blanc.

Serves 4

Editor's Note: Egg wash is an egg yolk or egg white mixed with a small amount of water or milk and is used to give the pastry color and gloss.

Café De France

Many honors have been awarded to this elegant French restaurant including the Four Diamond rating by AAA, the 1997 Reader's Choice of Gourmet magazine, and Best Food rating by Zagat Guide in 1999. Chef Marcel Keraval's palette of ingredients is hand chosen from the markets daily and is combined to create classic and creative French cuisine. Chef Marcel's desserts range from the freshest seasonal fruits and berries to decadent soufflés.

Sweet-and-Spicy Salmon

INGREDIENTS

½ cup (1 stick) unsalted butter
⅓ cup honey
⅓ cup packed brown sugar
2 tablespoons fresh lemon juice
1 teaspoon natural liquid smoke
¾ teaspoon crushed red pepper flakes
1 (2-pound) center-cut salmon fillet with skin

Combine the butter, honey, brown sugar, lemon juice, liquid smoke and red pepper flakes in a saucepan. Cook over medium heat for 5 to 7 minutes or until smooth, stirring constantly. Cool to room temperature.

Arrange the salmon in a baking dish just large enough to hold it. Pour the cooled marinade over the salmon. Let stand for 30 minutes, turning once.

Drain the salmon, discarding the marinade. Place skin side up on an oiled grill or broiler rack. Grill over medium-hot coals or in a broiler pan for 5 to 7 minutes. Turn over the salmon. Grill or broil for 5 to 7 minutes longer or until the salmon flakes easily. Arrange on a serving platter and serve immediately.

Serves 4

Grilled Tuna Steaks with Cantaloupe Salsa

CANTALOUPE
SALSA

¾ cup coarsely chopped cantaloupe or
    honeydew melon
¼ cup chopped onion
2 tablespoons chopped fresh cilantro
2 teaspoons olive oil
1 tablespoon fresh lime juice
1 teaspoon minced jalapeño pepper
Salt and pepper to taste

TUNA

2 (5- to 6-ounce) tuna steaks, ½ inch thick
2 teaspoons olive oil
Salt and pepper to taste

For the cantaloupe salsa, combine the cantaloupe, onion, cilantro, olive oil, lime juice and jalapeño pepper in a small bowl and mix well. Season with salt and pepper to taste. Let stand for 15 minutes.

For the tuna, brush the tuna on both sides with olive oil. Sprinkle with salt and pepper. Place on a greased grill rack. Grill over medium-high coals for 3 minutes per side or until just opaque in the center.

To serve, place the tuna on individual serving plates. Spoon the cantaloupe salsa beside the tuna.

Serves 2

Grilled Yellowfin Tuna "Fourchette"

FIO'S LA FOURCHETTE

TUNA	2 tablespoons mayonnaise
	1/2 tablespoon honey
	1/2 tablespoon brandy
	1/2 tablespoon lemon juice
	1/2 tablespoon chopped fresh rosemary
	4 (6- to 8-ounce) pieces thick-cut yellowfin tuna
	Salt and pepper to taste
SAUCE	2 garlic cloves, chopped
	2 tablespoons olive oil
	1 small onion, chopped
	2 green bell peppers, chopped
	3 medium tomatoes, chopped
	1/2 cup red wine
	1/2 cup tomato juice
	1 1/2 tablespoons chopped pitted Greek olives
	1 1/2 tablespoons capers, chopped
	2 tablespoons lemon juice
	Salt and pepper to taste
GARNISHES	Lemon slices
	Sprigs of fresh rosemary

For the tuna, blend the mayonnaise, honey, brandy, lemon juice and rosemary in a bowl. Brush generously over both sides of the tuna. Place in dish. Marinate in the refrigerator for 3 hours or longer. Drain the tuna, discarding the marinade. Season with salt and pepper. Place on a greased grill rack. Grill over hot coals until medium-rare, or to desired doneness.

For the sauce, sauté the garlic in the olive oil in a skillet for 30 seconds. Add the onion. Sauté for 3 minutes. Add the green peppers, tomatoes, red wine and tomato juice. Simmer for 5 minutes. Remove from heat. Add the olives, capers, lemon juice and salt and pepper to taste.

To serve, cover the bottom of the platter with the sauce. Arrange the tuna in the center. Garnish with lemon slices and sprigs of fresh rosemary. Serve immediately.

Serves 4

Fio's La Fourchette

For more than fifteen years, Fio Antognini and his wife, Lisa, have been delighting diners with his French-Swiss cuisine. The menu ranges from classic veal entrées and pâtés to low-fat dishes. During the season, wild game and other exotic fare can be found at Fio's. Irresistible dessert soufflés are always a must to finish off a truly enchanting evening.

Pan-Seared Yellowfin Tuna

INGREDIENTS

2 tablespoons butter or margarine
1 red bell pepper, cut into 1/4-inch strips
1 yellow bell pepper, cut into 1/4-inch strips
1 large red onion, cut into 1/4-inch strips
1/8 teaspoon cayenne pepper, or to taste
1 tablespoon honey
2 tablespoons olive oil
4 to 6 (8-ounce) yellowfin tuna steaks,
    1/2 to 3/4 inch thick
Salt and pepper to taste

Melt the butter in a skillet. Add the red pepper, yellow pepper and onion. Sauté for 5 minutes or until softened. Add the cayenne pepper and honey and mix well. Remove from heat. Cover and set aside.

Heat the olive oil in a 12-inch skillet over high heat. Season the tuna with salt and pepper. Place in the hot olive oil. Cook for 3 minutes per side or until the tuna flakes easily.

To serve, place the tuna on individual serving plates. Smother each with the warm vegetable mixture.

Serves 4 to 6

Crab Chantilly

INGREDIENTS

6 to 7 ounces frozen or canned snow crab meat
2 tablespoons chopped green onions
2 tablespoons butter
1 tablespoon flour
1/2 teaspoon salt
Cayenne pepper to taste
1 cup half-and-half or milk
1/4 cup mayonnaise
10 ounces asparagus spears, cooked, drained
1 tablespoon grated Parmesan cheese

Thaw the crab meat and cut into chunks. Sauté the green onions in the butter in a skillet until translucent but not brown. Stir in the flour, salt and cayenne pepper. Add the half-and-half. Cook until thickened, stirring constantly. Remove from heat. Stir in the mayonnaise. Fold in the crab meat.

Arrange the asparagus in a shallow 1 1/2-quart baking dish. Cover with the crab meat mixture. Sprinkle with Parmesan cheese. Broil 4 inches from the heat source for 5 minutes or until light brown and heated through.

Serves 4

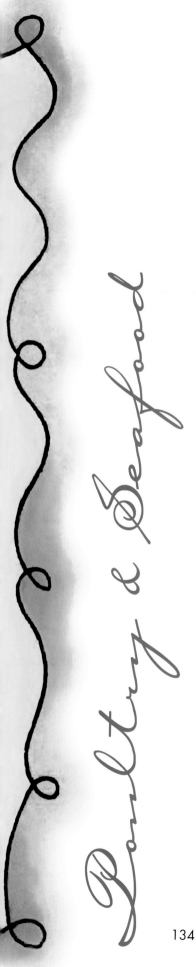

Poultry & Seafood

Crab in Curried Sour Cream and Brandy Sauce

INGREDIENTS

2 bunches green onions, sliced
1/2 cup (1 stick) butter
1/4 cup flour
3 ounces vermouth
1 1/2 ounces brandy
1/4 ounce sherry
1/8 teaspoon curry powder
1/8 teaspoon nutmeg
1/2 teaspoon salt
1 cup sour cream
1 pound fresh crab meat
Fresh bread crumbs
2 tablespoons butter
1 tablespoon lemon juice

Sauté the green onions in 1/2 cup butter in a skillet until tender. Add the flour and mix well. Add the vermouth, brandy, sherry, curry powder, nutmeg and salt. Simmer for 10 minutes. Remove from heat. Stir in the sour cream and crab meat. Place in small baking shells or ramekins. May cover and chill until ready to bake.

Sauté the bread crumbs in 2 tablespoons butter and lemon juice in a skillet. Sprinkle over the crab meat mixture. Bake at 400 degrees for 20 minutes or until brown and bubbly.

Serves 6

Maryland-Style Crab Cakes

JUNIOR LEAGUE OF ST. LOUIS GRILLE

This is one of the most popular dishes in the Junior League of St. Louis Grille.

INGREDIENTS

½ cup shredded yellow squash
½ cup shredded carrots
½ cup shredded zucchini
½ cup shredded red pepper
½ bunch scallions, minced
2 garlic cloves, minced
2 tablespoons minced fresh cilantro
1 teaspoon ginger
1 teaspoon garlic powder
1 teaspoon cumin
⅔ cup mayonnaise
3 egg whites
1 cup medium cracker meal
Juice of 1 lime
Salt and pepper to taste
1½ pounds lump crab meat

Combine the yellow squash, carrots, zucchini, red pepper, scallions, garlic, cilantro, ginger, garlic powder, cumin, mayonnaise, egg whites, cracker meal, lime juice and salt and pepper in a bowl and mix well. Let stand for 15 minutes.

Fold in the crab meat being careful to not break up the lumps. Shape into patties. Brown on both sides in a nonstick skillet. Place on a nonstick baking sheet.

Bake at 350 degrees for 10 minutes.

Serves 4 to 6

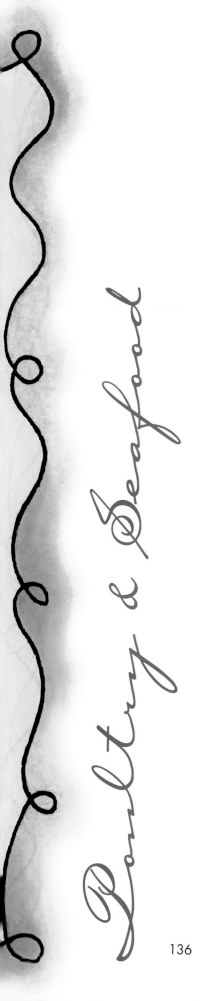

Poultry & Seafood

Shrimp Wrapped in Zucchini with Red Pepper Aioli

GIANFABIO RISTORANTE

RED PEPPER AIOLI	1 egg yolk
	½ tablespoon chopped garlic
	1 cup chopped roasted red bell peppers
	1 tablespoon Dijon mustard
	½ cup olive oil
	Fresh lemon juice to taste
	Salt and pepper to taste
	Tabasco sauce to taste
SHRIMP	16 large shrimp
	¼ cup dry white wine
	3 tablespoons olive oil
	1 teaspoon lemon zest
	1½ teaspoons chopped fresh oregano, or
	½ teaspoon dried
	1 teaspoon minced garlic
	1 tablespoon minced fresh parsley
	½ teaspoon red pepper flakes
	½ teaspoon kosher salt
	2 large zucchini
	Salt to taste
GARNISH	Lemon wedges

For the red pepper aioli, combine the egg yolk, garlic, red peppers and Dijon mustard in a food processor container. Add the olive oil in a fine stream, processing constantly until emulsified. The mixture should be thick but not stiff. Season with lemon juice, salt, pepper and Tabasco sauce to taste. Store, covered, in the refrigerator for up to 1 week.

For the shrimp, peel and devein the shrimp, leaving the tail intact. Combine the wine, olive oil, lemon zest, oregano, garlic, parsley, red pepper flakes and kosher salt in a bowl and mix well with a wire whisk. Add the shrimp and toss to coat. Marinate, covered, in the refrigerator for 1 hour.

Cut the zucchini into 16 very thin slices lengthwise. Blanch in lightly salted boiling water in a saucepan for 5 seconds. Remove and immediately plunge into cold water to stop the cooking process. Drain the zucchini and pat dry.

Soak the bamboo skewers in water. Drain the shrimp, discarding the marinade. Curl a zucchini slice around each shrimp and secure with a bamboo skewer. Place on a grill rack. Grill for 3 minutes or until the shrimp turn pink, turning once.

To serve, spoon a dollop of red pepper aioli on each shrimp. Garnish each serving with a lemon wedge.

Serves 4

Gianfabio Ristorante

This family-owned and -operated restaurant has been a landmark in the Chesterfield area since 1987. Gianfabio's addition of Il Formo Cafe three years ago has given its guests several dining options. For special occasions or a quiet evening out, one may choose the tranquility of the main dining room. Others will surely enjoy the casual atmosphere of the Cafe or Patio. Regardless of the environment, Gianfabio Ristorante will please any palate.

Spiced Orange Shrimp

Excellent served with wild rice or pilaf.

INGREDIENTS

4 cups freshly squeezed orange juice
1/4 cup hot sauce
2 tablespoons honey
2 tablespoons soy sauce
1 tablespoon minced garlic
3 dozen jumbo shrimp, peeled, deveined

Combine the orange juice, hot sauce, honey, soy sauce and garlic in a large skillet. Bring to a boil and reduce heat. Simmer for 5 minutes. Add the shrimp. Cook for 4 to 5 minutes or until the shrimp turn pink. Remove the shrimp to a warm serving bowl. Cook the remaining sauce in the skillet over high heat for about 3 minutes. Pour over the shrimp and serve immediately.

Serves 6

Grilled Shrimp in Pancetta with Asiago Cheese

INGREDIENTS

24 thin slices pancetta (Italian bacon)
24 jumbo shrimp, deveined, butterflied 1/4 inch
2 cups bread crumbs
2 cups grated asiago cheese
1/4 cup chopped fresh basil
2 tablespoons chopped fresh thyme
2 tablespoons pepper
1 cup (or more) olive oil

Wrap and twist the pancetta around the shrimp to form an "X" in the center; secure with wooden picks. Combine the bread crumbs, cheese, basil, thyme and pepper in a bowl and mix well. Moisten the bread crumbs with the olive oil until the mixture packs firmly. Dredge the shrimp in the crumb mixture and press lightly to coat evenly. Place on a grill rack. Grill for 4 minutes, turning frequently to prevent burning.

Serves 4

Pasta & Grains

Chef Dad

For forty-six years, my parents had a very traditional marriage: Dad went to work and Mom ran the house. It was a very satisfying arrangement until my mother was diagnosed with terminal cancer.

During the short time left to her, she taught my father how to pay bills, do the laundry, and take care of the house. But Mother only lived for five weeks after the diagnosis, and her time ran out before she could teach him to cook.

My dad had so little experience in the kitchen that once he spent fifteen minutes looking for the garbage disposal switch. He was accustomed to eating half a grapefruit every morning during the winter months, but hadn't the vaguest idea of how to use a grapefruit knife. At first, my sister and I tried to take care of his meals. When I visited him in Austin, Texas, I would spend a day cooking, then freezing and labeling individual portions with reheating instructions. For a while, my sister brought dinner to him every night, leaving it in the microwave. One night I called Dad to ask what he was eating and he answered, "Spaghetti sauce." He didn't know how to cook the pasta.

Dad soon realized that the situation had to change. He started by watching me cook and asking questions. I marked a few easy recipes in my mother's cookbooks. He began clipping recipes from the newspaper and experimenting. Within a year he had mastered enough recipes to hold a dinner party.

Now Dad entertains regularly, including luncheon for the bridge club, and shares his newfound recipes with me. We submitted five of his best recipes to *Bon Appétit* magazine and they were accepted for publication. Best of all, when he visits me, some of our happiest times are working together in the kitchen.

Gretchen Davis

Greek Isle Pastitsio

GROUND BEEF SAUCE	6 tablespoons butter or margarine
	¾ cup finely chopped yellow onion
	2 garlic cloves, crushed
	1¼ pounds ground beef
	1 (16-ounce) can peeled tomatoes, mashed
	½ cup canned tomato sauce
	½ cup water
	1 teaspoon salt
	½ teaspoon cinnamon
	⅛ teaspoon pepper
	⅛ teaspoon ground cloves
MACARONI	Salt to taste
	4 quarts water
	12 ounces uncooked Greek macaroni or medium Italian ziti
	¼ cup (½ stick) butter, melted
	6 eggs, beaten
	1 cup grated Parmesan or Romano cheese
WHITE SAUCE	6 tablespoons butter
	6 tablespoons flour
	2 cups warm milk
	3 eggs, beaten
	2 tablespoon dry sherry (optional)
	½ teaspoon nutmeg
	½ cup grated Parmesan cheese
	½ teaspoon salt
	⅛ teaspoon white pepper

For the ground beef sauce, melt the butter in a large skillet. Add the onion, garlic and ground beef. Cook until the ground beef is brown and crumbly, stirring constantly. Add the tomatoes, tomato sauce, water, salt, cinnamon, pepper and cloves and mix well. Simmer, uncovered, for 20 minutes or until the ground beef liquid is absorbed; should be thick.

For the macaroni, bring the salted water to a boil in a saucepan. Add the macaroni. Cook, uncovered, for 8 minutes; drain and rinse. Place in a large bowl. Add the butter, eggs and cheese and toss to coat well.

For the white sauce, melt the butter in a saucepan. Stir in the flour. Cook for 3 to 4 minutes or until blended, stirring constantly. Add the milk gradually, stirring constantly. Add ½ cup of the mixture to the beaten eggs; add the eggs to the mixture. Cook until thickened, stirring constantly. Add the sherry, nutmeg, Parmesan cheese, salt and white pepper. Cook until smooth, stirring constantly.

To assemble, layer ½ of the macaroni, ground beef sauce and remaining macaroni in a greased 9x9-inch baking pan. Pour the white sauce over the top. Bake at 350 degrees for 25 minutes or until the top is golden brown.

Serves 9

Pasta & Grains

Florentine-Stuffed Shells with Italian Sausage

INGREDIENTS

1 pound Italian sausage
1 medium onion, minced
1 garlic clove, minced
1 (8-ounce) can mushroom stems and pieces,
    drained
1 teaspoon basil
Salt and pepper to taste
2 (10-ounce) packages frozen spinach, cooked,
    drained
1 (10-ounce) can cream of mushroom soup
1 cup sour cream
10⅔ ounces large pasta shells, cooked
½ cup grated Parmesan cheese
½ cup shredded mozzarella cheese
1 cup 40% cream

Remove the casing from the sausage. Brown the sausage in a large skillet, stirring until crumbly; drain. Stir in the onion, garlic, mushrooms and basil. Season with salt and pepper. Add the spinach and soup and mix well. Stir in the sour cream.

Arrange the pasta shells in a single layer in a baking pan. Stuff the shells with the sausage mixture. Sprinkle with Parmesan cheese and mozzarella cheese. Pour a thin layer of the cream over the top. Bake at 350 degrees for 30 minutes.

Serves 4

Note: The cream will make a small amount of sauce. If more sauce is desired, add additional cream and thicken with cornstarch or flour.

Fusilli with Grilled Chicken and Summer Vegetables

INGREDIENTS

6 tablespoons olive oil
1/4 cup red wine vinegar
1/4 cup chopped red onion
3/4 cup chopped fresh basil
1/4 cup chopped fresh parsley
2 1/2 teaspoons salt
3/4 teaspoon pepper
2 cups seeded chopped tomatoes (about 2)
2 zucchini, cut lengthwise into 3 slices
2 yellow squash, cut lengthwise into 3 slices
Olive oil for brushing
1/8 teaspoon salt
1/8 teaspoon pepper
1 pound boneless skinless chicken breasts
1/8 teaspoon salt
1/8 teaspoon pepper
12 ounces fusilli
Salt to taste
Freshly ground pepper to taste

Combine 6 tablespoons olive oil, vinegar, red onion, basil, parsley, 2 1/2 teaspoons salt and 3/4 teaspoon pepper in a large bowl and mix well. Stir in the tomatoes.

Brush the zucchini and squash with olive oil. Sprinkle with 1/8 teaspoon salt and 1/8 teaspoon pepper. Place on a grill rack. Grill 3 to 6 inches from the heat source for 8 to 10 minutes or until brown, turning occasionally. Chop the zucchini and squash. Add to the tomato mixture.

Brush the chicken with olive oil. Sprinkle with 1/8 teaspoon salt and 1/8 teaspoon pepper. Place on a grill rack. Grill for 5 minutes per side or until cooked through. Cool for 5 minutes. Cut cross grain into slices. Add to the vegetable mixture and keep warm.

Cook the pasta in salted boiling water in a large saucepan for 13 minutes or until al dente; drain. Add to the chicken mixture and toss to mix well.

Season with salt and pepper to taste.

Serves 6

Spinach Fettuccini with Shrimp and Sun-Dried Tomatoes

INGREDIENTS

1 pound shrimp, peeled, deveined
1/4 cup (1/2 stick) butter
1/2 cup bourbon
1 1/2 cups heavy cream
2 teaspoons chopped fresh basil
1/8 teaspoon salt
1/8 teaspoon pepper
4 ounces chèvre
10 sun-dried tomatoes, rehydrated, chopped
1 pound spinach fettuccini, cooked
1/2 cup grated Parmesan cheese

Sauté the shrimp in the butter in a skillet for 2 minutes or until the shrimp turn pink; drain. Add the bourbon. Bring to a boil and reduce heat. Add the cream. Bring to a boil and reduce heat. Simmer until thickened, stirring constantly. Add the basil, salt, pepper, chèvre and tomatoes. Cook until the chèvre is melted, stirring constantly. Add to the hot pasta in a serving bowl and toss to coat. Sprinkle each serving with Parmesan cheese.

Serves 4

Rehydrating Sun-Dried Tomatoes

To quickly rehydrate sun-dried tomatoes, boil a cup of water in the microwave. Add the sun-dried tomatoes to the boiling water. Let stand for 5 to 10 minutes. Drain the tomatoes and let stand until cool.

Capellini with Spicy Shrimp

INGREDIENTS

1 pound capellini
1/4 cup olive oil
2 tablespoons chopped fresh parsley
2 garlic cloves, finely chopped
1/4 to 1/2 teaspoon crushed red pepper flakes
1/3 cup dry white wine
1/2 teaspoon freshly grated or ground nutmeg
12 ounces (26- to 30-count) shrimp, peeled, deveined

Cook the pasta using package directions. Heat the olive oil in a 4-quart Dutch oven or 12-inch skillet over medium-high heat. Add the parsley, garlic and red pepper flakes. Cook for 3 minutes. Stir in the wine, nutmeg and shrimp. Reduce heat. Simmer, covered, for 5 minutes or until the shrimp turn pink.

Drain the pasta. Add to the shrimp mixture and toss to mix well. Cook over medium heat for 2 minutes, stirring occasionally.

Serves 4

Linguini with Bay Scallops

INGREDIENTS

16 ounces linguini
2 tablespoons butter or margarine
1 pound bay scallops
¼ cup (½ stick) butter or margarine
1½ cups heavy cream
½ teaspoon salt
⅛ teaspoon nutmeg
⅛ teaspoon red pepper
1 cup freshly grated Parmesan cheese
½ cup chopped fresh basil, or 1 tablespoon dried
⅓ cup chopped fresh chives
⅓ cup chopped fresh parsley
1 tablespoon lemon zest

Cook the pasta using package directions; drain. Place in a large serving bowl and keep warm.

Melt 2 tablespoons butter in a Dutch oven. Add the scallops. Sauté for 3 minutes. Remove the scallops to a bowl using a slotted spoon and keep warm.

Add ¼ cup butter, cream, salt, nutmeg and red pepper to the Dutch oven. Bring to a boil over medium heat and reduce heat. Simmer for 15 minutes or until slightly reduced, whisking constantly. Add the Parmesan cheese, basil, chives and parsley. Simmer for 5 minutes, whisking frequently. Return the scallops to the Dutch oven. Simmer for 1 minute. Stir in the lemon zest. Remove from heat.

Stir ½ of the scallop mixture into the hot pasta. Top with the remaining scallop mixture.

Serves 6

Pasta & Grains

Layered Ziti with Asparagus and Prosciutto

A delicious make-ahead pasta dish suitable for company.

INGREDIENTS

1 pound asparagus, cut into 1-inch pieces
1/2 medium white onion, cut into long thin strips
2 garlic cloves, minced
1 (8-ounce) package frozen green peas
3 tablespoons olive oil
1/4 teaspoon red pepper flakes
1/2 cup white wine
1 1/2 cups chicken stock
1/2 cup heavy cream
Salt and pepper to taste
1 pound ziti, cooked, drained
4 ounces prosciutto, minced
8 ounces mozzarella cheese, shredded
2 ounces Parmesan cheese, grated
Bread crumbs

Sauté the asparagus, onion, garlic and green peas in the olive oil in a skillet over medium heat until tender. Add the red pepper flakes. Sauté for 4 to 5 minutes. Add the wine. Sauté for 3 minutes. Add the chicken stock and cream. Cook until the liquid is reduced by one-third. Season with salt and pepper. Add the pasta and mix well.

Layer the pasta mixture, prosciutto, mozzarella cheese and Parmesan cheese 1/2 at a time in a baking pan greased with olive oil. Sprinkle with bread crumbs. May prepare ahead and chill, covered, until serving time. Bake, uncovered, at 350 degrees for 25 to 30 minutes or until the top is brown and the cheeses are melted.

Serves 4

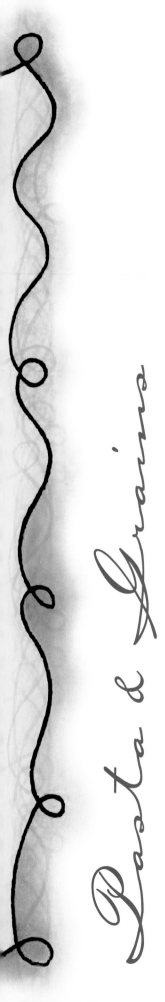

Vegetarian Pastitsio

A meatless variation of the classic Greek dish.

INGREDIENTS   1 pound mostaccioli or macaroni
Salt to taste
1½ cups (3 sticks) butter, melted
1 cup grated Romano cheese
1 cup grated Mitzithra cheese
1 cup crumbled feta cheese
4 eggs, beaten
2 cups milk
Salt and freshly ground white pepper to taste
8 sheets phyllo pastry

Cook the pasta in boiling salted water in a saucepan until tender; drain. Brush a 9x13-inch baking dish with some of the melted butter. Combine the pasta and ½ of the remaining butter in a large bowl. Add the Romano cheese, Mitzithra cheese and feta cheese and toss to mix well. Add the eggs, milk, salt and white pepper and toss to mix well. Spoon into the prepared dish. Cover and chill in the refrigerator for up to 1 day ahead of serving if desired.

Cover the pasta mixture with the phyllo pastry, brushing each sheet lightly with the remaining butter. Score the top 3 sheets with the tip of a knife. Bake at 350 degrees for 15 minutes. Reduce the oven temperature to 300 degrees. Bake for 35 minutes longer. Let stand for 15 minutes. Cut into squares and serve immediately.

Serves 8 to 10

Pasta with Creamy Walnut Sauce

INGREDIENTS

1 slice firm home-style white bread, crust trimmed
3 tablespoons milk
1 cup walnut pieces
1 tablespoon pine nuts
1 tablespoon virgin olive oil
1/4 cup (1/2 stick) butter
1/2 teaspoon minced garlic
1/2 teaspoon salt
1 1/4 cups heavy cream
1/8 teaspoon freshly grated nutmeg
Freshly ground pepper to taste
1/2 cup freshly grated Parmesan cheese
5 quarts water
1 tablespoon salt
12 ounces fusilli or tagliatelle
2 tablespoons chopped fresh basil
1/4 cup freshly grated Parmesan cheese

Place the bread in a small bowl. Add the milk. Let stand for a few minutes. Squeeze the milk from the bread. Tear the bread into small pieces.

Process the walnuts and pine nuts in a food processor fitted with a steel blade until finely chopped. Add the bread, olive oil, butter, garlic and 1/2 teaspoon salt. Process until of a paste consistency. Spoon into a small heavy nonaluminum saucepan. Stir in the cream, nutmeg and pepper. Cook over medium heat for 15 minutes, stirring occasionally. Stir in 1/2 cup Parmesan cheese. Reduce heat to low and keep warm.

Bring the water to a boil in a large stockpot. Add 1 tablespoon salt and pasta and stir to separate the pasta. Cook for 7 minutes or until al dente; drain and return to the stockpot. Add the basil and parsley and toss to mix well. Add the sauce and toss until coated. Divide among 4 serving plates. Serve with 1/4 cup Parmesan cheese.

Serves 4

Note: If fresh basil is not available, may substitute 1/2 teaspoon dried basil and 1 tablespoon chopped fresh parsley.

Olive Oil

Olive oils are classified by category from extra-virgin to pure. The categories are determined by the level of acidity contained in the oil. Extra-virgin olive oil has the lowest acidity. Its intense flavor and aroma derive from green olives. Extra-virgin olive oil is best used in salads, marinades, or with just-cooked vegetables. Virgin olive oil, higher in acidity, has a sweetish, nutty flavor. Pure olive oil is the most acidic of the olive oils. It is best used for cooking or frying.

Orzo with Fresh Vegetables

Substitute any fresh seasonal vegetables.

INGREDIENTS

2 large red bell peppers
2 pounds orzo
½ cup olive oil
2 large onions, finely chopped
2 garlic cloves, crushed
2 cups fresh whole baby carrots
2 cups trimmed snap pea halves
½ cup grated Parmesan cheese
Zest of 2 lemons
Salt and pepper to taste

Cut the red peppers into halves, discarding the ribs and seeds. Place skin side up on a rack in a broiler pan. Broil until the skin is black. Cover with foil or place in a nonrecycled paper bag. Let stand until cool. Remove and discard the skin. Chop the red peppers.

Cook the orzo using the package directions. Heat the olive oil in a skillet. Add the onions and garlic. Sauté until the onions are soft. Add the carrots and snap peas. Sauté until tender-crisp. Combine the orzo, sautéed vegetables, red peppers, Parmesan cheese, lemon zest, salt and pepper in a large bowl and toss to mix well.

Serves 8

Pasta & Grains

Farfalle with Basil and Sun-Dried Tomatoes

INGREDIENTS
    1 pound farfalle
    ½ cup (1 stick) butter
    1½ cups heavy cream
    1½ cups freshly grated Parmesan cheese
    ¼ teaspoon garlic salt
    6 sun-dried tomatoes, rehydrated, chopped
    ½ cup chopped fresh basil

Cook the pasta using the package directions; drain and keep warm. Melt the butter in a saucepan. Add the cream. Bring to a boil and reduce heat to low. Add the Parmesan cheese and garlic salt. Simmer for 4 to 5 minutes. Add the tomatoes. Pour over the pasta and toss to mix well. Spoon into a serving bowl. Sprinkle with basil. Serve immediately.

Serves 6

Black Bean Lasagna

INGREDIENTS
    6 lasagna noodles
    ¼ cup chopped green bell pepper
    ¼ cup chopped onion
    1 garlic clove, minced
    1 (15-ounce) can black beans, drained
    1 (15-ounce) can tomato sauce
    2 tablespoons snipped fresh cilantro
    ¼ teaspoon crushed red pepper
    4 ounces cream cheese or Neufchâtel cheese,
        softened
    ½ cup cottage cheese
    ¼ cup sour cream
    2 cups shredded Monterey Jack cheese

Cook the lasagna noodles using the package directions; drain. Combine the green pepper, onion and garlic in a skillet sprayed with nonstick cooking spray. Sauté over medium heat until tender but not brown. Add the black beans, tomato sauce, cilantro and red pepper. Cook until heated through.
    Combine the cream cheese, cottage cheese and sour cream in a large mixing bowl and beat well. Layer the lasagna noodles, black bean mixture, cream cheese mixture and Monterey Jack cheese ½ at a time in a 9x9-inch baking dish sprayed with nonstick cooking spray. Bake, covered, at 350 degrees for 40 minutes or until heated through. Let stand for 20 minutes before serving.

Serves 4 to 6

Basil

When cooking, use only the freshest basil available and avoid blackened drooping leaves. Store and use at room temperature. Never refrigerate this delicate herb. Always add basil at the end of the recipe to ensure the freshest flavor and fragrance.

Fiesta Mexican Lasagna

Serve this with traditional Mexican garnishments arranged in strips— diced tomatoes, diced green onions, shredded lettuce, sliced black olives, guacamole and sour cream piped from a pastry tube. Of course, don't forget a sombrero filled with tortilla chips.

INGREDIENTS

1 pound ground beef
1 onion, chopped
1 (10-ounce) can tomatoes with green chiles
1 (8-ounce) can tomato sauce
½ teaspoon cumin, or to taste
1 teaspoon salt
½ teaspoon pepper
4 ounces cream cheese, softened
½ cup sour cream
12 ounces shredded Colby-Monterey Jack cheese
3 large (10-inch) flour tortillas

Brown the ground beef with the onion in a skillet, stirring until the ground beef is crumbly; drain. Add the tomatoes with green chiles, tomato sauce, cumin, salt and pepper. Simmer for 15 minutes.

Mix the cream cheese and sour cream in a small bowl until smooth.

Reserve some of the ground beef mixture for the top. Spread ½ of the cream cheese mixture on 1 tortilla. Place in a 9x9-inch baking dish sprayed with nonstick cooking spray. Spread ½ of the remaining ground beef mixture over the cream cheese mixture. Sprinkle with ⅓ cup Colby-Monterey Jack cheese. Repeat the layers. Top with the remaining tortilla, reserved ground beef mixture and remaining Colby-Monterey Jack cheese. Bake at 350 degrees for 30 minutes.

Serves 6 to 8

Pasta & Grains

Mama Mia's Gourmet Lasagna

INGREDIENTS

1 1/2 pounds ground beef
2 cups chopped tomatoes
2 (6-ounce) cans tomato paste
1 cup water
1 garlic clove, minced
2 tablespoons parsley flakes
2 tablespoons basil
2 teaspoons salt
12 lasagna noodles
48 ounces large curd cottage cheese
2 eggs, beaten
1/2 cup grated Parmesan cheese
2 teaspoons parsley flakes
1 teaspoon pepper
1 1/2 pounds mozzarella cheese, sliced

Brown the ground beef in a skillet, stirring until crumbly; drain. Add the tomatoes, tomato paste, water, garlic, 2 tablespoons parsley flakes, basil and salt and mix well. Simmer for 45 minutes.

Cook the lasagna noodles using package directions. Place in cool water.

Combine the cottage cheese, eggs, Parmesan cheese, 2 teaspoons parsley flakes and pepper in a bowl and mix well.

Place 1/2 of the noodles in a single layer in a greased baking pan, tearing some of the noodles or overlapping to fit evenly. Layer the cottage cheese mixture, mozzarella cheese and ground beef mixture 1/2 at a time in the prepared dish. Bake, covered with foil, at 375 degrees for 30 minutes. Increase the oven temperature to 425 degrees. Bake, uncovered, for 15 minutes. Cool for 15 minutes before serving.

Serves 8

Garlic Lasagna

A piping hot piece of lasagna always brings to mind the special gourmet dinner my boyfriend prepared for me one cold, snowy winter several years ago. The table was set with his best china and silver, and candles glowed throughout the dining room. He proudly presented the main course to me: a pan of his own homemade lasagna. My first bite led me to believe something was terribly wrong. I asked, "Honey, how much garlic did you use?" He replied, "Two cloves", as he held up two whole bulbs of garlic! It was a meal neither of us will ever forget!

Tracey Hoffman

Seafood Lasagna

BÉCHAMEL SAUCE	⅓ cup margarine
	⅓ cup flour
	½ teaspoon salt
	⅛ teaspoon pepper
	3 cups milk
LASAGNA	8 ounces mushrooms, chopped
	1 tablespoon margarine
	1 pound fresh spinach, chopped, or
	1 (10-ounce) package frozen chopped spinach
	4 ounces cream cheese, softened
	8 ounces medium shrimp, peeled
	8 ounces bay scallops
	½ cup chopped onions
	2 garlic cloves, minced
	2 tablespoons olive oil
	1 tablespoon basil
	1½ teaspoons oregano
	¼ teaspoon salt
	⅛ teaspoon pepper
	¼ cup grated Parmesan cheese
	2 tablespoons dry sherry
	8 ounces lasagna noodles, cooked, drained
	4 cups shredded mozzarella cheese
	1 pound crab meat, cooked, flaked

For the béchamel sauce, melt the margarine in a saucepan. Stir in the flour, salt and pepper. Cook over low heat for 3 to 5 minutes or until blended. Add the milk gradually, stirring constantly. Cook until thickened, stirring constantly. Cover and keep warm.

For the lasagna, sauté the mushrooms in the margarine in a skillet until tender and the liquid has evaporated. Wilt the spinach in a skillet or thaw the frozen spinach and drain thoroughly. Add the cream cheese and mix well.

Cook the shrimp and scallops in a small amount of water in a saucepan until partially cooked; drain.

Sauté the onions and garlic in the olive oil in a skillet until tender. Stir in the basil, oregano, salt and pepper. Add 1½ cups of the béchamel sauce, Parmesan cheese, wine, shrimp and scallops. Remove from heat.

To assemble, spread ½ cup béchamel sauce in a greased 9x13-inch baking pan. Arrange 4 noodles in the prepared dish. Spread the shrimp mixture over the noodles. Sprinkle with ⅓ of the mozzarella cheese. Layer ½ of the remaining noodles, spinach mixture, ½ of the remaining mozzarella cheese, sautéed mushrooms and crab meat over the layers. Top with the remaining noodles and remaining béchamel sauce. Bake, covered, at 350 degrees for 30 minutes. Uncover and sprinkle with the remaining mozzarella cheese. Bake, uncovered, for 15 minutes. Let stand for 15 minutes before serving.

Serves 8

Autumn Chicken Risotto with Spinach and Apple

INGREDIENTS

6 cups chicken broth
2 tablespoons olive oil
1/3 cup chopped red bell pepper
2 green onions, chopped
1 1/2 cups uncooked arborio rice
8 ounces fresh spinach leaves, rinsed, trimmed, coarsely chopped
2 cups chopped cooked chicken
1 large Fuji, Braeburn or Cortland apple, cored, chopped
1/3 cup freshly grated Parmesan cheese
3 tablespoons butter
Salt and pepper to taste

Bring the chicken broth to a boil in a medium saucepan. Reduce the heat to low and keep the broth hot.

Heat the olive oil in a large saucepan or stockpot over medium heat. Add the red pepper and green onions. Sauté for 2 minutes or until softened. Add the rice. Cook for 2 minutes, stirring constantly. Add 1 cup of the hot broth. Reduce the heat to medium-low. Simmer for 1 minute or until the broth is completely absorbed, stirring frequently. Add 1 cup hot broth. Simmer for 3 minutes or until absorbed, stirring constantly. Continue adding the remaining hot broth 1/2 cup at a time, cooking until absorbed after each addition and stirring frequently. The rice should be tender, but still slightly firm in the center and have a creamy consistency. Stir in the spinach, chicken, apple and Parmesan cheese. Simmer until heated through, stirring constantly. Remove from heat. Stir in the butter. Sprinkle with salt and pepper.

Serves 4 to 6

Note: The total cooking time for the remaining broth to be absorbed is 20 to 30 minutes.

Risotto

Risotto is an Italian dish, typically using arborio rice. For the perfect risotto, do not rinse the rice before cooking it. The starch that coats each grain lends itself to a creamier dish. Both the broth added to the risotto and the rice should be kept at a lively simmer throughout preparation.

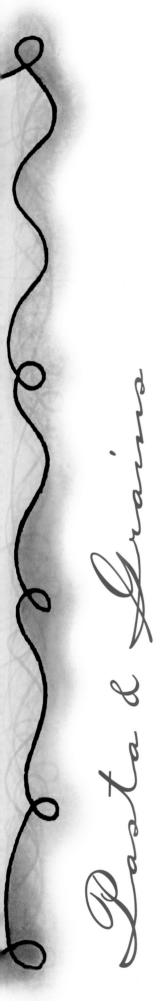

Tomato Basil and Chicken Risotto

INGREDIENTS

1 (14-ounce) can chicken broth
1 cup dry white wine
¾ cup water
2 garlic cloves, minced
3 tablespoons olive oil
1 pound boneless skinless chicken breasts, cut into
    bite-size pieces
Freshly ground pepper to taste
1 cup uncooked arborio rice
1 medium onion, chopped
1 large tomato, chopped
½ cup shredded asiago cheese
¼ cup finely shredded fresh basil

Heat the broth, wine and water in a medium saucepan over medium heat until the mixture is almost boiling. Reduce heat. Keep the mixture hot, but not boiling.

Heat the garlic in 1 tablespoon of the olive oil in a heavy 2-quart saucepan over medium-high heat. Add ½ of the chicken. Season with pepper. Cook for 4 minutes or until the chicken is cooked through, stirring frequently. Remove the chicken and set aside. Repeat with the remaining chicken and 1 tablespoon of the remaining olive oil.

Add the remaining 1 tablespoon olive oil to the saucepan. Stir in the rice and onion. Cook for 2 minutes. Stir in 1 cup of the hot broth mixture. Reduce the heat to medium-low. Continue adding the remaining broth mixture 1 cup at time and cooking until absorbed after each addition, stirring frequently. The rice should be tender and the mixture should have a creamy texture. Stir in the tomato and chicken. Cook until heated through. Stir in the cheese and basil. Serve immediately.

Serves 4

Shiitake Mushroom Risotto Cakes with Asparagus Relish

ANNIE GUNN'S

RISOTTO CAKES	4 cups chicken or vegetable broth
	1/2 cup canola oil
	2 tablespoons minced shallots
	2 tablespoons minced garlic
	1 cup uncooked arborio rice
	1 pound shiitake mushrooms
	1 cup grated Grana Padanoisan (Italian Mediterranean Parmesan cheese), or any grated Parmesan cheese
	2 tablespoons thyme
	1/2 cup extra-virgin olive oil
	Kosher salt to taste
	Cracked pepper to taste
ASPARAGUS RELISH	2 pounds asparagus, blanched
	Vegetable oil for coating
	8 ounces sweet red onion
	1/2 cup Champagne vinegar
	1 1/2 cups extra-virgin olive oil
	1 tablespoon thyme
	Kosher salt to taste
	Cracked pepper to taste

Annie Gunn's

Although Annie Gunn's was destroyed in the flood of 1993, this landmark, located in Chesterfield, came back and is better than ever. The hearty American cuisine includes smoked meats and fish served in a casual and relaxing atmosphere with an exceptional wine list.

For the risotto cakes, bring the chicken broth to a boil in a saucepan. Reduce the heat and simmer. Bring 1/2 cup canola oil just to the smoking point in a 6-quart stockpot. Add the shallots and garlic. Sauté until tender. Add the rice. Sauté until brown. Add the mushrooms. Sauté until tender. Add 1 cup of the simmering broth gradually, stirring constantly. Cook until most of the stock is absorbed. Repeat 2 times. Add the remaining 1 cup broth. Cook until the risotto is creamy. Add the Grana Padanoisan, thyme and extra-virgin olive oil. Season with kosher salt and pepper. Pour into a pan. Let stand until cool. Shape 2 tablespoonfuls of the risotto mixture at a time into patties. Sauté the patties in a nonstick skillet until golden brown.

For the asparagus relish, peel the asparagus. Coat the asparagus lightly with vegetable oil. Place on a grill rack. Grill until light brown. Cut diagonally into slices. Coat the onion lightly with vegetable oil. Place on a grill rack. Grill until light brown. Chop the onion finely. Blend the vinegar, olive oil and thyme in a bowl. Combine with the asparagus and onion in a bowl and mix well. Season with kosher salt and pepper.

To serve, spoon 2 tablespoonfuls of the asparagus relish on each risotto cake.

Serves 4 to 6

Spicy Rice Olé Casserole

INGREDIENTS

2 1/2 cups water
1 cup rice
2 tablespoons butter
1/2 teaspoon salt
1 small onion, chopped
2 tablespoons butter
3 (4-ounce) cans green chiles, chopped
1 pound Monterey Jack cheese, sliced
1 cup sour cream
2 cups shredded sharp Cheddar cheese

Bring the water to a boil in a saucepan. Add the rice, 2 tablespoons butter and salt and mix well; reduce heat. Simmer, covered, for 20 minutes.

Sauté the onion in 2 tablespoons butter in a skillet until translucent. Stir in the rice.

Layer the rice mixture, green chiles, Monterey Jack cheese and sour cream 1/2 at a time in a greased 1 1/2-quart baking dish. Sprinkle with Cheddar cheese. Bake at 350 degrees for 20 to 30 minutes or until bubbly.

Serves 4 to 6

Pasta & Grains

Barley Wild Rice Pilaf

The spinach, raisins and pine nuts add a real kick to this pilaf.

INGREDIENTS

1/2 cup pine nuts
2 quarts water
1 heaping cup uncooked wild rice (8 ounces)
1/4 cup (1/2 stick) unsalted butter or margarine
1 1/2 cups chopped onions
1 tablespoon chopped garlic
2 cups (or more) chicken stock
2 cups (or more) beef stock
1 1/2 cups pearl barley
1 teaspoon thyme
1 teaspoon salt
1/4 teaspoon freshly ground pepper
1/2 cup dark raisins
1 teaspoon lemon zest
1 1/2 tablespoons lemon juice
3 cups fresh spinach leaves, cut into 1/4-inch strips
1/2 teaspoon thyme (optional)
Salt and pepper to taste

Heat a small skillet over medium-high heat until hot. Add the pine nuts. Shake the skillet back and forth over the heat for 5 minutes or until the pine nuts are golden brown. Remove from heat and let cool.

Bring the water to a boil in a saucepan. Add the wild rice. Cook for 10 minutes or until slightly softened; drain well.

Heat the butter in a large saucepan. Add the onions. Sauté for 4 to 5 minutes. Add the garlic. Sauté for 1 minute. Add the chicken stock, beef stock, wild rice, barley, 1 teaspoon thyme, salt, pepper and raisins. Bring to a simmer and reduce heat. Cook, covered, for 35 minutes or until the liquid is absorbed, stirring several times toward the end of the cooking process to prevent sticking and adding 1/2 to 3/4 cup additional stock if liquid is absorbed too quickly. Remove from heat.

Stir in the toasted pine nuts, lemon zest and lemon juice. Add the spinach and stir until wilted and bright green. Season with 1/2 teaspoon thyme and salt and pepper to taste. Serve hot.

Serves 8 to 10

Note: Pilaf can be cooled, covered and refrigerated overnight before adding the pine nuts, etc. Reheat, covered, over medium heat, stirring frequently or bake in a preheated 400-degree oven for 15 minutes or until heated through.

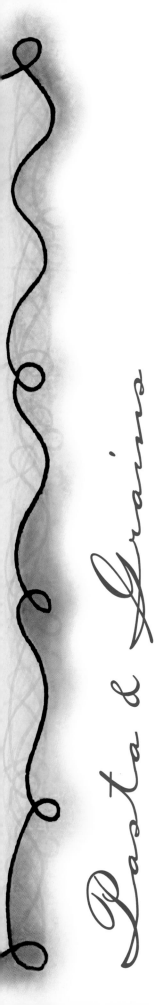

Persian Rice Pilaf

A savory, crunchy accompaniment to a lamb or poultry dish.

INGREDIENTS	1 cup chopped onions
	1 tablespoon butter
	1 cup uncooked rice
	1½ cups chicken broth
	½ cup light cream
	½ cup raisins
	1 teaspoon salt
	¼ teaspoon nutmeg
GARNISH	Toasted almonds

Sauté the onions in the butter in a skillet until tender. Add the rice. Cook for 2 minutes. Stir in the broth, cream, raisins, salt and nutmeg; cover. Bring to a boil and reduce heat.

Simmer for 20 minutes or until the rice is tender and the liquid is absorbed. Fluff with a fork. Garnish with toasted almonds.

Serves 6 to 8

Side Dishes

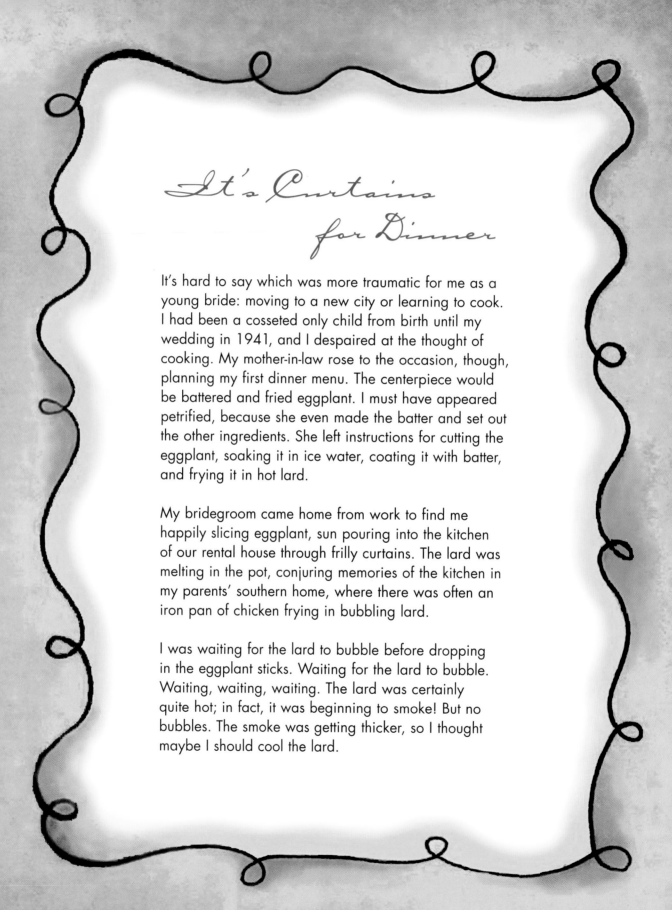

It's Curtains for Dinner

It's hard to say which was more traumatic for me as a young bride: moving to a new city or learning to cook. I had been a cosseted only child from birth until my wedding in 1941, and I despaired at the thought of cooking. My mother-in-law rose to the occasion, though, planning my first dinner menu. The centerpiece would be battered and fried eggplant. I must have appeared petrified, because she even made the batter and set out the other ingredients. She left instructions for cutting the eggplant, soaking it in ice water, coating it with batter, and frying it in hot lard.

My bridegroom came home from work to find me happily slicing eggplant, sun pouring into the kitchen of our rental house through frilly curtains. The lard was melting in the pot, conjuring memories of the kitchen in my parents' southern home, where there was often an iron pan of chicken frying in bubbling lard.

I was waiting for the lard to bubble before dropping in the eggplant sticks. Waiting for the lard to bubble. Waiting, waiting, waiting. The lard was certainly quite hot; in fact, it was beginning to smoke! But no bubbles. The smoke was getting thicker, so I thought maybe I should cool the lard.

I took it over to the sink, figuring a little cold water would do the trick. Whoomf!! The frilly curtains burst into flames. Fire, fire! The quick-witted bridegroom called the fire department, rushed into the kitchen and put a lid on the pot, then yanked down the curtains into running water.

The firemen were understanding, the bride had a good hysterical cry, and many hugs and pats later, the happy couple was off to the Parkmoor, a restaurant in Clayton, and to the tranquility of the Pevely Fountain for ice cream.

Ellen Jones

Morel and Asparagus Sauté

This dish is especially good with grilled steak or veal chops.

INGREDIENTS

4 ounces fresh morel mushrooms
8 ounces asparagus
1/4 cup (1/2 stick) unsalted butter
2 tablespoons minced shallots
2 tablespoons flour
1/2 cup beef consommé
1/2 cup water
Salt and pepper to taste

Cut the mushrooms into halves lengthwise or into quarters if the mushrooms are large. Rinse in cold water and drain on paper towels.

Trim the asparagus and cut diagonally into 1-inch long pieces.

Heat the butter in a 10-inch heavy skillet over medium heat until the foam subsides. Add the mushrooms, asparagus and shallots.

Sauté for 4 minutes or until the asparagus is tender-crisp. Sprinkle with flour. Sauté over medium-low heat for 2 minutes. Add the consommé and water. Bring to a boil and reduce heat, stirring constantly.

Simmer for 2 minutes, stirring constantly. Season with salt and pepper.

Serves 4

Oriental Cashew Asparagus

INGREDIENTS

1 pound fresh asparagus
1 1/2 cups quartered fresh mushrooms
1 medium onion, cut into thin wedges
1/4 cup chopped red bell pepper
2 tablespoons butter or margarine
1 teaspoon cornstarch
1/8 to 1/4 teaspoon pepper
1 tablespoon teriyaki sauce
1 tablespoon dry sherry
2 teaspoons water
2 tablespoons cashew halves

Trim the asparagus and cut on the bias into 1-inch-long pieces. Place in a steamer basket over but not touching gently boiling water in a saucepan. Cover and reduce heat. Steam for 2 minutes. Add the mushrooms, onion and red pepper. Steam, covered, for 2 to 5 minutes or until tender-crisp. Remove the basket and discard the liquid.

Melt the butter in the saucepan. Stir in the cornstarch and pepper. Add the teriyaki sauce, sherry and 2 teaspoons water. Cook until thickened and bubbly, stirring constantly. Add the steamed vegetables and toss until coated. Cook until heated through. Sprinkle each serving with cashews.

Serves 4

"Best of the Midwest" Baked Beans

The tart apple and golden raisins make this dish special.

INGREDIENTS

2 (16-ounce) cans pork and beans, drained
3/4 cup mesquite barbecue sauce
2 tablespoons golden raisins
1/2 small onion, chopped
1/2 cup packed brown sugar
3 slices bacon, chopped
1 tart apple, peeled, chopped
1/2 teaspoon liquid smoke
1/4 teaspoon ginger

Combine the pork and beans, barbecue sauce, raisins, onion, brown sugar, bacon, apple, liquid smoke and ginger in a bowl and mix well. Pour into a 2-quart baking dish. Bake, uncovered, at 350 degrees for 1 hour.

Serves 6

Bleu Cheese Broccoli

INGREDIENTS

1 1/2 pounds fresh broccoli
3 ounces cream cheese, softened
1/3 cup crumbled bleu cheese
2 tablespoons butter
2 tablespoons flour
1/4 teaspoon salt
1/4 teaspoon white pepper
1 cup milk
1/2 cup finely crushed butter crackers

Trim the broccoli. Cut into florets. Cut the stems into pieces. Steam the broccoli in a steamer until tender-crisp; drain.

Combine the cream cheese, bleu cheese, butter, flour, salt and white pepper in a saucepan and mix well. Add the milk. Bring to a boil, stirring constantly. Stir in the broccoli.

Spoon into a buttered 1-quart baking dish. Sprinkle with the cracker crumbs. Bake at 350 degrees for 3 minutes.

Serves 6

Feuilletée of Broccoli with Mushroom Sauce

BEURRE MANIE	1 tablespoon flour
	1 tablespoon butter, chilled
MUSHROOM SAUCE	3 tablespoons butter
	1 pound fresh mushrooms, sliced
	1½ cups heavy cream
	2 tablespoons finely minced fresh chives
	Salt and freshly ground white pepper to taste
BROCCOLI	Salt to taste
	1 large bunch broccoli, trimmed into florets
ASSEMBLY	6 to 8 puff pastry shells

For the buerre manie, place the flour in a baking pan. Bake at 350 degrees for 5 minutes or until medium brown. Let stand until cool. Combine the flour and butter in a bowl and mash to form a paste.

For the mushroom sauce, melt the butter in a large heavy skillet over medium-high heat. Add the mushrooms. Sauté until brown. Remove the mushrooms to a bowl. Add the cream to the skillet. Bring to a boil. Boil until the mixture is reduced by one-fourth. Add the buerre manie a small amount at a time, whisking constantly after each addition. Cook until the sauce heavily coats the back of a spoon, whisking constantly. Stir in the chives. Return the mushrooms to the skillet and mix well. Season with salt and white pepper.

For the broccoli, bring salted water to a boil in a large saucepan. Add the broccoli and reduce heat. Simmer, uncovered, until tender-crisp; drain.

To assemble, place the broccoli in the puff pastry shells. Spoon the mushroom sauce over the broccoli.

Serves 6 to 8

Side Dishes

Stir-Fried Broccoli and Romaine

This recipe is equally delicious as a side dish or a salad.

INGREDIENTS
1/2 bunch broccoli
1 medium head romaine or endive
4 slices bacon, chopped
1/4 cup water
1 teaspoon salt
1 teaspoon sugar

Remove the large leaves from the broccoli. Cut the broccoli into 1/2x2-inch pieces. Tear the romaine into bite-size pieces.

Fry the bacon in a skillet or wok over medium heat until crisp. Add the broccoli. Sauté until coated with the bacon drippings. Add the water. Cook, covered, for 4 minutes. Add the romaine, salt and sugar. Stir-fry for 3 minutes. Serve immediately.

Serves 4

Cinnamon Carrots

INGREDIENTS
2 pounds baby carrots
1/3 cup butter
1/2 cup sugar
1 tablespoon salt
1/3 teaspoon cinnamon, or to taste
1/2 cup boiling water

Place the carrots in a baking dish. Cut the butter into chunks and arrange over the carrots. Sprinkle with sugar, salt and cinnamon. Pour the boiling water over the top. Bake at 350 degrees for 1 1/2 hours or until tender.

Serves 8 to 10

Carrots Dijon

INGREDIENTS
- ½ cup water
- 2 pounds carrots, cut ¼ inch thick
- 2 tablespoons butter or margarine
- 2 tablespoons brown sugar
- 2 tablespoons Dijon mustard
- Snipped parsley to taste

Bring the water to a boil in a saucepan. Place the carrots in a steamer basket. Place in the saucepan. Cover and reduce heat. Simmer for 8 to 12 minutes or until tender. Remove the carrots from the saucepan and discard the water. Return the carrots to the saucepan.

Add the butter, brown sugar and Dijon mustard. Cook over medium heat for 1 to 2 minutes or until glazed, stirring constantly. Spoon into a serving dish. Sprinkle with parsley.

Serves 6 to 8

Honey Ginger Carrots Elegante

Serve this very festive-looking dish at Thanksgiving or any other holiday.

INGREDIENTS
- 1 pound carrots, thinly sliced
- ½ cup golden raisins
- ¼ cup (½ stick) margarine
- 3 tablespoons honey
- 1 tablespoon lemon juice
- ½ teaspoon ginger
- ¼ cup sliced almonds

Cook the carrots in ½ inch of boiling water in a large saucepan for 8 minutes; drain.

Combine the raisins, margarine, honey, lemon juice and ginger in a small microwave-safe bowl. Microwave on Medium for 1 minute or until the margarine is melted; mix well. Add to the carrots and toss to coat. Add the almonds and toss to mix well. Spoon into a 1-quart baking dish.

Bake, uncovered, at 375 degrees for 35 minutes, stirring occasionally.

Serves 4 to 6

Italian Green Beans

INGREDIENTS
1 pound green beans, trimmed, snapped
1 onion, sliced
1 garlic clove, minced
2 tablespoons vegetable oil
1 large tomato, peeled, seeded, chopped
1 tablespoon dry white wine
1 tablespoon each chopped green bell pepper,
    chopped celery and chopped parsley
1/2 teaspoon marjoram
1/2 teaspoon rosemary
Salt and pepper to taste
Freshly grated Parmesan cheese

Cook the green beans in boiling water in a large saucepan for 7 minutes; drain.

Sauté the onion and garlic in the oil in a skillet for 10 minutes or until soft but not brown. Add the tomato, wine, green pepper, celery, parsley, marjoram, rosemary and salt and pepper to taste. Simmer for 10 minutes. Add the green beans. Cook for 5 minutes. Sprinkle with Parmesan cheese. Serve immediately.

Serves 4 to 6

Green Beans Caesar

INGREDIENTS
1 1/2 pounds fresh green beans, trimmed
2 tablespoons vegetable oil
1 tablespoon white wine vinegar or tarragon
    vinegar
1 tablespoon minced onion
1 garlic clove, crushed
1/4 teaspoon salt
1/8 teaspoon pepper
2 tablespoons dry bread crumbs
2 tablespoons grated Parmesan cheese
1 tablespoon butter or margarine, melted
Paprika to taste

Cut the green beans into 1-inch pieces. Cook in a small amount of water in a saucepan for 15 to 20 minutes or until tender-crisp; drain.

Combine the oil, white wine vinegar, onion, garlic, salt and pepper in a bowl and mix well. Add the green beans and toss to mix. Spoon into an ungreased 1-quart baking dish.

Mix the bread crumbs, Parmesan cheese and butter in a bowl. Sprinkle over the green beans. Sprinkle paprika over the top. Bake at 350 degrees for 30 minutes or until heated through.

Serves 6

Wild Mushroom Bread Pudding

INGREDIENTS

3 tablespoons olive oil
6 ounces shiitake mushrooms
6 ounces oyster mushrooms
6 ounces cremini mushrooms
2 portobello mushrooms
4 teaspoons garlic
1 tablespoon chopped fresh basil
1 tablespoon chopped fresh parsley
1 teaspoon sage
1 teaspoon thyme
Salt and pepper to taste
5 large eggs
2 cups heavy cream
1 cup milk
1/4 cup freshly grated Parmesan cheese
3/4 teaspoon salt
1/2 teaspoon pepper
6 cups trimmed 1-inch dry French bread cubes
2 tablespoons freshly grated Parmesan cheese

Heat the oil in a large heavy saucepan over medium-high heat. Add the mushrooms, garlic, basil, parsley, sage and thyme. Sauté for 15 minutes or until the mushrooms are tender and brown. Remove from heat. Season with salt and pepper to taste.

Whisk the eggs, cream, milk, 1/4 cup Parmesan cheese, 3/4 teaspoon salt and 1/2 teaspoon pepper in a large bowl. Add the bread cubes and toss to coat. Let stand for 15 minutes.

Stir in the sautéed mushrooms. Spoon into a lightly buttered 8x8-inch glass baking dish. Sprinkle with 2 tablespoons Parmesan cheese. Bake at 350 degrees for 1 hour. Serve warm.

Serves 6

Note: Do not use skim or low-fat milk in this recipe.

Side Dishes

Magnificent Mushrooms

This dish could be baked in small ramekins as individual appetizers or first-course servings.

INGREDIENTS	½ cup (1 stick) butter or margarine
	1 pound fresh mushrooms, sliced
	2 cups bread crumbs (made from dry French bread)
	Salt and pepper to taste
	1 cup sour cream
	⅓ cup dry sherry

Melt the butter in a 1½-quart baking dish. Pour the butter into a small bowl.

Arrange ⅓ of the mushrooms in the prepared baking dish. Sprinkle with ⅓ of the bread crumbs. Drizzle with ⅓ of the butter. Season with salt and pepper. Spread ½ of the sour cream over the layers. Continue layering with ½ of the remaining mushrooms and ½ of the remaining bread crumbs. Drizzle with ½ of the remaining butter. Season with salt and pepper.

Spread the remaining sour cream over the layers. Continue layering with the remaining mushrooms and bread crumbs. Drizzle with the remaining butter. Pour the wine over the layers. Bake, covered, at 325 degrees for 25 minutes.

Serves 6

Grilled Portobello Mushrooms

INGREDIENTS	2 large portobello mushrooms
	½ cup extra-virgin olive oil
	Juice of 1 large lemon
	½ teaspoon kosher salt
	½ teaspoon cracked black pepper
	1 garlic clove, chopped
	2 tablespoons chopped fresh parsley
GARNISH	2 teaspoons grated Parmesan cheese

Clean and gill the mushrooms, removing and discarding the stems. Combine the oil, lemon juice, kosher salt, pepper, garlic and parsley in a bowl and mix well. Add the mushrooms. Marinate for 15 to 20 minutes or until soaked through; drain.

Place the mushrooms on a grill rack. Grill for 2 to 5 minutes or until tender. Place on a serving plate. Garnish with Parmesan cheese.

Serves 2 to 4

Basiled Peas

INGREDIENTS

2 (10-ounce) packages frozen green peas
Boiling water
1/2 cup sliced green onions with tops
2 1/2 tablespoons butter
2 tablespoons chopped parsley
1 tablespoon sugar
1 teaspoon salt
1/2 teaspoon crushed basil
1/8 teaspoon pepper

Place the green peas in a colander. Pour boiling water over the peas to separate.

Sauté the green onions in the butter in a large skillet until tender. Stir in the peas, parsley, sugar, salt, basil and pepper. Cook, uncovered, for 5 minutes.

Serves 8

Chile Potatoes

INGREDIENTS

3 1/2 pounds small red potatoes
2 tablespoons olive oil
2 large onions, chopped
1 garlic clove, finely chopped
1 to 2 tablespoons butter
Salt and pepper to taste
1/2 cup chopped green chiles
1/2 cup shredded Monterey Jack cheese

Boil the potatoes in water to cover in a large saucepan until just tender; drain. Let stand until cool. Cut into 1-inch chunks.

Heat the olive oil in a large skillet. Add the onions. Sauté until soft. Add the garlic. Sauté briefly. Add the potatoes and butter. Season with salt and pepper. Sauté until the potatoes are brown and crisp. Stir in the green chiles. Cook for 2 minutes. Spread the potatoes evenly in the skillet. Sprinkle with the cheese and cover tightly. Turn off heat. Let stand for 2 to 3 minutes or until the cheese melts.

Serves 8

Side Dishes

Potato Horseradish Gratin with Caramelized Onions

POTATOES	2 1/2 pounds baking potatoes
	1/2 teaspoon salt
	1/2 teaspoon pepper
	2 cups half-and-half
	1/2 cup prepared horseradish
CARAMELIZED	1/4 cup (1/2 stick) butter
ONIONS	2 large onions, thinly sliced
	1 teaspoon sugar
	1/2 teaspoon salt
	1/2 teaspoon pepper
	1 tablespoon balsamic vinegar
	1 cup shredded Swiss cheese
	2 tablespoons chopped parsley
GARNISH	2 tablespoons chopped parsley

For the potatoes, boil the potatoes in water to cover in a saucepan for 20 minutes or until almost tender. Drain and cool slightly. Peel the potatoes and cut into 1/4-inch-thick slices. Arrange in a lightly greased 9x13-inch baking dish. Sprinkle with the salt and pepper. Blend the half-and-half and horseradish in a bowl. Pour over the potatoes. Bake, covered, at 400 degrees for 40 minutes.

For the caramelized onions, melt the butter in a large skillet over medium heat. Add the onions, sugar, salt and pepper. Cook for 5 to 8 minutes or until caramelized, stirring occasionally. Stir in the balsamic vinegar. Cook for 2 minutes or until the liquid evaporates. Remove from heat. Cool for 5 minutes. Fold in the Swiss cheese and parsley.

To assemble, uncover the potatoes and top with the caramelized onions. Reduce the oven temperature to 350 degrees. Bake for 30 minutes. Garnish with the parsley.

Serves 8

Crunchy Potato Casserole

POTATOES   2 pounds frozen hash brown potatoes
$\frac{1}{2}$ cup chopped onion
1 teaspoon salt
$\frac{1}{4}$ teaspoon pepper
1 (10-ounce) can cream of chicken soup
10 ounces mild Cheddar cheese, shredded
$\frac{1}{2}$ cup (1 stick) butter or margarine, melted
2 cups sour cream

TOPPING   2 cups crushed cornflakes
$\frac{1}{4}$ cup ($\frac{1}{2}$ stick) butter or margarine, melted

For the potatoes, combine the potatoes, onion, salt, pepper, soup, cheese, butter and sour cream in a large bowl and mix well. Pat into a greased 9x13-inch baking dish. Bake, covered with foil, at 350 degrees for 45 minutes.

For the topping, mix the cornflakes and butter in a bowl. Spoon over the potato mixture. Bake, uncovered, for 25 minutes.

Serves 12 to 15

Sautéed New Potatoes

INGREDIENTS   3 tablespoons butter
3 tablespoons olive oil
40 small white new potatoes, peeled
1 cup chopped fresh parsley
Salt and pepper to taste

Heat the butter and olive oil in a large skillet over high heat. Add the potatoes. Sauté for 15 minutes, shaking the skillet frequently to avoid sticking. Add the parsley, salt and pepper. Reduce the heat to medium-low. Cook for 15 minutes or until the potatoes are brown and tender in the middle, shaking the skillet occasionally.

Serves 8

Side Dishes

Sweet Potatoes Supreme

INGREDIENTS
3 large sweet potatoes
1/2 cup (1 stick) butter
2 eggs, beaten
1/4 cup sugar
1 tablespoon cinnamon
1 teaspoon nutmeg
3 tablespoons butter, softened
1/2 cup packed brown sugar
3 tablespoons flour
1/2 cup chopped pecans

Cut the sweet potatoes into quarters. Boil the sweet potatoes in water to cover in a saucepan until tender; drain. Remove the skins from the sweet potatoes. Place the sweet potatoes in a large bowl and mash until smooth. Add 1/2 cup butter, eggs, sugar, cinnamon and nutmeg and beat until smooth. Spoon into an 1 1/2-quart baking dish.

Cut the butter into the brown sugar and flour in a bowl until crumbly. Stir in the pecans. Sprinkle over the sweet potato mixture. Bake at 350 degrees for 30 minutes.

Serves 8

Crunchy Potato Strips

INGREDIENTS
2 tablespoons cornstarch
2 tablespoons soy sauce
4 cups cold water
4 baking potatoes

Combine the cornstarch, soy sauce and water in a large bowl and mix well. Peel the potatoes and cut into strips. Add to the soy sauce mixture. Soak for 1 hour; drain. Pat dry using paper towels.

Place the potatoes in a single layer on a baking sheet. Bake at 375 degrees for 20 minutes. Turn over the potatoes. Bake for 20 minutes longer or until golden brown.

Serves 4

Sweet Potatoes

Sweet potatoes are at their best during the months of August through October. When choosing sweet potatoes, look for those that are firm, heavy, and without bruises or cuts. The darker the skin, the sweeter and moister the pulp of the potato.

Savory Summer Vegetable Tart

EGGPLANT SAUCE	¼ cup olive oil
	3 large garlic cloves, minced
	1 medium green bell pepper, chopped
	1 medium eggplant, cut into ½-inch chunks
	1 large onion, chopped
	1 teaspoon thyme
	Salt and pepper to taste
	3 tablespoons tomato paste
TART	Olive oil
	10 sheets phyllo pastry, thawed
	10 teaspoons grated Parmesan cheese
	1½ cups grated provolone cheese
	6 Roma tomatoes, cut into ¼-inch slices
	2 medium zucchini, cut into ¼-inch slices
	Salt and pepper to taste
	2 teaspoons grated Parmesan cheese

For the eggplant sauce, heat the olive oil in a large nonstick skillet over medium-high heat. Add the garlic. Sauté for 2 minutes. Add the green pepper, eggplant, onion and thyme. Season generously with salt and pepper. Sauté for 10 minutes or until the vegetables begin to soften. Reduce heat to low. Cook, covered, for 10 minutes or until the eggplant is tender, stirring occasionally. Stir in the tomato paste. Cook, uncovered, for 3 minutes or until the liquid evaporates. Spoon into a strainer placed over a bowl. Let stand until cool. Discard the liquid in the bowl. Pour the eggplant sauce into a container with a lid. Store, covered, in the refrigerator for up to 24 hours before preparing the tart, if desired.

For the tart, brush a 9-inch tart pan with a removable bottom with olive oil. Stack the phyllo sheets on a work surface. Cut the phyllo stack into 11-inch circles. Line the prepared pan with 1 phyllo circle, allowing the side to extend above the rim of the pan and keeping the remaining phyllo sheets covered with a damp cloth to prevent drying out. Brush the phyllo circle with olive oil and sprinkle with 1 teaspoon Parmesan cheese. Top with another phyllo circle, brushing with olive oil and sprinkling with 1 teaspoon Parmesan cheese. Continue the stacking process with remaining phyllo circles and remaining 8 teaspoons Parmesan cheese.

Spoon the eggplant sauce over the phyllo layers. Sprinkle provolone cheese evenly over the top. Arrange the tomato slices and zucchini slices in alternating overlapping concentric circles over the provolone cheese. Brush with olive oil. Season with salt and pepper. Sprinkle with 2 teaspoons Parmesan cheese. Bake at 350 degrees for 1 hour or until the crust is golden brown. Let stand until cool before serving.

Serves 8

Side Dishes

Vegetables Glazed with Balsamic Vinegar

INGREDIENTS

2 tablespoons olive oil
1 red bell pepper, cut into strips 1/4 inch wide
1 yellow bell pepper, cut into strips 1/4 inch wide
1 small onion, thinly sliced
2 zucchini, cut into 1/2-inch slices
2 yellow squash, cut into 1/2-inch slices
2 tablespoons balsamic vinegar
Salt and pepper to taste

Heat the olive oil in a large heavy nonstick skillet over medium-high heat. Add the bell peppers and onion. Sauté for 5 minutes or until the vegetables begin to soften. Add the zucchini and yellow squash. Sauté for 8 minutes or until tender. Add the vinegar. Boil for 2 minutes or until the liquid is reduced to a glaze consistency, tossing constantly to coat the vegetables. Season with salt and pepper.

Serves 4

Sophisticated Spinach Bake

INGREDIENTS

2 (10-ounce) packages frozen chopped spinach
1/4 cup (1/2 stick) butter
1/4 cup chopped onion
1 tablespoon flour
8 ounces cream cheese, softened
1 1/2 teaspoons salt
1/8 teaspoon pepper
1/8 teaspoon nutmeg
2 cups seasoned croutons

Prepare the spinach using the package directions; drain. Melt the butter in a skillet over medium heat. Add the onion. Sauté until tender. Blend in the flour. Add the spinach, cream cheese, salt, pepper and nutmeg. Heat until the cream cheese melts, stirring constantly. Place in a serving dish. Sprinkle with croutons.

Serves 6

Note: May make ahead, refrigerate and reheat when ready to serve. Sprinkle with croutons just before serving.

Balsamic Vinegar

Balsamic vinegar is a fragrant wine-based vinegar made in Northern Italy. It can be used in salads, sprinkled on cold meats or over hot vegetables, or used to deglaze a pan. Balsamic vinegar is also delicious sprinkled over a quality extra-virgin olive oil and used in place of butter as a dipping sauce for crusty French or Italian bread.

Spicy Green Enchiladas

TORTILLA ROLL-UPS	1/2 cup vegetable oil
	12 corn tortillas
	3 cups shredded Monterey Jack cheese
	1 cup chopped onion
GREEN CHILE SAUCE	1/4 cup (1/2 stick) butter or margarine
	1/4 cup flour
	2 cups chicken broth
	1 cup sour cream
	1 (4-ounce) can chopped green chiles, drained

For the tortilla roll-ups, heat the oil in a skillet. Add 1 tortilla. Heat for 1 minute or until soft enough to roll. Remove from the skillet. Sprinkle with 1/4 cup of the cheese and 4 teaspoons of the onion. Roll up to enclose the filling. Place seam side down in a 9x13-inch glass baking dish. Repeat with the remaining tortillas.

For the green chile sauce, melt the butter in a saucepan. Stir in the flour. Cook for 1 to 2 minutes or until blended, stirring constantly. Add the chicken broth, sour cream and green chiles. Cook until thickened, stirring constantly.

To assemble, pour the green chile sauce over the tortilla roll-ups. Bake, covered, at 350 degrees for 15 minutes. Bake, uncovered, for 5 minutes longer. Let stand for 10 to 15 minutes before serving.

Serves 6

Note: May add additional cheese and onion to the sauce.

Sautéed Cherry Tomatoes

These are particularly attractive when served in fried grated potato baskets.

INGREDIENTS

6 tablespoons butter
1 garlic clove, minced
4 to 5 dozen cherry tomatoes, rinsed, stemmed
2 tablespoons chopped fresh parsley
1 tablespoon chopped fresh dill
Salt and pepper to taste

Melt the butter in a skillet. Add the garlic. Sauté until soft. Add the tomatoes, parsley, dill, salt and pepper. Cook for 3 minutes, shaking the skillet until the tomatoes are coated. Serve immediately.

Serves 6 to 8

Blushing Applesauce

INGREDIENTS

4 pounds Granny Smith or other tart apples, peeled, cored, thinly sliced (about 8)
1½ cups apple juice
1 cup cranberries
3 strips lemon peel
3 tablespoons fresh lemon juice
1½ cups sugar

Combine the apples, apple juice, cranberries, lemon peel and lemon juice in a Dutch oven. Bring to a boil and reduce heat to low. Simmer, uncovered, for 10 minutes. Stir in the sugar. Return to a boil and reduce heat to medium or low. Cook, partially covered, for 1 hour, stirring occasionally. Spoon into jars or a covered container. Store in the refrigerator for up to 3 weeks.

Makes about 4 cups

Grand Marnier Cranberries

A wonderful addition to Thanksgiving dinner, it is also good served cold from the refrigerator.

INGREDIENTS

1 (12-ounce) package cranberries
2 cups sugar
2 tablespoons thawed orange juice concentrate
2 ounces Grand Marnier

Rinse the cranberries and place in a baking dish. Sprinkle with the sugar. Drizzle with orange juice concentrate and 1/2 of the Grand Marnier. Bake, covered, at 350 degrees for 1 hour. Drizzle with the remaining Grand Marnier. Chill, covered, for 12 to 36 hours. Place in a cold oven. Bake, covered, at 325 degrees for 45 to 50 minutes. Let stand for 5 minutes before serving.

Serves 6 to 8

Side Dishes

Sweet Endings

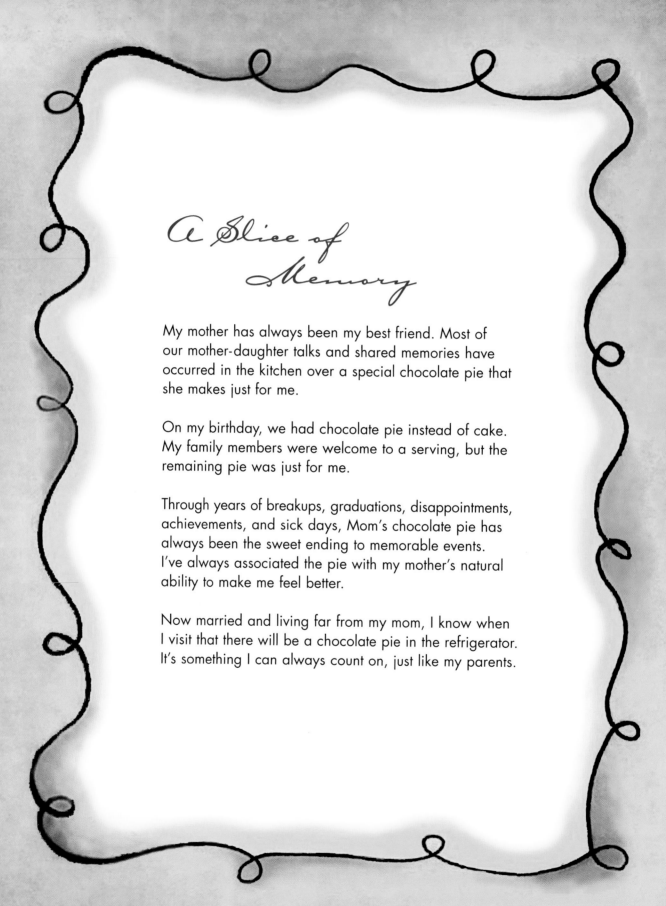

A Slice of Memory

My mother has always been my best friend. Most of our mother-daughter talks and shared memories have occurred in the kitchen over a special chocolate pie that she makes just for me.

On my birthday, we had chocolate pie instead of cake. My family members were welcome to a serving, but the remaining pie was just for me.

Through years of breakups, graduations, disappointments, achievements, and sick days, Mom's chocolate pie has always been the sweet ending to memorable events. I've always associated the pie with my mother's natural ability to make me feel better.

Now married and living far from my mom, I know when I visit that there will be a chocolate pie in the refrigerator. It's something I can always count on, just like my parents.

I make the pie on my own now for my husband, and I hope one day I can share this special memory with a child of my own. I love Mom's chocolate pie, but not near as much as I love her.

Stacy Wells

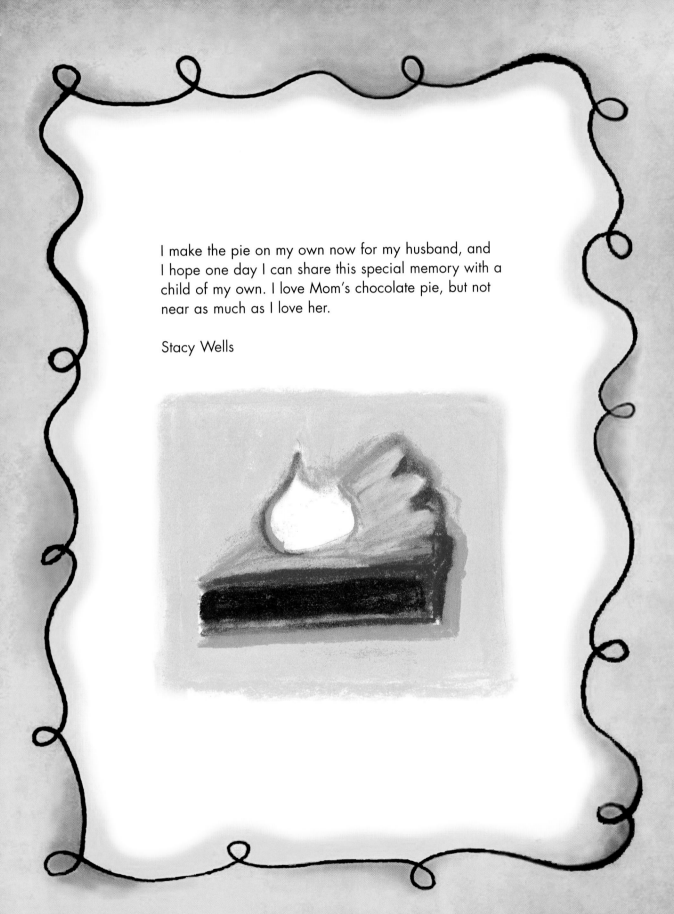

Chocolate Almond Dip

INGREDIENTS   2¼ ounces blanched sliced almonds
8 ounces bittersweet chocolate, broken into pieces
1½ cups heavy cream
2 tablespoons sugar
½ teaspoon vanilla extract
Fresh strawberries, banana slices, mandarin
     oranges and/or pound cake cubes

     Process the almonds in a food processor until finely chopped.
Microwave the chocolate in a heavy microwave-safe bowl on High for
30 seconds; stir. Continue to microwave at 30-second intervals until melted,
stirring after each interval.
     Combine the cream, sugar and vanilla in a heavy saucepan. Bring
to a low boil over medium heat. Boil until the sugar is dissolved, stirring
constantly. Remove from heat and cool slightly. Pour over the chocolate,
whisking constantly until blended, discarding any chocolate lumps. Stir in
the almonds. Spoon into a serving bowl. Chill, covered, for 2 hours or
longer. Bring to room temperature before serving. Serve with fresh
strawberries, banana slices, mandarin oranges and/or pound cake cubes.

Makes 1½ to 2 cups

Citrus Lime Dip

INGREDIENTS   1 cup sour cream
2 tablespoons fresh lime juice
2 tablespoons sugar
1½ teaspoons lime zest
Fresh sliced fruit, such as cantaloupe, honeydew
     melon, strawberries or kiwifruit

GARNISHES   Mint or herb leaves
Twist of lime

     Combine the sour cream, lime juice, sugar and lime zest in a small
bowl and mix well. Spoon into a small serving bowl. Place in the center of
a large platter. Surround the bowl with fresh sliced fruit. Garnish the dip
with mint or herb leaves and a twist of lime.

Makes about 1 cup

Apple Berry Salsa with Cinnamon Chips

CINNAMON CHIPS
2 tablespoons sugar
1/2 teaspoon cinnamon
8 (7-inch) flour tortillas
Melted butter

APPLE BERRY SALSA
8 medium Granny Smith apples, peeled, cored, sliced
1 cup sliced strawberries
6 kiwifruit, peeled, quartered
1/4 cup packed brown sugar
1/4 cup apple jelly

For the cinnamon chips, combine the sugar and cinnamon in a small bowl. Brush the tortillas lightly with melted butter. Sprinkle with the cinnamon-sugar. Cut each tortilla into 8 wedges. Place in a single layer on an ungreased baking sheet.

Bake at 400 degrees for 10 minutes or until light brown and crisp. Remove to a wire rack to cool.

For the apple berry salsa, process the apples, strawberries and kiwifruit in a food processor until chopped. Add the brown sugar and jelly and mix well.

To serve, pour the apple berry salsa into a serving bowl. Serve with the cinnamon chips.

Serves 6 to 8

Apple Blueberry Crumble

Serve this dish warm with vanilla bean ice cream.

FILLING	3 (6-ounce) containers fresh blueberries (about 3 cups)
	6 to 8 Granny Smith or other tart apples, peeled, cored, cut into 1/3-inch slices
	3/4 cup sugar
	6 tablespoons orange juice
	3 tablespoons cornstarch
TOPPING	1 cup flour
	1/2 cup packed brown sugar
	1/2 cup (1 stick) unsalted butter, cut into pieces

For the filling, combine the blueberries, apples, sugar, orange juice and cornstarch in a large bowl and toss gently. Spoon into an 8x8-inch glass baking dish. Place on a baking sheet. Bake at 375 degrees for 45 minutes or until the fruit begins to soften and bubble slightly.

For the topping, mix the flour and brown sugar in a medium bowl. Cut in the butter until crumbly.

To assemble, sprinkle the topping over the filling. Bake for 35 minutes or until the apples are tender and the topping is crisp. Cool slightly before serving.

Serves 6

Apple Pecan Crisp

INGREDIENTS

2 tablespoons flour
1¼ teaspoons baking powder
⅛ teaspoon salt
1 egg
¾ cup sugar
½ cup chopped pecans
1 apple, peeled, cored, finely chopped
1 teaspoon vanilla extract
1 cup whipping cream, whipped

Mix the flour, baking powder and salt together. Beat the egg in a mixing bowl until light. Add the sugar gradually, beating constantly until fluffy. Add the flour mixture and beat well. Stir in the pecans, apple and vanilla. Spread evenly in a buttered pie plate. Bake at 350 degrees for 35 minutes. Serve hot with the whipped cream.

Serves 4

Gooey Chocolate Cobbler

INGREDIENTS

2 cups (4 sticks) unsalted butter
10 ounces semisweet chocolate, chopped
4 cups sugar
8 large eggs
1 teaspoon vanilla extract
1⅔ cups flour
1 teaspoon salt
2½ cups walnuts, chopped, lightly toasted
Vanilla ice cream

Melt the butter and chocolate in a large heavy saucepan over medium-low heat until melted and smooth, stirring constantly. Remove from heat. Whisk in the sugar. Whisk in the eggs 1 at a time. Whisk in the vanilla, flour and salt. Stir in the walnuts. Spoon into a buttered 10x15-inch baking dish. Bake at 350 degrees for 50 minutes or until the top is crisp and a tester inserted into the center comes out with wet crumbs attached. Cool for 15 minutes. Serve warm with the vanilla ice cream.

Serves 10 to 12

The Finishing Touch to that Special Dinner

Amaretto—almond-flavored liqueur

Chambord—raspberry-flavored liqueur

Crème de Menthe—peppermint-flavored liqueur

Frangelico—toasted hazelnut-flavored liqueur

Grand Marnier—orange-flavored liqueur

Kahlúa—coffee-flavored liqueur

Café au Lait Cheesecake

CRUST
:   1¾ cups chocolate wafer crumbs
    (about 30 cookies)
    ⅓ cup butter, melted

FILLING
:   2 ounces semisweet chocolate, chopped
    2 tablespoons water
    1½ tablespoons instant coffee granules
    2 tablespoons coffee liqueur
    24 ounces cream cheese, softened
    1 cup sugar
    2 tablespoons flour
    1½ teaspoons pure vanilla extract
    4 eggs, lightly beaten

For the crust, combine the wafer crumbs and butter in a bowl and mix well. Press on the bottom and 2 inches up the side of an ungreased 8-inch springform pan. Place the pan on a baking sheet. Chill in the refrigerator.

For the filling, combine the chocolate, water and coffee granules in a small saucepan. Cook over low heat until the chocolate begins to melt, stirring constantly. Remove from heat and stir until smooth. Stir in the liqueur. Let stand until cool.

Beat the cream cheese, sugar, flour and vanilla at medium speed in a mixing bowl until smooth. Add the eggs and beat at low speed until just blended. Do not overbeat. Reserve 2 cups of the cream cheese mixture. Chill, covered, in the refrigerator.

Add the cooled chocolate coffee mixture to the remaining cream cheese mixture and stir until blended.

To assemble, remove the reserved cream cheese mixture from the refrigerator and let stand for 10 minutes. Pour the chocolate mixture into the prepared crust.

Bake at 350 degrees for 30 minutes or until the side is set. The center will be soft set. Pull the oven rack gently from the oven. Pour the reserved cream cheese mixture in a ring over the outside edge of the chocolate filling. Spread gently over the entire surface.

Bake for 20 to 25 minutes or until the center appears nearly set when gently shaken. Cool for 10 minutes on a wire rack. Remove the side. Cool completely. Chill, covered, for 24 hours before serving.

Serves 12

Sweet Endings

Apple Raisin Cheesecake

HANK'S CHEESECAKES

CRUST
8 graham crackers
2 tablespoons sugar
1/8 teaspoon apple pie spice or cinnamon
2 1/2 tablespoons butter

FILLING
24 ounces cream cheese, softened
3/4 cup sugar
1/2 teaspoon apple pie spice
1/8 teaspoon salt
1/2 cup sour cream
1 teaspoon vanilla extract
3 eggs
3/4 cup raisins
1 3/4 cups apple pie filling

TOPPING
1/2 cup flour
1/3 cup sugar
1 teaspoon apple pie spice or cinnamon
1/4 cup (1/2 stick) butter
1 cup walnut halves

For the crust, process the graham crackers, sugar, apple pie spice and butter in a food processor until crumbly. Press into a 9-inch springform pan. Chill, covered, in the refrigerator.

For the filling, beat the cream cheese, sugar, apple pie spice and salt in a mixing bowl until smooth and creamy. Add the sour cream and vanilla and blend well. Add the eggs 1 at a time, beating well at low speed after each addition. Stir in the raisins. Chop up the largest pieces of apple in the apple pie filling. Stir into the cream cheese mixture.

For the topping, combine the flour, sugar and apple pie spice in a food processor container. Add the butter and process until crumbly. Add the walnuts and mix well. This makes enough topping for 3 cheesecakes; store remaining topping in an airtight container in the refrigerator.

To assemble, pour the filling into the cooled crust. Sprinkle 2/3 cup of the topping over the filling. Bake at 350 degrees for 1 1/2 hours. Cool on a wire rack for 1 to 2 hours. Chill, covered, in the refrigerator for 8 to 12 hours. Cut into slices using a hot knife and place on serving plates. Store any leftovers in the refrigerator.

Serves 12

Note: Do not use light or reduced-fat cream cheese in this recipe.

Hank's Cheesecakes

Yes, there really is a Hank. Hank Krussel began creating his outstanding cheesecakes in 1983. Since then, Hank's Cheesecakes has become famous in St. Louis as THE place to get cheesecake. There are well over thirty cheesecakes from which to choose and each one is individually hand-crafted. Hank's cheesecakes are "to die for"!

Raspberry Chocolate Cheesecake

You may substitute strawberry preserves and fresh strawberries for an equally delicious dessert.

CRUST	34 chocolate sandwich cookies, crushed ¼ cup (½ stick) butter, melted
FILLING	18 ounces cream cheese, softened ¾ cup sugar 3 eggs ¾ teaspoon vanilla extract
TOPPING	1½ teaspoons unflavored gelatin 1½ tablespoons cold water ½ cup seedless raspberry preserves 1 cup whipping cream 2 tablespoons sugar
ASSEMBLY	Fresh raspberries

For the crust, combine the cookie crumbs and butter in a bowl and mix well. Pat into an 8-inch springform pan.

For the filling, beat the cream cheese, sugar, eggs and vanilla at medium speed in a mixing bowl until blended.

For the topping, soften the gelatin in cold water in a small microwave-safe bowl. Stir and let stand for 1 minute. Microwave on High for 1 minute. Stir in the preserves. Chill, covered, in the refrigerator for 15 minutes. Beat the whipping cream in a mixing bowl. Add the sugar gradually, beating until soft peaks form. Add the preserve mixture. Beat at low speed until blended.

To assemble, pour the filling into the crust. Bake at 350 to 375 degrees for 40 minutes or until the cheesecake is set and slightly cracked on top. Cool on a wire rack. Spread the topping on the cooled cheesecake. Sprinkle with fresh raspberries.

Serves 8

Peppermint Marble Cheesecake

Try this dessert on St. Patrick's Day, or substitute red food coloring for a Valentine's Day treat.

CRUST	3/4 cup chocolate wafer crumbs
	1 tablespoon butter or margarine, melted
FILLING	16 ounces light cream cheese, softened
	12 ounces cottage cheese, at room temperature
	1/2 cup sugar
	2 teaspoons vanilla extract
	6 ounces white chocolate baking bar, melted, cooled
	4 egg whites, stiffly beaten
ASSEMBLY	1/4 teaspoon peppermint extract
	2 to 4 drops green food coloring
CHOCOLATE SHAMROCKS	1 ounce semisweet chocolate
	1 ounce white chocolate

For the crust, combine the chocolate wafer crumbs and butter in a bowl and mix well. Press into a 9-inch springform pan sprayed with nonstick cooking spray. Bake at 325 degrees for 8 minutes.

For the filling, purée the cream cheese and cottage cheese in a food processor fitted with a steel blade. Add the sugar and vanilla and blend well. Add the melted white chocolate and process just until blended. Add a small amount of the egg whites and process until blended. Add the remaining egg whites and process just until blended. Reserve 1 cup of the filling.

To assemble, pour the remaining filling into the prepared crust. Add peppermint flavoring and food coloring to the reserved filling and blend well. Drop by teaspoonfuls onto the filling, forming 5 or 6 dollops. Swirl with a knife to marbleize. Bake at 325 degrees for 40 to 50 minutes or until the edge is set and the center is almost set. Turn off the oven. Let the cheesecake stand in the oven with the door ajar for 30 minutes. Remove from the oven to a wire rack. Run a knife around the edge of the pan. Cool to room temperature. Chill, covered, for 24 hours.

For the chocolate shamrocks, place semisweet chocolate in a sealable plastic freezer bag. Immerse in very hot water to melt the chocolate. Cool slightly. Cover a baking sheet with waxed paper. Cut a shamrock pattern out of paper and place under the waxed paper. Make a small snip in the corner of the plastic bag. Pipe a chocolate shamrock following the pattern. Repeat with the white chocolate.

To serve, remove the cheesecake from the refrigerator and remove the side of the pan. Garnish the cheesecake with the chocolate shamrocks.

Serves 12

Pumpkin Cheesecake

CRUST

2 cups graham cracker crumbs
1 cup pecans, finely chopped
1/2 cup sugar
1/2 teaspoon cinnamon
1/2 teaspoon ginger
1/4 teaspoon nutmeg
1/2 cup (1 stick) butter, melted

PUMPKIN FILLING

24 ounces cream cheese, softened
1 1/4 cups packed light brown sugar
6 eggs
1 (16-ounce) can solid-pack pumpkin
1 teaspoon orange extract
1 teaspoon rum extract
1 teaspoon cinnamon
1 teaspoon ginger
1/4 teaspoon nutmeg

TOPPING

1 1/2 cups sour cream
1/3 cup packed light brown sugar
1 teaspoon rum extract
1/8 teaspoon nutmeg
1/3 cup coarsely chopped pecans

For the crust, combine the graham cracker crumbs, pecans, sugar, cinnamon, ginger, nutmeg and butter in a large bowl and mix well. Press over the bottom and halfway up the side of a 10-inch springform pan. Place on a baking sheet.

For the pumpkin filling, beat the cream cheese in a mixing bowl until creamy. Add the brown sugar and beat until smooth. Add the eggs, pumpkin, flavorings, cinnamon, ginger and nutmeg and beat until smooth.

Pour into the prepared crust. Bake at 350 degrees for 1 hour or until the center is set. Cool on a wire rack for 20 minutes. Increase the oven temperature to 450 degrees.

For the topping, combine the sour cream, brown sugar, rum flavoring and nutmeg in a small bowl and blend well. Spread evenly over the cooled cheesecake. Sprinkle with pecans. Bake for 10 minutes. Watch carefully; do not burn. Cool on a wire rack. Chill, covered, for 8 to 12 hours before serving.

Serves 12

Sweet Endings

Lemon Meringue Ice Cream Pie with Blueberry Sauce

GRAHAM CRACKER CRUST	2 cups graham cracker crumbs 1/2 cup sugar 1 teaspoon cinnamon 1/2 cup (1 stick) butter, melted
LEMON ICE CREAM FILLING	2 quarts French vanilla ice cream, softened Zest and juice of 6 lemons 2 to 4 drops yellow food coloring
MERINGUE	2 cups egg whites 4 cups sugar
BLUEBERRY SAUCE	2 cups sugar 1 cup water Zest and juice of 2 lemons 1 pint fresh blueberries

For the graham cracker crust, combine the graham cracker crumbs, sugar, cinnamon and butter in a bowl and mix well. Press into a buttered 9-inch pie plate. Freeze in the freezer until firm.

For the lemon ice cream filling, combine the ice cream, lemon zest and lemon juice in a bowl and mix well. Tint with food coloring. Spoon into the graham cracker crust. Freeze until firm.

For the meringue, mix the egg whites and sugar in a stainless steel mixing bowl over a hot water bath. Heat to 110 degrees on a candy thermometer to dissolve the sugar. Beat at high speed until stiff peaks form. Spread over the pie, sealing to the edge. Freeze in the freezer.

For the blueberry sauce, bring the sugar, water, lemon zest and lemon juice to a boil in a saucepan. Boil for 20 minutes. Remove from heat. Add the blueberries and mix well until the blueberries begin to turn light, split and color the sauce. Let stand until cool.

To serve, broil the frozen pie at 500 degrees for 3 minutes or until the meringue is light brown. Watch carefully. Cut into slices and place on serving plates. Spoon the blueberry sauce over each serving.

Serves 8

Meringue Topping

When topping a pie or other dessert with meringue, be sure to coat the entire top surface with at least 3/4-inch thickness of meringue, bringing it right down to the outside lip of the dish and making sure all edges are completely sealed. To decorate, pull a knife upward through the meringue to make tall peaks or place some of the meringue in a pastry bag and pipe on fluted edges or patterns.

To brown the meringue, preheat the broiler to 500 degrees and place the dish under the broiler for about 3 minutes, allowing the edges and peaks of the meringue to turn light brown. Watch closely, as the meringue can burn quickly.

Cranberry Swirl Ice Cream Cake

CRUST	1 1/2 cups finely ground chocolate wafers (about 28) 1/4 cup (1/2 stick) butter, melted
CRANBERRY PURÉE	1 1/2 cups cranberries 1/2 cup light corn syrup 1/3 cup sugar 1/3 cup water
ASSEMBLY	1 1/2 pints vanilla ice cream, softened
TOPPING	1/2 cup shelled pistachios, finely chopped 1/4 teaspoon salt 1 tablespoon butter 1 cup whipping cream 3 tablespoons confectioners' sugar 1 teaspoon vanilla extract
GARNISH	Chocolate curls or grated chocolate

For the crust, combine the chocolate wafer crumbs and melted butter in a bowl and mix well. Pat over the bottom and 1 inch up the side of a greased 9-inch springform pan. Freeze for 30 minutes.

For the cranberry purée, combine the cranberries, corn syrup, sugar and water in a saucepan. Simmer, covered, for 10 minutes or until the cranberries are soft. Purée in a food processor. Chill, covered, for 1 hour.

To assemble, reserve 1/3 cup of the cranberry purée. Spread 1/2 of the ice cream in the prepared crust. Drizzle with the remaining cranberry purée. Spread the remaining ice cream over the top. Swirl with a knife to marbleize; smooth the top. Freeze for 30 minutes or until firm. Spread the reserved cranberry purée evenly over the top. Freeze for 15 minutes or until the top is firm.

For the topping, sauté the pistachios with salt in the butter in a skillet over medium heat for 1 minute. Beat the whipping cream in a mixing bowl until soft peaks form. Beat in the confectioners' sugar and vanilla. Fold in the pistachios. Spread over the dessert. Freeze for 30 minutes or until the top is firm. Freeze, covered with plastic wrap and foil, for 4 hours longer.

To serve, remove the side of the pan and place on a serving plate. Garnish with chocolate curls or grated chocolate. Cut into wedges with a knife dipped in hot water.

Serves 8 to 10

Note: This dessert may be made up to 5 days ahead of time.

Old-Fashioned Southern Bread Pudding in Bourbon Caramel Sauce

9TH STREET ABBEY

BREAD PUDDING	2 tablespoons bourbon
	1/3 cup raisins
	1/3 cup dried apricots, cut into 1/4-inch pieces
	3 cups milk
	1 1/2 cups half-and-half
	3 eggs, lightly beaten
	1 1/2 cups sugar
	3 tablespoons butter, melted
	1 1/2 tablespoons vanilla extract
	1/2 teaspoon cinnamon
	1 1/2 pounds dry bread, cut into 1-inch cubes
BOURBON CARAMEL SAUCE	1/2 cup bourbon
	1 tablespoon lemon juice
	3 cups sugar
	3 cups heavy cream
WHIPPED CREAM	1 cup whipping cream
	Sugar to taste
	1/2 teaspoon vanilla extract

For the bread pudding, pour the bourbon over the raisins and apricots in a bowl. Let stand for 30 minutes. Combine the milk, half-and-half, eggs, sugar, butter, vanilla and cinnamon in a bowl and mix well. Pour over the bread in a large bowl and mix well. Let stand for 20 to 30 minutes. Stir in the raisin mixture. Pour into a greased 9x12-inch baking dish. Bake at 325 degrees for 1 hour or until set.

For the bourbon caramel sauce, combine the bourbon, lemon juice and sugar in a heavy 2-quart saucepan. Cook over medium-high heat for 10 minutes or until a rich caramel color, brushing crystals from the side of the pan with a pastry brush dipped in water. Watch carefully and do not burn. The mixture will change color quickly. Remove from heat. Add the cream gradually, whisking constantly after each addition. Be careful; the mixture will steam and sputter. Return to medium heat. Cook until smooth. The sauce is also delicious served over ice cream.

For the whipped cream, pour the whipping cream into a chilled mixing bowl. Add the sugar and vanilla. Beat with chilled beaters until stiff peaks form.

To serve, cut the hot bread pudding into pieces and place on serving plates. Spoon the bourbon caramel sauce over the bread pudding. Dollop with the whipped cream.

Serves about 10

Note: The bread pudding can be made ahead and reheated in the microwave. May use any combination of breads, muffins or sweet rolls.

9th Street Abbey

In the heart of historic Soulard resides Patty Long's 9th Street Abbey. The old church now occupied by the 9th Street Abbey has a long history, which began circa 1850. Over the years this site encountered a catastrophic tornado, fire, and finally abandonment. Purchased in 1992 by Patty Long Catering, the old church was rehabbed, now providing nourishment of the palate in a place formerly dedicated to restoration of the soul.

Lemon Meringue à la Champagne

INGREDIENTS
- 1 cup sugar
- ½ cup water
- 4 egg whites, at room temperature
- 2 pints lemon sherbet, softened
- 1 bottle champagne

GARNISH
- Sprigs of fresh mint

Combine the sugar and water in a medium saucepan. Cook over medium heat to 238 degrees on a candy thermometer, soft-ball stage. Beat egg whites at high speed in a large mixing bowl until soft peaks form. Add the hot syrup in a fine stream, beating constantly. Stir in the sherbet. Spoon into 12 freezer-proof stem glasses, filling ⅔ full. Freeze, covered, until firm or up to 1 week before serving.

To serve, remove from the freezer. Fill glasses to the top with champagne. Garnish with a sprig of fresh mint.

Serves 12

Peaches and Cream

INGREDIENTS
- 1 (29-ounce) can sliced peaches in heavy syrup
- ¾ cup flour
- 1 teaspoon baking powder
- ½ teaspoon salt
- 1 (4-ounce) package vanilla pudding and pie filling mix
- ½ cup milk
- 1 egg
- 8 ounces cream cheese, softened
- ½ cup plus 1 tablespoon sugar
- ½ teaspoon cinnamon

Drain the peaches, reserving 3 tablespoons syrup. Combine the flour, baking powder, salt, pudding mix, milk and egg in a large bowl and mix well. Pour into a 2-quart baking dish. Arrange the peach slices over the batter.

Beat the cream cheese, ½ cup of the sugar and reserved syrup in a mixing bowl until smooth. Spoon over the peaches, spreading to within 1 inch of the edges. Sprinkle with a mixture of the remaining 1 tablespoon sugar and cinnamon. Bake at 350 degrees for 30 to 35 minutes or until bubbly.

Serves 8

Strawberry Soufflé with Sliced Strawberries

INGREDIENTS

3 tablespoons sugar
2 (12-ounce) containers strawberries, hulled
3 tablespoons sugar
1 tablespoon cornstarch
¾ teaspoon orange zest
1 tablespoon sugar
4 egg whites, at room temperature
3 tablespoons sugar

Spray a 6-cup soufflé dish with nonstick cooking spray. Dust the dish with 3 tablespoons sugar to coat, shaking out any remaining sugar.

Process ½ of the strawberries, 3 tablespoons sugar and cornstarch in a food processor until coarsely puréed. Spoon into a saucepan. Cook over medium heat for 3 minutes or until the mixture boils and thickens, stirring constantly. Whisk in the orange zest. Cool completely.

Slice the remaining strawberries into a medium bowl. Add 1 tablespoon sugar and toss to coat.

Beat the egg whites in a large mixing bowl until soft peaks form. Add 3 tablespoons sugar gradually, beating constantly until stiff peaks form. Fold in the puréed strawberries ⅓ at a time. Spoon into the prepared dish.

Bake at 400 degrees for 18 minutes or until puffed and golden brown. Serve with the sliced strawberries.

Serves 8

Citrus Cake with Fresh Blueberries

CAKE

1 (2-layer) package lemon cake mix
1/2 cup orange juice
1/2 cup water
1/3 cup vegetable oil
3 eggs
1 1/2 cups fresh blueberries
1 tablespoon fresh orange zest
1 tablespoon fresh lemon zest

CITRUS FROSTING

3 ounces cream cheese, softened
1/4 cup (1/2 stick) butter, softened
3 cups sifted confectioners' sugar
2 tablespoons orange juice
1 cup whipping cream, whipped
1 tablespoon fresh lemon zest
1 tablespoon fresh orange zest

For the cake, combine the cake mix, orange juice, water, oil and eggs in a large mixing bowl. Beat at low speed for 30 seconds. Beat at medium speed for 2 minutes. Fold in the blueberries, orange zest and lemon zest. Spoon into 2 greased and floured 8- or 9-inch round cake pans. Bake at 350 degrees for 35 to 40 minutes or until a wooden pick inserted in the center comes out clean. Cool in the pans on wire racks for 10 minutes. Invert onto wire racks covered with clean dish towels to cool completely.

For the citrus frosting, beat the cream cheese and butter in a medium mixing bowl until light and fluffy. Add the confectioners' sugar and orange juice and beat until smooth. Add the whipped cream, lemon zest and orange zest. Beat at low speed until blended.

To assemble, spread the citrus frosting between the layers and over the top and side of cake. Store, covered, in the refrigerator.

Serves 12 to 16

Cream Cheese Pound Cake

INGREDIENTS

1 1/2 cups (3 sticks) butter
8 ounces cream cheese, softened
3 cups sugar
6 large eggs
3 cups flour
1 teaspoon vanilla extract

Cream the butter and cream cheese in a mixing bowl. Add the sugar and beat well. Add 2 of the eggs and beat until fluffy. Add the flour and remaining eggs alternately, beating well after each addition. Stir in the vanilla. Pour into a greased and floured tube pan. Bake at 300 degrees for 1 hour and 30 minutes to 1 hour and 40 minutes or until a wooden pick inserted in the center comes out clean. Cool completely in the pan on a wire rack. Invert onto a serving plate.

Serves 16

Flourless Chocolate Torte

JUNIOR LEAGUE OF ST. LOUIS GRILLE

The Junior League shares this easy and rich dessert recipe.

INGREDIENTS

Butter
1 pound bittersweet chocolate
8 ounces hazelnut paste
8 eggs, at room temperature

Butter an 8-inch round cake pan. Line the bottom with waxed paper. Butter the waxed paper.

Melt the chocolate and hazelnut paste in a double boiler. Cool slightly.

Beat the eggs in a mixing bowl until tripled in volume. Add to the chocolate mixture and stir to blend. Pour into the prepared pan. Place in a larger pan. Fill the larger pan with enough water to come halfway up the side of the smaller pan. Bake in the water bath at 425 degrees for 10 minutes. Bake, covered, for 6 minutes. Cool completely before removing to a serving plate.

Serves 8 to 12

Happy Birthday, Mommy

Some years ago, I got quite a surprise when I came home from work to find the kitchen a disaster. There, all by herself and standing on a chair by the counter, was my five-year-old daughter, Angie. Flour, sugar, eggs, pots, pans, and spoons were everywhere. Surprised, I exclaimed, "Angie, what in the world are you doing?!? Clean up this mess!" She turned around with a smile and said, "But Mommy, I'm making you a birthday cake." I felt about six inches tall. All I could think to say was, "Let me help you with that mixer."

Ann Brubaker

Decadent Flourless Chocolate Cake

Try substituting crème de menthe liqueur at Christmastime.

INGREDIENTS

14 ounces bittersweet chocolate
¾ cup plus 2 tablespoons unsalted butter
¾ cup sugar
10 egg yolks
10 egg whites
½ cup sugar
2 tablespoons orange-flavored liqueur
1 tablespoon vanilla extract
1 cup walnuts, finely chopped
Confectioners' sugar

Melt the chocolate and butter in a double boiler, stirring occasionally. Stir in ¾ cup sugar. Heat until the sugar is almost dissolved, stirring constantly.

Beat the egg yolks in a mixing bowl. Add a small amount of the hot chocolate mixture to the egg yolks, beating constantly. Continue adding the chocolate mixture a small amount at a time, beating constantly. Return to the double boiler. Heat until slightly thickened, stirring constantly.

Beat the egg whites in a mixing bowl until medium peaks form. Add ½ cup sugar 1 tablespoon at a time, beating constantly until stiff peaks form.

Stir the liqueur and vanilla into the chocolate mixture. Scrape the chocolate mixture onto the stiffly beaten egg whites using a rubber spatula; fold the egg whites carefully into the chocolate. Fold in the walnuts.

Spoon into a buttered and floured 12-inch springform pan. Bake at 250 degrees for 2 hours. Cool to room temperature. Chill, covered, in the refrigerator. Dust with confectioners' sugar before serving.

Serves 12

Note: May serve with whipped cream and fresh berries.

Chocolate Peanut Butter Passion Cake

CAKE	1 (2-layer) package devil's food cake mix
PEANUT BUTTER MOUSSE FILLING	2/3 cup heavy cream 1 (10-ounce) package peanut butter chips 2 teaspoons vanilla extract 1 1/3 cups whipping cream
CHOCOLATE ICING	4 3/4 cups sifted confectioners' sugar 1/2 cup baking cocoa 1/2 cup (1 stick) butter, softened 1/3 cup boiling water 1 teaspoon vanilla extract
ASSEMBLY	1/4 cup chopped roasted peanuts

For the cake, prepare the cake mix using the package directions for three 8-inch round cake pans. Cool in the pans for 10 minutes. Invert onto wire racks to cool completely.

For the peanut butter mousse filling, combine 2/3 cup cream with peanut butter chips in a small saucepan. Cook over low heat until smooth, stirring constantly. Remove from heat. Stir in the vanilla. Let cool for 30 minutes. Beat 1 1/3 cups whipping cream at high speed in a mixing bowl until soft peaks form. Fold in the peanut butter mixture.

Spread the peanut butter mousse filling between the cake layers. Chill, covered, for 1 hour or longer before icing the cake.

For the chocolate icing, combine the confectioners' sugar and baking cocoa in a mixing bowl. Add the butter, boiling water and vanilla. Beat at low speed until combined. Beat at medium speed for 1 minute. Cool, if needed.

To assemble, spread the chocolate icing over the top and side of cake. Sprinkle with the peanuts.

Serves 12 to 16

Autumn Pumpkin Cake Roll

CAKE	¾ cup flour
	1 teaspoon baking powder
	2 teaspoons cinnamon
	1 teaspoon ginger
	½ teaspoon nutmeg
	½ teaspoon salt
	3 eggs
	1 cup sugar
	⅔ cup pumpkin
	1 teaspoon lemon juice
	1 cup chopped walnuts
	Confectioners' sugar
CREAM CHEESE FILLING	6 ounces cream cheese, softened
	4 teaspoons butter or margarine, softened
	½ teaspoon vanilla extract
	1 cup confectioners' sugar
GARNISHES	Mint leaves
	Whipped cream

For the cake, mix the flour, baking powder, cinnamon, ginger, nutmeg and salt together. Beat the eggs at high speed in a mixing bowl for 5 minutes. Add the sugar gradually, beating constantly. Stir in the pumpkin and lemon juice. Fold in the flour mixture. Spread in a greased and floured 10x15-inch cake pan. Sprinkle with walnuts.

Bake at 375 degrees for 15 minutes. Invert onto a clean towel sprinkled with confectioners' sugar. Roll up the towel and cake together, beginning at the narrow end. Let stand until cool.

For the cream cheese filling, beat the cream cheese, butter and vanilla in a mixing bowl until creamy. Add the confectioners' sugar and beat until smooth.

To assemble, unroll the cake. Spread the cream cheese filling over the cake. Reroll the cake and place on a serving plate. Chill in the refrigerator until ready to serve.

To serve, cut the cake roll into slices 1 inch thick. Garnish with mint leaves and dollops of whipped cream.

Serves 8

Seven-Up Cake with Pineapple Icing

CAKE
1 (2-layer) package yellow cake mix
4 eggs
1 (4-ounce) package pineapple or vanilla instant
    pudding mix
¾ cup vegetable oil
1 (10-ounce) bottle 7-Up

PINEAPPLE ICING
1½ cups sugar
1 tablespoon flour
2 eggs, beaten
½ cup (1 stick) margarine, melted
1 cup undrained juice-pack crushed pineapple
1 (3½-ounce) can shredded coconut

For the cake, combine the cake mix, eggs, pudding mix and oil in a mixing bowl and beat until light and fluffy. Add the 7-Up and beat well. Pour into a lightly greased 9x13-inch cake pan. Bake at 350 degrees for 40 minutes or until the cake tests done.

For the pineapple icing, mix the sugar and flour in a saucepan. Add the eggs, margarine and pineapple and mix well. Cook until thickened, stirring constantly. Stir in the coconut.

To assemble, pour the pineapple icing immediately over the hot cake. Cool completely before serving.

Serves 15

Note: May store in the refrigerator.

Turtle Cake

INGREDIENTS

1 (2-layer) package German chocolate cake mix
1 (14-ounce) package caramels
1/2 cup evaporated milk
3/4 cup margarine, melted
1 1/2 cups chopped pecans
1 cup chocolate chips
Confectioners' sugar

Prepare the cake mix using the package directions. Pour 1/2 of the batter into a greased and floured 9x13-inch cake pan. Bake at 350 degrees for 15 minutes.

Combine the caramels, evaporated milk and margarine in a saucepan. Heat until the caramels are melted, stirring constantly. Pour over the baked layer. Sprinkle with pecans and chocolate chips. Pour the remaining cake batter over the top.

Bake for 25 minutes or until the cake tests done. Cool in the pan on a wire rack. Sprinkle with confectioners' sugar.

Serves 15

Sugar and Cinnamon Pecans

INGREDIENTS

1/2 cup sugar
1/2 teaspoon cinnamon
1/4 teaspoon salt
1 egg white
1 tablespoon cold water
1 pound pecan halves

Mix the sugar, cinnamon and salt together. Beat the egg white and water in a mixing bowl until frothy. Add the pecans and stir to coat well. Add the sugar mixture and stir until coated and absorbed by the pecans. Spread in a single layer on a buttered baking sheet. Bake at 225 degrees for 1 hour, stirring every 15 minutes with a fork to prevent sticking or browning too much in one spot.

Makes 1 pound

Easy Chocolate Toffee

INGREDIENTS

2 ounces sliced almonds
½ cup (1 stick) butter
1 cup sugar
½ cup water
¼ teaspoon salt
4 ounces milk chocolate bars (about 3 bars)

Butter a baking sheet on the bottom and sides. Sprinkle with almonds. Combine the butter, sugar, water and salt in a microwave-safe bowl. Microwave on High for 7 to 10 minutes or until light brown, stirring occasionally. Drizzle over the almonds.

Place the chocolate bars in a microwave-safe bowl. Microwave on Medium for 2 to 3 minutes or until melted. Pour over the toffee mixture. Freeze for 20 to 30 minutes. Remove from the freezer. Break apart the candy and store in an airtight container.

Makes about 1 pound

Gooey Butter Cookies

This is a twist on St. Louis' own Gooey Butter Cake.

INGREDIENTS

½ cup (1 stick) butter, softened
8 ounces cream cheese, softened
1 egg
¼ teaspoon vanilla extract
1 (2-layer) package butter-recipe yellow cake mix
1 to 2 cups confectioners' sugar

Beat the butter, cream cheese, egg and vanilla in a mixing bowl until light and fluffy. Stir in the dry cake mix. Chill, covered, for 30 minutes.

Drop the dough by teaspoonfuls into a bowl of confectioners' sugar and roll into balls. Arrange on cookie sheets lightly coated with nonstick cooking spray. Bake at 350 degrees for 12 minutes or until golden brown. Cool on wire racks.

Makes 3 dozen

Butter Cookies with Walnut Meringue

DOUGH	1 cup (2 sticks) butter, softened
	1½ cups sugar
	4 egg yolks
	2 tablespoons milk
	1 teaspoon vanilla extract
	4 cups sifted flour
	1 teaspoon salt
EGG WASH	1 egg yolk
	1 tablespoon water
WALNUT MERINGUE	2 large egg whites
	1½ cups sugar
	½ cup ground walnuts

For the dough, beat the butter, sugar, egg yolks, milk and vanilla in a mixing bowl until creamy. Add a mixture of the flour and salt gradually, using clean hands to combine. Handle as little as possible. Wrap the dough until ready to roll.

For the egg wash, beat the egg yolk and water in a bowl until blended.

For the walnut meringue, beat the egg whites in a mixing bowl until foamy. Add the sugar gradually, beating constantly until stiff peaks form. Fold in the walnuts.

To assemble, roll the dough ⅛ inch thick. Cut with a flower-shaped cookie cutter or as desired. Place on lightly greased cookie sheets. Brush with the egg wash. Place ½ to ¾ teaspoon of the walnut meringue in the middle of each.

Bake at 375 degrees for 10 to 12 minutes or until light brown around the edges. Watch carefully. Cool on wire racks.

Makes 25 large or 40 small cookies

Chocolate Chip Brownies

INGREDIENTS

1/2 cup (1 stick) unsalted butter
2 ounces unsweetened chocolate
1 cup sugar
1/2 cup sifted flour
1/2 cup chopped pecans or walnuts (optional)
1/2 teaspoon baking powder
1 teaspoon vanilla extract
2 eggs, lightly beaten
1 cup semisweet chocolate chips

Melt the butter and unsweetened chocolate in a double boiler. Remove from heat and blend well. Combine with the sugar, flour, pecans, baking powder and vanilla in a bowl and mix well using a wooden spoon. Add the eggs and mix well. Stir in the chocolate chips.

Pour into a buttered 8x8-inch glass baking dish. Bake at 350 degrees for 30 to 40 minutes or until a wooden pick inserted in the center comes out clean. Do not overcook. Brownies should be moist. Cool completely. Cut into squares.

Makes 16 brownies

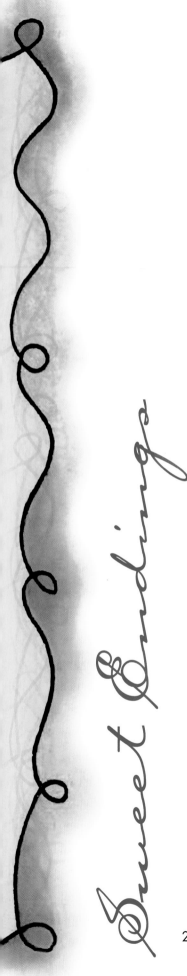

Triple Espresso Brownies

BROWNIES	1 (21-ounce) package fudge brownie mix
	½ cup water
	¼ cup vegetable oil
	1 egg
	2 teaspoons instant espresso coffee granules
	1 teaspoon vanilla extract

CHOCOLATE ESPRESSO FILLING	¼ cup (½ stick) butter or margarine, softened
	½ cup packed brown sugar
	1 egg
	2 teaspoons instant espresso coffee granules
	1 teaspoon vanilla extract
	1 cup coarsely chopped walnuts (optional)
	3 (4-ounce) bars sweet dark or bittersweet chocolate, chopped

CHOCOLATE ESPRESSO GLAZE	½ cup semisweet chocolate chips
	1 tablespoon butter or margarine
	⅛ teaspoon instant espresso coffee granules
	1 to 2 teaspoons milk or whipping cream

For the brownies, combine the brownie mix, water, oil, egg, coffee granules and vanilla in a large bowl. Beat 50 strokes by hand. Spread in a greased 9x13-inch baking pan. Bake at 350 degrees for 30 minutes.

For the chocolate espresso filling, beat the butter and brown sugar in a mixing bowl until light and fluffy. Add the egg, coffee granules and vanilla and blend well. Combine the walnuts and chopped chocolate in a medium bowl. Add the brown sugar mixture and mix well. Spoon over the partially baked brownies and spread carefully to cover. Bake for 17 to 20 minutes or until light brown.

For the chocolate espresso glaze, melt the chocolate chips and butter in a small saucepan over low heat, stirring constantly until smooth. Remove from heat. Add the coffee granules and enough milk to make of the desired drizzling consistency, whisking constantly.

To assemble, drizzle the chocolate espresso glaze over the warm brownies. Cool completely. Cut into bars.

Makes 3 to 4 dozen

Cinnamon Chocolate Chip Bars

DOUGH
2 cups sifted flour
1 teaspoon baking powder
1 cup sugar
1 tablespoon cinnamon
1/2 cup (1 stick) butter, softened
1/2 cup shortening
1 egg
1 egg yolk
1 egg white

TOPPING
1 cup chocolate chips
1/2 cup sugar
1 teaspoon cinnamon

For the dough, mix the flour, baking powder, sugar and cinnamon in a bowl. Beat the butter, shortening, egg and egg yolk in a mixing bowl until light and fluffy. Add the flour mixture and mix well. Press evenly in a greased 9x13-inch baking pan. Beat the egg white in a mixing bowl until fluffy. Brush over the dough.

For the topping, combine the chocolate chips, sugar and cinnamon in a bowl and toss to mix well.

To assemble, sprinkle the topping over the dough. Bake at 350 degrees for 30 to 35 minutes. Cut into bars.

Makes 3 dozen

Chocolate Graham Squares

INGREDIENTS
½ cup (1 stick) butter
2 cups chocolate chips
2 cups graham cracker crumbs
8 ounces cream cheese, softened
1 (14-ounce) can sweetened condensed milk
1 egg
1 teaspoon vanilla extract

Melt the butter and chocolate chips in a saucepan, stirring constantly. Remove from heat. Stir in the graham cracker crumbs. Reserve ½ cup of the crumb mixture. Spread the remaining crumb mixture in a greased 9x13-inch baking pan.

Beat the cream cheese, condensed milk, egg and vanilla in a bowl until smooth. Spread over the crumb mixture. Crumble the reserved crumb mixture over the top. Bake at 325 degrees for 25 to 30 minutes or until light brown. Cool and cut into squares.

Makes 3 dozen

Magic Cookie Bars

INGREDIENTS
½ cup (1 stick) butter, melted
1 cup graham cracker crumbs
2 cups chocolate chips
2 cups butterscotch chips (optional)
1 cup shredded coconut
1 cup pecan pieces
1 (14-ounce) can sweetened condensed milk

Layer the ingredients in the order listed in a 9x12-inch baking dish. Bake at 350 degrees for 30 minutes or until light brown on top. Cool and cut into bars.

Makes 3 dozen

Chocolate Raspberry Bars

INGREDIENTS

1 cup (2 sticks) butter, softened
2 cups flour
1/2 cup packed light brown sugar
1/4 teaspoon salt
1 cup semisweet chocolate chips
1 (14-ounce) can sweetened condensed milk
1/3 cup seedless raspberry jam
1/2 cup semisweet chocolate chips
1/2 cup white chocolate chips

Beat the butter in a large bowl until creamy. Add the flour, brown sugar and salt and beat well. Press 1 3/4 cups of the crumb mixture into a greased 9x13-inch baking pan. Bake at 350 degrees for 10 to 12 minutes or until the edges are golden brown.

Combine 1 cup chocolate chips and condensed milk in a small saucepan. Cook over low heat until melted, stirring constantly. Spread over the hot crust.

Sprinkle the remaining crumb mixture over the chocolate layer. Drop the jam by 1/2 teaspoonfuls over the crumb mixture. Sprinkle 1/2 cup chocolate chips and white chocolate chips over the top. Bake for 25 to 30 minutes or until the center is set. Cool completely on a wire rack. Cut into bars.

Makes 3 dozen

German Chocolate Cookies

INGREDIENTS

1 cup sugar
1/2 cup (1 stick) butter, melted
1 cup evaporated milk
3 egg yolks
1 teaspoon vanilla extract
1 1/2 cups flaked coconut
1 1/2 cups pecans, chopped
1 (2-layer) package German chocolate cake mix
1/3 cup butter, melted

Combine the sugar, 1/2 cup butter, evaporated milk, egg yolks and vanilla in a saucepan and blend well. Cook over medium heat for 10 to 13 minutes or until thickened and bubbly, stirring constantly. Stir in the coconut and pecans. Remove from heat. Let stand until cool.

Combine the cake mix, 1/3 cup butter and 1 1/4 cups of the coconut mixture in a large bowl and stir until moist. Shape into 1-inch balls. Place on nonstick cookie sheets. Make an indentation in the center of each. Fill each indentation with the remaining coconut mixture.

Bake at 375 degrees for 10 to 13 minutes. Cool on the cookie sheets for 5 minutes. Remove to wire racks to cool completely.

Makes about 2 dozen

Ultimate Toffee Bars

INGREDIENTS

Whole graham crackers
1 cup (2 sticks) butter
1 cup packed brown sugar
1 cup chopped pecans
6 (1.5-ounce) milk chocolate bars

Line a 10x15-inch baking pan with foil. Line the prepared pan with enough graham crackers to cover the entire surface, cutting the graham crackers as needed to fit the edges and corners.

Combine the butter, brown sugar and pecans in a saucepan. Bring to a boil over medium heat. Boil for 2 minutes, stirring constantly. Pour over the graham crackers.

Bake at 350 degrees for 10 minutes. Arrange the milk chocolate bars immediately over the top. Let stand until the chocolate bars are shiny and softened.

Spread the chocolate evenly over the top of the bars. Let stand until still slightly warm. Cut into bars. Chill in the refrigerator until firm. Store in an airtight container.

Makes 4 dozen

Soft Ginger Cookies

INGREDIENTS

2 cups sifted flour
2 teaspoons baking soda
1 teaspoon cinnamon
1 teaspoon ginger
1 teaspoon ground cloves
1/4 cup dark molasses
3/4 cup unsalted butter, softened
1 cup sugar
1 egg, beaten
Sugar

Sift the flour, baking soda, cinnamon, ginger and cloves together. Bring the molasses to a boil in a saucepan. Let stand until cool.

Cream the butter and 1 cup sugar in a mixing bowl until light and fluffy. Add the egg and beat well. Beat in the cooled molasses. Add the flour mixture gradually, beating constantly. Drop by scoopfuls into sugar in a bowl using a trigger-handled cookie scoop. Roll in the sugar until coated. Place 2 inches apart on greased cookie sheets.

Bake at 350 degrees for 8 to 10 minutes or until the tops lightly crack. Do not overbake. Remove to wire racks to cool.

Makes 3 dozen

Country Club Cookies

INGREDIENTS

1 cup (2 sticks) butter, softened
1 cup sugar
1 cup packed brown sugar
2 eggs
1 teaspoon vanilla extract
2 1/2 cups flour
1 teaspoon baking soda
1 teaspoon baking powder
1/2 teaspoon salt
1 1/2 cups rolled oats
1 large Hershey's Symphony Bar with almonds
    and toffee, chopped into bite-size pieces
4 (2-ounce) Butterfinger bars, chopped into
    bite-size pieces

Cream the butter, sugar and brown sugar in a mixing bowl until light and fluffy. Add the eggs and vanilla and beat well. Add the flour, baking soda, baking powder and salt and mix well using a wooden spoon. Add the oats and mix well. Stir in the candy pieces.

Drop 2- to 3-tablespoon-size portions onto cookie sheets sprayed with nonstick cooking spray. Bake at 350 degrees for 10 minutes or until set and light brown. Do not overbake. Cool on wire racks.

Makes about 2 dozen

Cowboy Cookies

INGREDIENTS

2 cups flour
1 teaspoon baking powder
1 teaspoon baking soda
1 teaspoon salt
½ cup (1 stick) butter, softened
½ cup (1 stick) margarine, softened
1 cup sugar
1 cup packed brown sugar
2 eggs
1 teaspoon vanilla extract
3 cups rolled oats
1 cup shredded coconut

Sift the flour, baking powder, baking soda and salt together. Cream the butter, margarine, sugar and brown sugar in a mixing bowl until light and fluffy. Add the eggs 1 at a time, mixing well after each addition. Stir in the vanilla. Beat in the flour mixture. Add the oats and coconut and mix well.

Roll into small balls. Place 2 inches apart on greased cookie sheets; press to flatten with a fork.

Bake at 375 degrees for 10 minutes. Cool on wire racks.

Makes 2 dozen

Cranberry Oatmeal Cookies with White Chocolate Chips

INGREDIENTS

1 cup (2 sticks) butter, softened
1 cup packed brown sugar
2 eggs
2 cups rolled oats
2 cups flour
1 teaspoon baking soda
½ teaspoon salt
1½ cups sweetened dried cranberries
1 cup white chocolate chips

Cream the butter and brown sugar in a mixing bowl until light and fluffy. Add the eggs 1 at a time, mixing well after each addition. Add the oats, flour, baking soda and salt and mix well. Stir in the cranberries and white chocolate chips. Drop by rounded teaspoonfuls onto ungreased cookie sheets.

Bake at 375 degrees for 10 to 12 minutes or until golden brown. Cool on wire racks.

Makes 2½ dozen

Pumpkin Spice Cookies

A delightful fall cookie–wonderful if you love pumpkin!

COOKIES
- 2 cups flour
- 1 teaspoon baking soda
- 1/2 teaspoon salt
- 1 teaspoon cinnamon
- 1/2 teaspoon allspice
- 1/2 cup (1 stick) butter, softened
- 1/2 cup packed brown sugar
- 1/2 cup sugar
- 1 egg
- 2 tablespoons maple syrup
- 1 (16-ounce) can pumpkin
- 1 teaspoon orange zest
- 1 teaspoon vanilla extract
- 1 cup raisins

ORANGE GLAZE
- 1 cup confectioners' sugar
- 4 teaspoons orange juice
- 1/2 teaspoon orange zest
- 2 drops of orange food coloring

For the cookies, mix the flour, baking soda, salt, cinnamon and allspice together. Cream the butter, brown sugar and sugar in a mixing bowl until light and fluffy. Beat in the egg and maple syrup. Blend in the pumpkin, orange zest and vanilla. Add the flour mixture and beat well. Stir in the raisins.

Drop by rounded tablespoonfuls onto nonstick cookie sheets. Bake at 350 degrees for 12 minutes. Cool on wire racks.

For the orange glaze, combine the confectioners' sugar, orange juice, orange zest and food coloring in a bowl and mix well.

To assemble, drizzle the cooled cookies with the orange glaze.

Makes 3 dozen

White Chocolate Strawberry Wedges

Try this with kiwifruit, raspberries, peaches, or any combination of fresh fruits.

INGREDIENTS

1 unbaked refrigerator pie pastry
1 tablespoon sugar
8 ounces cream cheese, softened
1/4 cup sugar
1/2 teaspoon vanilla extract
1 egg
3 cups fresh strawberry halves
1/4 cup white chocolate chips
1 teaspoon vegetable oil

Let the pastry stand at room temperature for 15 to 20 minutes. Unfold and place on a cookie sheet or pizza pan. Prick with a fork. Sprinkle with 1 tablespoon sugar. Bake at 400 degrees for 8 to 10 minutes or until light brown. Cool slightly. Reduce oven temperature to 375 degrees.

Beat the cream cheese, 1/4 cup sugar and vanilla in a mixing bowl until creamy. Add the egg and beat until smooth. Spread over the baked crust to within 1/2 inch of the edge. Bake for 13 to 18 minutes or until set in the center and light brown around the edge. Let stand until cool.

Arrange the strawberries over the cooled layer. Combine the white chocolate chips and oil in a microwave-safe dish. Microwave on Low for 1 to 2 minutes. Stir until smooth. Drizzle over the strawberries. Cut into wedges. Store, covered, in the refrigerator.

Serves 8

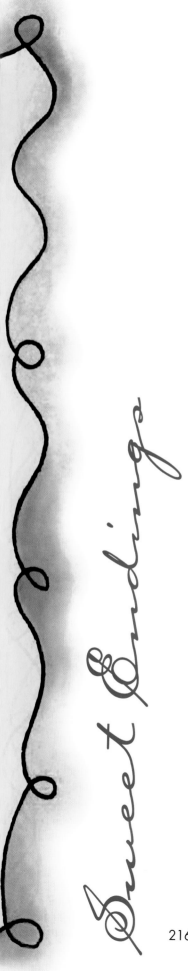

Sweet Endings

Mississippi Mud Pie

CRUST	1 package chocolate wafers, crushed ½ cup (1 stick) butter, melted
ICE CREAM LAYER	2 pints coffee or mocha ice cream, softened
CHOCOLATE SAUCE	⅓ cup baking cocoa ⅔ cup sugar ⅓ cup heavy cream 3 tablespoons butter 1 teaspoon vanilla extract
WHIPPED CREAM	1 cup whipping cream 2 tablespoons sugar 1 teaspoon vanilla extract
GARNISH	2 ounces unsweetened chocolate, shaved

For the crust, mix the chocolate wafers and butter in a bowl. Press into a 9-inch pie plate. Bake at 375 degrees for 10 minutes. Cool.

For the ice cream layer, spread the ice cream into the cooled crust. Freeze for 1½ hours or until firm.

For the chocolate sauce, bring the baking cocoa, sugar, cream and butter to a boil in a saucepan over medium heat. Cook until smooth, stirring constantly. Remove from heat. Stir in the vanilla. Cool slightly. Pour over the ice cream layer. Freeze for 1½ hours or longer.

For the whipped cream, beat cream and sugar in a mixing bowl until soft peaks form. Add the vanilla and mix well. Spread over the pie. Garnish with chocolate shavings.

Serves 8

Heavenly Coconut Cream Pie

INGREDIENTS

¼ cup flour
2 tablespoons cornstarch
3 cups milk
3 egg yolks
½ cup sugar
⅛ teaspoon salt
3 tablespoons butter
1 teaspoon vanilla extract
1 (3.5-ounce) can flaked coconut
1 baked (9-inch) pie shell
1 recipe meringue or whipped cream

Mix the flour and cornstarch with ⅓ cup of the milk in a bowl to form a smooth paste. Scald the remaining milk in a saucepan.

Beat the egg yolks in a mixing bowl. Add the sugar and salt and beat well. Add a small amount of the scalded milk to the flour paste and mix well. Add a small amount of the scalded milk to the egg mixture and mix well. Add the flour paste mixture and egg mixture to the scalded milk gradually, stirring constantly.

Cook until thickened, stirring constantly. Remove from heat. Add the butter, vanilla and coconut and mix well. Pour into the pie shell. Top with meringue or whipped cream.

Serves 8

Apple Tart Tatin

CAFÉ DE FRANCE

INGREDIENTS

1 cup (2 sticks) butter
1 cup sugar
3 Granny Smith apples
Sugar
1/2 sheet puff pastry
1 egg, beaten

Combine the butter and 1 cup sugar in a large skillet. Cook over high heat until the mixture begins to brown. Remove from heat. Pour into 4 individual tart pans, evenly covering the bottom of each.

Peel the apples and cut into halves. Cut each half into 1/4-inch slices. Arrange in the prepared tart pans. Sprinkle with sugar. Place on a baking sheet.

Cut the puff pastry into 4 circles the same diameter as the tart pans. Place the pastry over the apples, tucking the edges into the tart pans. Brush with the beaten egg. Prick the top of the pastries. Bake at 375 degrees for 15 to 20 minutes or until the pastry is golden brown. Cool for 10 minutes. Invert the tarts onto serving plates.

Serves 4

Café De France

Many honors have been awarded to this elegant French restaurant including the Four Diamond rating of AAA, the 1997 Reader's Choice of Gourmet magazine, and Best Food rating by Zagat Guide in 1999. Chef Marcel Keraval's palette of ingredients is hand chosen from the markets daily and are combined to create classic and creative French cuisine. Chef Marcel's desserts range from the freshest seasonal fruits and berries to decadent soufflés.

Very Berry Chocolate Chip Pie

INGREDIENTS

18 ounces refrigerator chocolate chip cookie dough
8 ounces light cream cheese, softened
¼ cup sugar
1 teaspoon vanilla extract
1 pound strawberries (about 20 to 25 medium berries)
¼ cup semisweet chocolate chips

Spray a 9-inch pie plate with nonstick cooking spray. Cut the cookie dough into slices. Arrange evenly in the prepared pie plate. Bake at 350 degrees for 22 minutes or until the center is set. Cool on a wire rack.

Beat the cream cheese, sugar and vanilla in a medium bowl until smooth using a wooden spoon. Chill, covered until serving time.

To serve, rinse the strawberries and remove the caps. Spread the cream cheese mixture over the cooled crust. Arrange the strawberries upright in the cream cheese mixture.

Place the chocolate chips in a sealable freezer plastic bag; seal the bag. Microwave on High for 1½ to 2 minutes or until softened. Snip ⅛ inch from the corner of the bag. Drizzle the chocolate over the strawberries. Serve immediately.

Serves 8

Bumbleberry Pie

MISS AIMEE B'S TEA ROOM

INGREDIENTS

Flour
2 prepared pie pastries
1/2 cup blueberries
1/2 cup whole strawberries
1/2 cup sliced rhubarb
1/2 cup raspberries
1/3 cup flour
1 cup sugar
2 Granny Smith apples, peeled, thinly sliced
1 tablespoon lemon juice
Milk
Sugar to taste
Ice cream

Spray a deep-dish pie plate with nonstick cooking spray and dust with flour. Line the prepared pie plate with 1 of the pie pastries. Trim the edge, reserving the pastry. Cut the reserved pastry into leaf and berry shapes to use on the top pastry.

Combine the blueberries, strawberries, rhubarb and raspberries in a large bowl. Add 1/3 cup flour, 1 cup sugar, apples and lemon juice and toss to mix well. Spoon into the prepared pie plate.

Top with the remaining pie pastry, sealing and fluting the edge and cutting vents. Arrange the leaf and berry pastry cutouts over the top. Brush with milk and sprinkle with sugar to taste. Place the pie plate on a baking sheet with sides.

Bake at 400 degrees for 15 minutes. Reduce the oven temperature to 350 degrees. Bake for 30 minutes or until the juice is thickened and bubbly. Serve warm with ice cream.

Serves 8

Miss Aimee B's
Tea Room

Miss Aimee B's is named in remembrance of a laudable first lady of St. Charles. The tearoom resides in a historic home built in 1865 and listed on the National Register of Historic Places. Creative recipes, gracious hospitality, and charming surroundings allow guests to enjoy the sights, smells, and sounds of a time gone-by.

Key Lime Pie with Chocolate Crust

CHOCOLATE CRUST	1½ (8½-ounce) packages chocolate wafers
	1½ teaspoons Key lime zest
	3 tablespoons cold butter
	3 tablespoons sugar

KEY LIME FILLING	3 egg yolks
	2¼ cups sweetened condensed milk
	4 teaspoons Key lime zest
	¾ cup plus 2 tablespoons fresh Key lime juice

| GARNISHES | Whipped cream |
| | Key lime slices |

For the chocolate crust, lightly grease the bottom and side of a 9-inch springform pan. Process the wafers in a food processor with a metal blade to form coarse crumbs. Add the lime zest, butter and sugar and process until mixed. Press into the prepared pan. Bake at 350 degrees for 12 minutes. Let stand until cool.

For the Key lime filling, beat the egg yolks in a medium mixing bowl until thick and pale yellow. Add the condensed milk, whisking until blended. Add the lime zest and lime juice gradually, whisking constantly. Pour into the cooled crust. Bake at 350 degrees for 15 to 20 minutes or until set. Let stand until cool. Chill, covered, in the refrigerator.

To serve, remove the side of the pan. Garnish with piped whipped cream and lime slices.

Serves 10 to 12

Fresh Raspberry Tart

PASTRY
1 1/4 cups flour
1/4 teaspoon salt
1/3 cup shortening
4 to 5 tablespoons cold water

CREAM CHEESE
FILLING
16 ounces cream cheese, softened
1 cup sugar
2 teaspoons vanilla extract
2 eggs
2 tablespoons flour

RASPBERRY GLAZE
1/3 cup seedless red raspberry jam
1 tablespoon water

ASSEMBLY
2 cups fresh raspberries

For the pastry, combine the flour and salt in a bowl. Cut in the shortening until crumbly. Sprinkle 1 tablespoon of the water over part of the mixture; toss gently with a fork. Push to the side of the bowl. Repeat with the remaining water 1 tablespoon at a time until moistened. Shape into a ball. Roll into a 13-inch circle on a lightly floured surface. Line a 9- or 9 1/2-inch tart pan with a removable bottom with the pastry, trimming the edge. Prick the bottom and side with a fork. Bake at 425 degrees for 10 to 12 minutes or until golden brown. Cool on a wire rack.

For the filling, beat the cream cheese, sugar and vanilla at medium speed in a mixing bowl until smooth. Add the eggs and flour. Beat at low speed until combined. Spread evenly in the prepared crust. Bake at 350 degrees for 35 to 40 minutes or until the center appears nearly set when shaken. Cool on a wire rack.

For the raspberry glaze, combine the jam and water in a saucepan. Heat over low heat until melted, stirring constantly.

To assemble, drizzle 1/2 of the glaze over the tart, allowing some of the filling to show through. Top with the raspberries. Drizzle with the remaining glaze. Chill, covered, for up to 24 hours before serving.

Serves 10 to 12

Cookbook Committee

CO-CHAIRS:	Millicent Dohr
	Becky Eggmann
CO-VICE CHAIRS:	Tracee Holmes
	Lisa Price
TREASURER:	Laurie Zeveski
STORY EDITORS:	Leslie Hollander
	Katheryn Stalker

SPECIAL EVENTS COMMITTEE:

Carole Bartnett	Sarah Fobes
Caroline Bean	Becky Haukap
Katrina Biermann	Ronda Helton
Eleanor Burns	Bettina Joist
Judy Dude	Alison Pass
MaryBelle Eggers	Bridget Leitch Steinhart

DISTRIBUTIONS COMMITTEE:

Todd Higley
Laurie Zeveski

SALES COMMITTEE:

Ann Brubaker	Karen Shafer
Todd Higley	Ginny Shields
Leslie Hollander	Natalie Stathis
Lisa Price	

PUBLIC RELATIONS/ MARKETING COMMITTEE:

Carrie McCartney
Amy McDermott
Glory Sumka-Stack
Vicki Wilding

LEAGUELINKS COMMITTEE CHAIRS:

Cyndi Michalak
Mary Ann Schwartz

1998–1999 CHAIR: Carey Johnson

Story Contributors

Christine Blazevic
Karen Boehme
Sharon Boranyak
Kathleen Brandt
Kittie Brown
Ann Brubaker
Vicki Carius
Jenni Chambers-Smith
Jenifer Corbin
Gretchen Davis
Claire Devoto
MaryBelle Eggers
Janice Eickhorst
Michelle Harrell
Lynda Hetlage

Tracey Hoffman
Ellen Jones
Sally Jones
Amy Kottmeyer
Jodi Luetkemeyer
Terrie Magruder
Amy Mayfield
Darlene Miller
Genie Mueller
Laura Murphy
Julie Novak
Sue Schneider
Bridget Leitch Steinhart
Stacy Wells

Recipe Contributors

Beverly Wade Aach
Christy Adams
Helen Allen
Betty Amelotti
Merline P. Anderson
Sylvia Akin
Melissa Archer
Kelly Arciszewski
Ethel Armstrong
Nancy Auld
Laura Dierberg Ayers
Janice Darrow Baker
Molly Baker
Peggy Baker
Mary "Mickey" Bange
Barbara Barrett
Susan Mansfield Bartlett
Cathy Bartling
Wendy L. Beach
Pamela Kisling Bearden
Joan Bechtold
Gail Beck
Jenny Bell
Sally Berglund
Kathi Biesinger
Laura A. Bing
Marge Bock
Elizabeth Bohlman
Sharon Boranyak
Kathleen Brandt

Gale Braswell
Janet Brault
Carol Lynne Briggs
Andrea Brodsky
Kittie Brown
Wendy Brown
Kaye Browning
Ann Brubaker
Ginger Sperandeo Brune
Joyce Bryan
Patti Bubash
Grace Sunn Bush
Denise Butts
Moira Pons Byrd
Frances A. Byrnes
Allyson Bowen Callison
Cindy Capatosta
Patti Careklas
Josephine Carus
Carmen Censky
Carmen Cervantes
Chrissy Chapo
Margaret M. Chatham
Laura Cialdella
Jinny Coleman
Audrey Coyle
Mary Suzanne Crockett
Rhonda Cross
Mary Cruz
Cathy D'Alessandro

Merilee Dauster
Gretchen G. Davis
Sue Davis
Michelle Sokol Dean
Lisa Debo
Mimi Denes
Vonna Despotis
Cathy DeVille
Maria Diekneite
Lynn Diestelkamp
Melanie McVay DiLeo
Debra Tashjian Dockins
Millicent Akin Dohr
Virginia Donofan
Beth Downey
Tracie L. Drake
Julie Dubray
Judy Palmquist Dude
Pat Hupp Dunaway
Sue Duval
Kim Dwyer
Ruth Hanks Edwards
Dr. Anita K. Eftimoff
MaryBelle Eggers
Becky Rowe Eggmann
Ann Eisel
Sandy Ellis
Cathy Ely
Mary Beth Engler
Joanne Montell Erblich
Jean L. Ewell
Mrs. Web Federspiel
Sue Felling
Sharon Fenoglio
Barbara Ferman
Julie Hardesty Ferman
Theresa Fiala
Cindy Fisher
Felecia Fleishman
Dayna Flint
Anne Marie Flora
Deborah L. Franklin
Mrs. Earl T. Franzen
Phyllis Freiberger
Stephanie Gallagher
Amanda Gauer
Debbie Genung
Gretchen Gerber
Carole Germain
Amanda George

Jean Gibbs
Elizabeth A. Goad
Nancy Bolton Grable
Marilyn Grens
Kris Grigsby
Rheta Grisham
Mrs. Robert J. Ground
Suzy Gunter
Sally Hall
Bethany Hamilton
Mitch Hanneken
Tammy Kahre Hardesty
Marie Harrington
Debbie Harris
Gregory T. Harris
Mrs. Edward H. Heinz
Laura M. Heitland
Vicki Henderson
June Herman
Jennifer Parfield Hess
Lynda M. Hetlage
Sally Higgins
Todd Higley
Ann Hiller
Doris Hindman
Mrs. Jack H. Hipps
Karen Hoeman
Susan Hoffman
Joseph M. Hogen
Leslie Hollander
Angela Hollingshead
Tracee J. Holmes
Roxane Holtzman
Donna Hostetter
Margaret House
Mary Beth Hughes
Elsa M. Hunstein
Lisa C. Hunt
Lawrence J. Hutti
Christy Jansen
Carey Johnson
Lodell Johnson
Susan Johnson
Teresa Johnson
Ellen Jones
Helen Jones
David Kaiser
Mrs. Franck Hyatt Kaiser
Joni Karandjeff
Sue Kelly

Missy Kent
Joella Ketcherside
Pat King
Susie Kinsella
Melinda Klinghammer
Jessie Koch
Madeleine A. Koch
Diane Kohn
Phyllis Konold
Patty Korn
Amy Kottmeyer
Karen Koury
Janet Krekeler
Meredith Krenzel
Maxine Kunkel
Bonnie L. Kupferer
Bea Kuzmich
Anne Lamb
Berry Lane
Sandra Lauschke
Kelly LeGard
Catherine Lemcovitz
Zoe Lemcovitz
Kim Lindley
Marge Littleton
Janice M. Lynch
Theresa Lynch
Sharon Lyons
Pam Mahoney
Julie Maire-Turner
Julia D. Major
Kellie Mandry
Patricia Marshall
Veletta Martin
Amy Mayfield
Marjorie McFarland
Cheryl S. McKinley
Katheryn McWard
Deborah Romo Medley
Blythe Meisinger
Christina Merriman
Cathy Meyer
Katie Meyers
Candy Miller
Darlene Miller
Debbie Monterubio
Shelby Moody
Gay Moppert
Genie Mueller
Wendy M. Mueller

Sarah J. Mullen
Emily Mulvihill
Nellie Nicholson
Kim Niemuth
Virginia Noe
Carleton Norton
Christine L. Norton
Marilyn S. Norton
Julie Novak
Ann T. Kinney O'Brien
Susan Olendorff
Jacqueline Olson
Leigh Ann O'Neil
Amy O'Neill
Mrs. Doris Palmer
Mrs. Leslie H. Palmer
Angie Panos
Jenny Pappas
Liz Parker
Ethel Parrington
Bernice Peukert
Rosemary N. Pickle
Tyann Proffer
Rosemary M. Quigley
Jean Racowsky
Anne Ragland
Mary E. Raizman
Emily B. Rapp
Sally Rash
Diane Rau
Carol Recklein
Dorothy Rhodes
Susan Richardson
Karen Ridgeway
Annette Ritchie
Sharon Robinson
Jean Roessler
Catherine Roestel
Marge Roman
Anne Rosenberg
Kelly Rosenblatt
Judy Ross
Lee Quelsh Ross
Carol Rosse
John W. Rowe
Marcia C. Rowe
Ann Rowley
Mrs. Louis W. Rubin
Myrtle Louise Sampson
Jane Hoyt "GiGi" Sanders

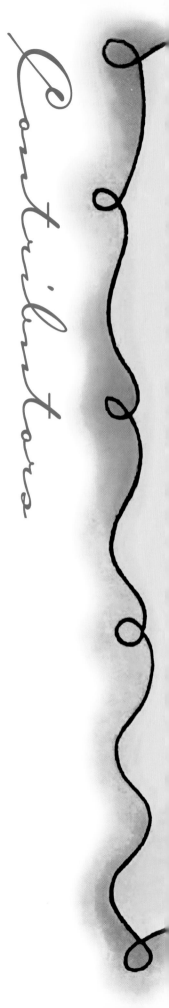

Heather Kirkpatrick Scherer
David Schlortt
Rochelle Blaschke Schlortt
Laura Hays Schlueter
Paul Schlueter
Phyllis Schneider
Sue Schneider
Nancy G. Schnoebelen
Shirley Schuehmann
Ruth Scott
Janice Seele
Pat Sewell
Kathy Sewing
Karen Shafer
Dolly Sherwood
Jacqueline J. Short
Victoria Siegel
Ann Simmons
Patty Simpson
Nancy Sinclair
Jean Sippy
Connie Smith
Gloria M. Smith
Vernona O. Smith
Sally F. Snavely
Kathryn Snodgrass
Donna M. Sondag
Bonnie Sparks
Beverly Spiller
Mrs. Kaye E. Stabler
Lisa Stein
Bridget Leitch Steinhart
Julia Steurer
Emily Stickle
Suzanne Stolar
Mrs. L. K. Stringham
Charlotte Sulltrop
Glory Sumka-Stack
Myra Tener
Linda M. Thomas
Laura E. Thompson
Teresa L. Thompson
Mary-Ellen Tobin

Mildred "Toots" Tobin
Carolyn Token
Vicki Tsiaklides
Sue Tubbesing
Sonia M. Tumialan
Mrs. Donald Tyree
Sue Vesser
Cristin Viebranz
Hetha B. Wagner
Mary Pillsbury Wainwright
Joan Walsh
Kathryne Walsh
Tammy Walsh
Alice Walther
Ann C. Wandishin
Sharon Ward
Nancy Warner
Lauren Watson
Phyllis Weidman
Suzanne Weintraub
Gail Weller
Stacy K. Wells
Robin Wenneker
Davin S. Wenner
Judy Werner
Holly Wertz
Ann White
Lesley Whitener
Nicole Wight
Vicki L. Wilding
Daniel Wilke
Betty Williamson
Marion M. Wilson
Marjorie C. Wilson
Heather Winsby
Stephanie Wollard
Elizabeth Woodworth
Karen R. Wright
Karen Wucher
Ann Y. Wyrick
Laurie Zeveski
Katherine Ziegler
Susan Zimmermann

Restaurant Recipe Contributors

Annie Gunn's
Busch's Grove
Café Campagnard
Café De France
Fio's La Fourchette
Gianfabio Ristorante
Hank's Cheesecakes
Junior League of St. Louis Grille

Kemoll's
Miss Aimee B's Tea Room
9th Street Abbey
St. Louis Steakhouse
Soulard's Restaurant
Super Smokers BBQ
Tony's
Vivian's Vineyards

Recipe Testers

Christy Adams
Heather Akred
Amy Alt
Betty Amelotti
Becky Arendt
Kathy Barnes
Katie Barrett
Carole Bartnett
Ann Basler
Elizabeth Basler
Anne Bearden
Diane Beaver
Susan Becher
Christine Bell
Suzanne Billhymer
Eva Bischoff
Christine Blazevic
Sharon Boranyak
Karen Boyle
Kathleen Brandt
Trina Bremerkamp
Janet Brennan
Anne Bresnahan
Anne Brewster
Cheryl Brinkmeyer
Donna Brown
Janine Brown
Kittie Brown
Wendy Brown
Eleanor Burns
Sarah Butler
Cindy Capatosta
Sally Carpenter
Barbara Carswell
Coleen Cavanagh
Angela Cerutts
Jenni Chambers-Smith

Kim Chulick
Mary Ann Clifford
Tricia Cline
Jenifer Corbin
Wendy Cordia
Kim Crocker
Cathy D'Alissandro
Yvonne D'Amore
Gretchen G. Davis
Tracy Deater
Vonna Despotis
Millicent Akin Dohr
Julie Dubray
Chris Duda
Judy Palmquist Dude
Dorcas Dunlop
Ruth Hanks Edwards
MaryBelle Eggers
Becky Rowe Eggmann
Mark Ellis
Sandy Ellis
Cathy Ely
Sherry Fafoglia
Margo Farley
Sue Felling
Linda Finerty
Sarah Fobes
Kate Fox
Mandy French
Debbie Genung
Marissa Gilbert
Stacey Lohr Graves
Nancy Bolton Grable
Nancy Gray
Luisa Greenlaw
Elizabeth Grob
Angela Grupas

Recipe Testers

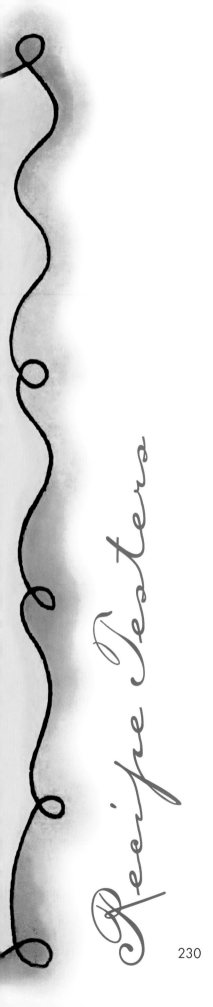

Sue Hammann
Randi Hanpeter
Meredith Harvath
Becky Haukap
Laurie Hegeman
Ronda Helton
Leslie Hendrix
June Herman
James C. Hetlage
Lynda M. Hetlage
Jennifer Heyl
Todd Higley
Amy Hillemann
Tracey Hoffman
Leslie Hollander
Tracee J. Holmes
Amy Hunt
Lisa Iannazzone
Laura Jacoby
Carey Johnson
Cathy S. Johnson
Elaine Johnson
Teresa Johnson
Bonnie Johnston
Ellen Jones
Sally Jones
Sharon Kaiser
Missy Kent
Lynn Koeneman
Stephanie Komen
Nancy Kopsky
Karyn Koury
Kathy Kummetz
Anne Lamb
Jan Lane
Larry Larson
Karen Leeker
Catherine Lemcovitz
Jamie Love
Jodi Luetkemeyer
Carol Maddock
Genie Magruder
Terrie Magruder
Pam Mahoney
Marla Malony
Kellie Mandry
Ginger Marecek
Peggy Martin
Amy Mayfield
Carrie McCartney

Amy McDermott
Martha "Mirth" McMahon
Susan McNary
Dianne Meine
Joan Mendoza
Darlene Miller
Shelby Moody
Nila Morris
Genie Mueller
Laura Murphy
Jessica Nagar
Barbara Nance
Mary Newmaster
Leslie Davis Niemoeller
Barbara Nikolychik
Joy Noonan
Julie Novak
Linda Oberlin
Heidi Oberman
Ann T. Kinney O'Brien
Heather O'Keefe
Jacqueline Olson
Carolyn Parham
Alison Pass
Megan Philip
Debora Poe
Lisa Price
Jane Quinn
Suzanne Rackers
Suzanne Randolph
Tammy Rasche
Carol Rechlein
Renee Ribble
Susan Robben
Nancy Rodgers
Terry Romine
Kelly Rosenblatt
Anne Rosenberg
Judy Ross
Marcia C. Rowe
Angela Ruggeri
Jane Hoyt "Gigi" Sanders
Rochelle Blaschke Schlortt
Sue Schneider
Angela Schnieders
Patricia Seeler
Kathy Sewing
Karen Shafer
Victoria Siegel
Susan Small

Sally Snavely
Elizabeth Southern
Gretchen Spalt
Katheryn Stacker
Susie Stackle
Jill Stafford
Quinn Stahl
Bridget Leitch Steinhart
Julie Steurer
Becky Stits
Barbara Swantner
Kristi Tacony
Peggy Taylor
Julie Thomas
Teresa L. Thompson
Mary-Ellen Tobin
Anne Troupis
Nancy Umbeck
Gloria Ventura

Dawn Von Rohr
Mary Warburton
Judy Ward
Judy Werner
Ann White
Vicki L. Wilding
Allison Wilson
Marjorie Wilson
Heather Winsby
Stephanie Wolf
Leigh Wooten
Jennifer Wulfers
Kathy Wunderlich
Lorna Wurm
Karen Zeigler
Laurie Zeveski
Susan Zimmermann
Junior League of St. Louis Kitchen

Index

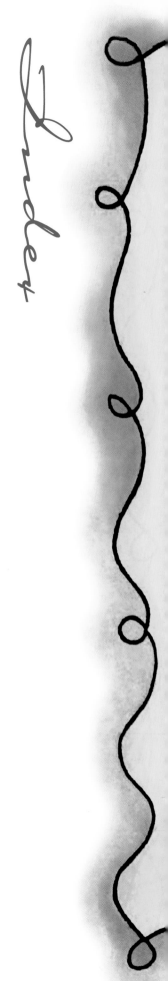

Meet Us
IN THE
Kitchen

Junior League of St. Louis
1630 Des Peres Road, Suite 150
St. Louis, MO 63131
314-822-2344   www.jlsl.org

Please send _____ copies of *Meet Us in the Kitchen*

@ $22.95 per book $ _____

Postage and Handling @ $4.50 per book $ _____

Total $ _____

Name _____

Address _____ Phone _____

City _____ State _____ Zip _____

[   ] Check enclosed. Make check payable to Junior League of St. Louis.
[   ] Charge to: [   ] VISA   [   ] MasterCard

Account Number _____

Expiration Date _____

Cardholder Name _____

Signature _____

How did you find out about *Meet Us in the Kitchen*?
[   ] Friend or family member
[   ] League member
[   ] Bookstore
[   ] Newspaper
[   ] Catalog
[   ] Other _____

Photocopies accepted.